D1649765

Higher
History
Practice Papers for SQA Exams

Claire Wood
Simon Wood

Contents

HODDER
GIBSON
AN HACHETTE UK COMPANY

The Publishers would like to thank the following for permission to reproduce copyright material:

Acknowledgements: p.5 (Source B) © Michael Lynch (Pimlico 1991) *Scotland: A New History*; (Source C) Fiona Watson (1998) *Under the Hammer: Edward I and Scotland, 1286–1307* - reproduced with permission of Birlinn Ltd through PLSclear; **p.6** (Source D) Colm McNamee (1997) *The Wars of the Bruces* - reproduced with permission of Birlinn Ltd through PLSclear; **p.7** (Source B) Eds. Croft Dickinson, Donaldson, Milne (1958) *A Source Book of Scottish History, Volume 2, 1424 to 1567*, Thomas Nelson & Sons; (Source C) © Michael Lynch (Pimlico 1991) *Scotland: A New History*; **p.8** (Source D) Ian B. Cowan (1960), *Blast and Counterblast; contemporary writings on the Scottish Reformation* – used with permission of The Saltire Society; **p.10** (Source D) © Michael Lynch (Pimlico 1991) *Scotland: A New History*; **p.11** (Source A) *Scotland and the Americas, c.1650–c.1939* (2002) eds. MacInnes, Harper and Fryer, Scottish History Society; (Source B) Murdoch Rodgers, 'The Lanarkshire Lithuanians' from *Complete Odyssey: Voices From Scotland's Recent Past* (ed. Billy Kay, 1994) - reproduced with permission of Birlinn Ltd through PLSclear; **p.12** (Source C) Murdoch Rodgers, used by permission © History Today; (Source D) *Complete Odyssey: Voices From Scotland's Recent Past* (ed. Billy Kay, 1994) - reproduced with permission of Birlinn Ltd through PLSclear; **p.13** (Source B) Ewen A. Cameron (2010), *Impaled Upon A Thistle* - reproduced with permission of Edinburgh University Press Ltd through PLSclear; (Source C) Trevor Royle (2006) *The Flowers of the Forest: Scotland and the First World War* - reproduced with permission of Birlinn Ltd through PLSclear; **p.14** (Source D) Iain.G.C. Hutchison (2000), *Scottish Politics in the Twentieth Century* – used with permission of Palgrave Macmillan; **p.25** (Source C) Colm McNamee (1997) *The Wars of the Bruces* - reproduced with permission of Birlinn Ltd through PLSclear; **p.26** (Source D) Geoffrey W.S. Barrow, *Robert Bruce and the Community of the Realm of Scotland* (3rd rev. ed. 1988) - reproduced with permission of Edinburgh University Press Ltd through PLSclear; **p.27** (Source A) Eds. Croft Dickinson, Donaldson, Milne (1958) *A Source Book of Scottish History, Volume 2, 1424 to 1567*, Thomas Nelson & Sons; (Source C) Eds., B. Harris, A. MacDonald (2007) *Scotland: The Making and Unmaking of the Nation c.1100-1707 Volume 2 Early Modern Scotland: c.1500-1707* - reproduced with permission of Edinburgh University Press Ltd through PLSclear; **p.28** (Source D) Ian B. Cowan (1960), *Blast and Counterblast; contemporary writings on the Scottish Reformation* – used with permission of The Saltire Society; **p.29** (Source A) Copyright © T.M. Devine *Scotland's Empire 1600-1815* (Penguin Books, 2004); (Source C) William Ferguson (1965) *Edinburgh History Of Scotland - Scotland 1689 to the Present* - reproduced with permission of Birlinn Ltd through PLSclear; **p.30** (Source D) Approximately one hundred and thirty-nine (139) words from *The Scottish Nation: 1700-2000* by T.M. Devine (Penguin Books, 2000). Copyright © T.M. Devine, 1999, 2006, 2012; **p.31** (Source A) Murdoch Rodgers, 'Italiani in Scozzia' from *Complete Odyssey: Voices From Scotland's Recent Past* (ed. Billy Kay, 1994) - reproduced with permission of Birlinn Ltd through PLSclear; (Source B) *Scotland and the Americas, c.1650–c.1939* (2002) eds. MacInnes, Harper and Fryer, Scottish History Society; (Source C) Esther Breitenbach (2009), *Empire and Scottish Society: The Impact of Foreign Missions at Home, c. 1790 to c. 1914*, reproduced with permission of Edinburgh University Press Ltd through PLSclear; **p.32** (Source D) Copyright © T.M. Devine *To the Ends of the Earth: Scotland's Global Diaspora, 1750-2010* (Penguin Books, 2011); **p.33** (Source A) Trevor Royle (2006) *The Flowers of the Forest: Scotland and the First World War* - reproduced with permission of Birlinn Ltd through PLSclear; (Source B) Ed. Ian MacDougall (1995) *Voices from War: Personal Recollections of War in Our Century* - reproduced with permission of Birlinn Ltd through PLSclear; (Source C) Iain.G.C. Hutchison (2000), *Scottish Politics in the Twentieth Century* – used with permission of Palgrave MacMillan; **p.34** (Source D) Ewen A. Cameron (2010), *Impaled Upon A Thistle* - reproduced with permission of Edinburgh University Press Ltd through PLSclear; **p.43** (Source A) Geoffrey W.S. Barrow, *Robert Bruce and the Community of the Realm of Scotland* (3rd rev. ed. 1988) - reproduced with permission of Edinburgh University Press Ltd through PLSclear; (Source C) © Michael Lynch (Pimlico 1991) *Scotland: A New History*; **p.45** (Source A) Gordon Donaldson (1994) *Edinburgh History Of Scotland - Scotland: James V–James VII* - reproduced with permission of Birlinn Ltd through PLSclear; (Source B) © Michael Lynch (Pimlico 1991) *Scotland: A New History*; (Source C) A.R. MacDonald (1998), *The Jacobean Kirk, 1567–1625*, reproduced with permission of Routledge; **p.47** (Source A) Christopher A. Whatley (1998) 'The Union of 1707' from *Modern Scottish History 1-Transformation Of Scotland* - reproduced with permission of Birlinn Ltd through PLSclear; (Source B) © T.M. Devine *Scotland's Empire 1600-1815* (Penguin Books, 2004); (Source C) © Michael Lynch (Pimlico 1991) *Scotland: A New History*; **p.48** (Source D) Document 11: Ed. D Szechi (1989) *Letters of George Lockhart of Carnwath, 1698–1732, Edinburgh* (Scottish History Society); **p.49** (Source A) Marjory Harper (2003), *Adventurers & Exiles: The Great Scottish Exodus*, used with permission of Profile Books; (Source B) Copyright © T.M. Devine *To the Ends of the Earth: Scotland's Global Diaspora, 1750-2010* (Penguin Books, 2011); **p.50** (Source C) Copyright © T.M. Devine *To the Ends of the Earth: Scotland's Global Diaspora, 1750-2010* (Penguin Books, 2011); (Source D) Murdoch Rodgers 'Glasgow Jewry' from *Complete Odyssey: Voices From Scotland's Recent Past* (ed. Billy Kay, 1994) - reproduced with permission of Birlinn Ltd through PLSclear; **p.51** (Source A) Derek Young (2006), *Scottish Voices From the Great War*, used with permission by The History Press; (Source B) Ewen A. Cameron (2010), *Impaled Upon A Thistle* - reproduced with permission of Edinburgh University Press Ltd through PLSclear; (Source C) Clive H. Lee 'The Scottish Economy' from *Scotland and the Great War*; eds. Catriona M. M. Macdonald and E. W. McFarland (1999) - reproduced with permission of Birlinn Ltd through PLSclear; **p.52** (Source D) Ed. Ian MacDougall (1995) *Voices from War: Personal Recollections of War in Our Century* - reproduced with permission of Birlinn Ltd through PLSclear;

Exam rubrics at the start of each paper and extract from Higher SQP Marking Instruction Copyright © Scottish Qualifications Authority

Every effort has been made to trace all copyright holders, but if any have been inadvertently overlooked the Publishers will be pleased to make the necessary arrangements at the first opportunity.

Hachette UK's policy is to use papers that are natural, renewable and recyclable products and made from wood grown in sustainable forests. The logging and manufacturing processes are expected to conform to the environmental regulations of the country of origin.

Orders: please contact Bookpoint Ltd, 130 Park Drive, Milton Park, Abingdon, Oxon OX14 4SE. Telephone: (44) 01235 827720. Fax: (44) 01235 400454. Lines are open 9.00–5.00, Monday to Saturday, with a 24-hour message answering service. Visit our website at www.hoddereducation.co.uk. Hodder Gibson can be contacted direct on: Tel: 0141 333 4650; Fax: 0141 404 8188; email: hoddergibson@hodder.co.uk.

First published in 2017 by
Hodder Gibson, an imprint of Hodder Education
An Hachette UK Company
211 St Vincent Street
Glasgow G2 5QY

Impression number   5 4 3 2 1
Year   2021 2020 2019 2018 2017

Cover photo © Aliaksandr Zabudzko – 123RF
Typeset in Din Regular,12/14.4 pts. by Aptara, Inc.
Printed in the UK

A catalogue record for this title is available from the British Library

ISBN: 978 1 5104 1500 3

Introduction

Higher History

This book is intended to help you achieve as good a performance in the Higher History examination as you can. The examination is where the bulk of marks are gained in Higher History. The rest of the marks are achieved in the Assignment, which you will complete in school under examination conditions.

It is important that you know what you are doing when you arrive in the examination hall. The Higher History exam is 2 hours and 20 minutes in length. There are three sections to the exam paper: Scottish, British, and European and World.

Section 1 is the Scottish part of the paper. This section is where you answer three questions based on four presented sources. You must answer all of the questions from this part of the exam paper. Five periods of Scottish history are examined. You will answer questions on ONE of these periods.

Sections 2 and 3 are both based on writing one essay, or extended response, to each section. Section 2 is the British part of the exam paper. Five periods of British history are examined. Each period of history has three essay questions You will answer one essay question from ONE of the periods of history.

Section 3 is the European and World part of the exam paper. Nine periods of European and World history are examined. Each period of history has three essay questions. You will answer one essay question from ONE of the periods of history.

Tips for examination success

Get started on revision as soon as possible. It is no good putting it off as you will only create more problems by doing so. There are three stages to effective revision.

Step 1: review your material. This is where you make sure that you have the notes and detail that are needed to successfully answer three source questions and two essay questions in the exam. You will need to know the entire Scottish period you have studied as questions can come from any of the four areas that each period covers. The British, and European and World sections are organised around six essay topics per period of history. You will, therefore, need to know at least four of the essay topics from each period you have studied. This will ensure that you are able to complete at least one essay. However, we would recommend that you know at least five of the topics as this will mean you have a choice of questions you can answer in the examination.

Are your notes detailed in terms of knowledge and do you understand the arguments that surround each topic? If your notes lack detail or you do not fully understand the arguments, then you need to speak to your teacher/lecturer in order to ensure that you complete your notes and do understand the arguments.

Step 2: revise your topics. This is where you make sure that the detail of your notes is embedded in your brain. It is not enough simply to read through the notes in front of you as you will rapidly forget the information. You need to do something with the notes, preferably creatively, to make them stick. For example, you could make up your own revision cards for each topic. Change how the information is recorded by drawing spider diagrams. Work with another person and test your knowledge on each other. Above all, be active in your revision as this is the effective way to retain information.

Step 3: Practise, practise, practise! This is where this book comes in very handy. The more you practise answering questions in a timed way, the better you will become at answering the different questions. The biggest problem that history examiners see when marking work is students who simply write an answer about the topic of the question, rather than tackling the issue that the question is asking them to address. By practising, you make sure that you are adaptable in your use of the information that you know. Also, only through practising will you learn how to organise the topic information you know and, above all, learn how to analyse and evaluate what is needed to directly answer the question in front of you.

This book contains three specially created examination papers with their relevant marking schemes. This book enables you to practise how to evaluate, contextualise and compare sources, as well as answer different types of exam essay questions.

You will have 2 hours and 20 minutes in the examination. Practise writing essays in 40–45 minutes and each source question in around 20 minutes.

Revision guide

You can use this book in three main ways.

1   Work your way through an entire practice paper.

2   Concentrate on questions on a certain topic.

3   Concentrate on certain types of questions. (This is easy to do for the source questions, but is more difficult for the essay type questions.)

1 Work your way through an entire practice paper

There are three Higher History Practice Papers in this book. Remember in the exam you can only answer questions on ONE Scottish period, and the periods that your examination centre has chosen from the British and European and World essays. It is important that you complete ONE essay from a British period and ONE essay from a European and World period.

2 Concentrate on questions on a certain topic

Remember that the Scottish source section of the exam paper is based on a selection of three topic areas from four subject content areas and the British and European extended responses are based on a selection of three essay topics from six possible areas.

Section 1 – Scottish

Questions on the following periods can be found on the pages indicated in the table on page vii:

A   The Wars of Independence, 1249–1328

B   The Age of the Reformation, 1542–1603

C   The Treaty of Union, 1689–1740

D   Migration and Empire, 1830–1939

E   The Impact of the Great War, 1914–1928

Section 2 – British

Questions on the following periods can be found on the pages indicated in the table on page vii:

A   Church, State and Feudal Society, 1066–1406

B   The Century of Revolutions, 1603–1702

C   The Atlantic Slave Trade

D   Britain, 1851–1951

E   Britain and Ireland, 1900–1985

Section 3 – European and World

Questions on the following periods can be found on the pages indicated in the table opposite:

A   The Crusades, 1071–1204

B   The American Revolution, 1763–1787

C   The French Revolution, to 1799

D   Germany, 1815–1939

E   Italy, 1815–1939

F   Russia, 1881–1921

G   USA, 1918–1968

H   Appeasement and the Road to War, to 1939

I   The Cold War, 1945–1989

For additional advice and examples of different question types, please see the following pages in the Hodder Gibson *How to Pass Higher History* book.

For further advice on/examples of …	See HTP Higher History pages
Evaluate the usefulness of Source … *In making a judgement you should refer to:* • *The origin and possible purpose of the source* • *The content of the source* • *Your own knowledge.*	3–5; 35; 36–37; 46; 57
Compare the views of Sources X and Y … *Compare the content overall and in detail.*	5–7; 35–36; 46–47; 47–48; 58
How fully does **Source X** explain … *Use the source and your own knowledge.*	7–9; 37; 47; 58; 59–60
'Quotation' How valid is this view?	9–14; 20–26; 66; 69; 78; 86; 88; 99; 104; 110; 115; 125; 129; 131; 144; 149; 151; 154; 156; 162; 165; 168; 171; 174; 177; 178–179
To what extent …?	9–14; 20–26; 64; 69; 72; 75; 86; 88; 95; 99; 100–101; 104; 107; 110; 113; 119; 120–121; 125; 129; 131; 134; 137; 140; 140–141; 144; 147; 149; 151; 154; 156; 157–158; 165; 171
How important …?	9–14; 20–26; 64; 72; 79–80; 83; 92; 95; 107; 113; 115; 119; 137; 162; 168; 174; 177

3 Concentrate on certain types of questions

Examples of the following types of question can be found on the pages indicated:

Question type	The Wars of Independence, 1249–1328	The Age of the Reformation, 1542–1603	The Treaty of Union, 1689–1740	Migration and Empire, 1830–1939	The Impact of the Great War, 1914–1928	Church, State and Feudal Society, 1066–1406	The Century of Revolutions, 1603–1702	The Atlantic Slave Trade	Britain, 1851–1951	Britain and Ireland, 1900–1985	The Crusades, 1071–1204	The American Revolution, 1763–1787	The French Revolution, to 1799	Germany, 1815–1939	Italy, 1815–1939	Russia, 1881–1921	USA, 1918–1968	Appeasement and the Road to War, to 1939	The Cold War, 1945–1989
To what extent …	–	8, 28, 46	10, 30, 48	12, 32, 50	–	15, 35, 53	15, 35, 53	35, 53	15, 35, 53	16, 36, 54	17, 37, 55	17, 37, 55	17, 37	17, 37, 55	18, 38, 56	18, 38, 56	18, 38, 56	18, 38, 56	19, 38, 57
How important …	–	–	–	–	–	35, 53	15, 35, 53	15, 35, 53	35	16, 36, 54	17, 37, 55	17, 37, 55	17, 37, 55	17, 37, 55	18, 38, 56	38	18, 38, 56	18, 38	19, 38, 57
'Quotation' How valid is this view?	–	8, 28, 46	10, 30, 48	–	–	15, 35, 53	15, 35, 53	15, 35, 53	15, 35, 53	16, 36, 54	37, 55	17, 37, 55	17, 37, 55	17, 37, 55	18, 38, 56	18, 38, 56	18, 38, 56	18, 38, 56	19, 38, 57
Evaluate the usefulness …	6, 26, 44	8, 28, 46	10, 30, 48	12, 32, 50	14, 34, 52	–	–	–	–	–	–	–	–	–	–	–	–	–	–
Compare the views …	6, 26, 44	8, 28, 46	10, 30, 48	12, 32, 50	14, 34, 52	–	–	–	–	–	–	–	–	–	–	–	–	–	–
How fully …	6, 26, 44	8, 28, 46	10, 30, 48	12, 32, 50	14, 34, 52	–	–	–	–	–	–	–	–	–	–	–	–	–	–

Higher History

Duration: 2 hours and 20 minutes

Total marks: 60

Section 1 – Scottish – 20 marks

Attempt ONE part.

Section 2 – British – 20 marks

Attempt ONE question from the part you have chosen.

Section 3 – European and World – 20 marks

Attempt ONE question from the part you have chosen.

In the exam, you must write your answers clearly in the answer booklet provided and clearly identify the question number you are attempting.

Use **blue** or **black** ink.

Section 1 – Scottish

Attempt ONE part.

Parts

Section 2 – British

Attempt ONE part.

Parts

A

Section 1 – Scottish – 20 marks

Part A – The Wars of Independence, 1249–1328

> Study the sources below and attempt the questions which follow.

Source A from the speech of Roger Brabazon, Edward I's representative, Norham, May 1291

Source A

Our king, seeing that the peace of the kingdom of Scotland has been disturbed by the deaths of the king Alexander and of his children who were relatives of our king. He is greatly distressed by their deaths. Wishing to do justice to all who can lay any claim to the inheritance of the kingdom of Scotland and to keep the peace among the people, he has asked you, the good people of the realm, to come here because of something he wishes to explain to you. He himself has come here so that he may restore firm peace to the kingdom of Scotland. So that this matter may be concluded satisfactorily our lord king asks for your agreement and for recognition of his overlordship; he wishes to act with your advice in doing and effecting justice.

Source B from Michael Lynch, *Scotland: A New History* (1991)

Source B

The international crisis which engulfed Edward in 1293–4 brought about the actual split between England and Scotland. War with France coincided with the outbreak of a rising in Wales in September 1294. The Welsh revolt had been caused by Edward's demands for military support. A similar demand, framed in terms of personal service, had been sent in June 1294 to the King of Scots, ten of his earls and sixteen barons. This may have provoked the decision made at a parliament held in Stirling in July 1295 to give control to a council of twelve, made up equally of bishops, earls and barons. Balliol was still king, but in effect a form of Guardianship had been restored. It was the reluctance of the Scots to become involved in the English war effort which drove them into an alliance with France.

Source C from Fiona Watson, *Under the Hammer: Edward I and Scotland, 1286–1307* (1998)

Source C

The breakdown of Anglo-French relations provided exactly the catalyst the Scots needed in order to make their bid for freedom. The demand for military service in France was a powerful reminder, not just to the Scots, but also to the recently conquered Welsh of Edward's success in extending and formalising English authority throughout the British Isles. The failure of the Welsh revolt set the seal on Edward's conquest of Wales. The Scots did not rush to follow, partly because they wisely intended to play a card denied to the Welsh: an alliance with France. Also because Balliol was reluctant to commit himself to an all-out war with England. In order to get round this reluctance, the political community adopted an extraordinary policy: they sidelined the king and installed a caretaker government of twelve guardians.

Source D from Colm McNamee, *The Wars of the Bruces* (1997)

Source D

The Scots entered Northumberland at Norham and marched the length of the county to Newburn on the Tyne, where they stayed three days, devastating, burning and intimidating Newcastle. The Lanercost Chronicle goes on to say that they crossed into Durham, but there they did not burn much because the inhabitants bought them off. They crossed into Richmondshire then, gathering together their forces, they turned north-west into Swaledale 'and other valleys' following the old Roman road. At Stainmore they carried off yet more cattle; but at the Reycross they met with resistance organised by Andrew Harclay of the Carlisle garrison. In the account of the King's receiver of victuals at Carlisle it is recorded that the garrison lost 16 horses in an action there on 4th August 1314, a loss which suggests Harclay's detachment came off worse.

Attempt all of the following questions.

1   Evaluate the usefulness of **Source A** as evidence of the succession problem, 1286–1292.

   In making a judgement you should refer to:
   - *the origin and possible purpose of the source*
   - *the content of the source*
   - *your own knowledge.*

6

2   Compare the views of **Sources B** and **C** about the relationship between King John of Scotland and Edward I of England.

   Compare the content overall and in detail.

5

3   How fully does **Source D** explain the reasons for the rise and triumph of Robert Bruce?

   Use the source and your own knowledge.

9

[Now go to Section 2]

Section 1 – Scottish – 20 marks

Part B – The Age of the Reformation, 1542–1603

> Study the sources below and attempt the questions which follow.

Source A from a speech by Archbishop Hamilton addressing the dean of Christianity of the Merse (Scottish Borders), 9 April 1556

Source A

During our last visit from St Andrews, we toured many parishes situated in the Merse [Scottish Borders]. We discovered and saw with our own eyes that a great many of the parish churches – their choirs as well as their naves – were wholly collapsed and, as it were, levelled to the ground. Others were partly ruined or threatened collapse with weak walls or missing roofs. Many of the churches did not even have a baptismal font, suitable clothing for the priests and instructions for the celebration of mass. This meant that their parishioners could not hear the divine services or masses as a good Christian should. The fault for this belongs to the parishioners as well as the parsons.

Source B from eds. W. Croft Dickinson, G. Donaldson, I.A. Milne, *A Source Book of Scottish History, Volume 2, 1424 to 1567* (1958)

Source B

The revolution of 1560 had been carried through while Mary, Queen of France since July 1559, seemed likely to remain in France. On 5 December 1560, however, Francis II died, and it was soon evident that Mary would return to Scotland to rule in person. Splits between moderate and extreme reformers arose afresh over the attitude to be adopted towards Mary. There were those, including Knox and the Hamiltons, to whom a Catholic princess could not be acceptable, while a more moderate group, headed by Lord James Stewart and Maitland of Lethington, sought compromise. They believed that if Mary were allowed the private exercise of her own religion she might be guided into acknowledgement of the reformed church and the English alliance. Mary was allowed to accept the Catholic Mass, but it must be done in private.

Source C from Michael Lynch, *Scotland: A New History* (1991)

Source C

In December 1560 Francis II died suddenly and Mary's reign as Queen Consort of France ended. Within a month, it was clear to more astute diplomats amongst the Congregation, such as Maitland of Lethington, that she would return to Scotland. By March 1561, the bargaining about the details of her future personal reign had begun. A climate of compromise established itself and Lord James's advice to Mary was to act carefully. The nature of the careful bargains struck before her reign became evident just five days later: on this first Sunday Mary and her household attended mass in her private chapel at Holyrood and Lord James barred the door against Protestant protesters. Knox preached a sermon on the following Sunday that one mass was more dangerous than the landing of ten thousand armed enemies and Mary's rule was not acceptable.

Source D from ed. Ian B. Cowan, *Blast and Counterblast; Contemporary Writings on the Scottish Reformation* (1960)

Source D

One of the most serious criticisms levelled against the pre-Reformation Church was its failure to provide an educated priesthood. Therefore, it is not surprising that the Protestants laid great stress upon education and insisted that all Ministers should be examined as to their qualifications. Particular emphasis was laid upon literacy and the use of books. The Protestants had ambitious plans for the provision of educational facilities. Although Medieval Scotland possessed three universities; there was much room for improvement in the provision of schools, while university education urgently required an overhaul. Lack of finance proved to be an insurmountable obstacle to the realisation of these ambitious plans. Most of the funds the Protestants had earmarked for education fell into other hands, although certain revenues from friaries were utilised by schools and universities.

Attempt all of the following questions.

4 Evaluate the usefulness of **Source A** as evidence of the reasons for the Reformation of 1560.

In making a judgement you should refer to:

- *the origin and possible purpose of the source*
- *the content of the source*
- *your own knowledge.*

6

5 Compare the views of **Sources B** and **C** about the reign of Mary, 1561–1567.

Compare the sources overall and in detail.

5

6 How fully does **Source D** explain the impact of the Reformation on Scotland, to 1603?

Use the source and your own knowledge.

9

[Now go to Section 2]

Section 1 – Scottish – 20 marks

Part C – The Treaty of Union, 1689–1740

Source A from the Act anent (concerning) Peace and War, 1703, Edinburgh, Scottish Parliament

Source A

Our sovereign lady, with advice and consent of the estates of parliament, declares that after her majesty's death, and failing heirs of her body, no person being king or queen of Scotland and England shall have the sole power of making war with any prince or state without the consent of parliament. Also that no declaration of war without consent shall be binding on the subjects of this kingdom, declaring always that this shall not stop the sovereign of this kingdom to call forth, command and employ their subjects to suppress any insurrection within the kingdom or reject any invasion from abroad; and also declaring that everything which relates to treaties of peace, alliance and commerce is left to the wisdom of the sovereign, with consent of the estates of parliament who shall declare the war.

Source B from a petition from Stirling Town Council against the proposed incorporating union, 18 November 1706

Source B

Though we are desirous that true friendship be cultivated with our neighbours in England up on just and honourable terms, we judge going into this Treaty will bring an insupportable burden of taxation upon this land, which all the grants of freedom of trade will never counterbalance being uncertain while under the regulations of the English in the parliament of Britain, who may if they please discourage our trade, if it in any way interfered with their own. That it will prove ruining to our manufactures. That it will expose our Religion, Laws and Liberties and consequently all that's valuable in our country, to be overthrown by England. Thereby one of the most ancient nations so long and gloriously defended by our worthy patriots will be ended and with fatal consequences of which we tremble to think about.

Source C from a speech to the Scottish Parliament, 2 November 1706, by Lord Belhaven

Source C

I think I see the Honest Industrious Trades-man loaded with new Taxes and Impositions, disappointed of the Equivalents, drinking Water in Place of Ale, eating his saltless Pottage, Petitioning for Encouragement to his Manufactures, and Answered by counter-petitions. But above all, My Lord, I think I see our ancient country of Scotland, looking round about Her, seeing Her religious and legal freedoms threatened by England. These are worrying times My Lords. Are we deaf and blind to the threats that face us from England? Where is our heart and our voice to defend ourselves? That in this our day, we should not mind the things that concern the very existence and well-being of our Ancient Kingdom, before they be hid from our Eyes.

Source D from Michael Lynch, *Scotland: A New History* (1991)

Source D

The free trade area which opened up after 1707 brought prosperity only to a few Scots. The most obvious symbol of economic success in post-Union Britain were the Glasgow tobacco lords, who by the 1750s controlled almost half of all Scotland's imports; yet the tobacco trade until the mid-1720s grew not through the opportunities offered by free trade, but through the long-honed skills of Scottish merchants of carrying on an illicit trade evading customs regulations. The worst forecasts of the swamping of Scottish manufactures after 1707 did not happen, but such industries found at best only sluggish demand for their produce in the new English market, both domestic and colonial. In the most important sector of the Scottish economy, in which eight or nine out of every ten Scots were still employed – in agriculture – the effects of Union were marginal.

Attempt all of the following questions.

7 Evaluate the usefulness of **Source A** as evidence of worsening relations between Scotland and England.

In making a judgement you should refer to:
- *the origin and possible purpose of the source*
- *the content of the source*
- *your own knowledge.*

6

8 Compare the views of **Sources B** and **C** about the arguments against union between Scotland and England.

Compare the content overall and in detail.

5

9 How fully does **Source D** explain the effects of the Union to 1740?

Use the source and your own knowledge.

9

[Now go to Section 2]

Section 1 – Scottish – 20 marks

Part D – Migration and Empire, 1830–1939

Study the sources below and attempt the questions which follow.

Source A from an account by John Will in 1994 from the 'Ellis Island Oral History Collection'

Source A

When First World War ended my father tried to get his farming equipment business back in Fife, but the economic conditions as a result of First World War in Scotland were very poor. The farmers were not making any money and they were not hardly buying anything new. So, his business wasn't successful, and he was going broke. He had another thought in mind and that was the education of his kids. Scots people are traditionally very educational minded and it didn't look like much opportunity for his kids. He had read a lot about California, the orange groves, the climate, land of opportunity – he decided we should emigrate to Southern California. The primary reason for emigrating was better economic conditions abroad. I might add that all my brothers and sisters did very well in our new country.

Source B from Murdoch Rodgers, 'The Lanarkshire Lithuanians' in *Odyssey: Voices From Scotland's Recent Past* (1980), ed. Billy Kay

Source B

The ultimate destination of most of the emigrants was the United States and Scotland, initially, was probably no more than a stepping stone. With cheap shipping routes between, for example, Hamburg or Bremen and Leith and Dundee, Scotland was easily accessible from the continent. Recruitment took place, either at home or abroad and it solved three of the most immediate problems facing the immigrants; accommodation, money and communication. Firstly, employment with the large companies in the Lanarkshire area such as Baird, Merry and Cuninghame included provision of company owned housing. Secondly, wages in Scotland were high by Lithuanian standards and could only be substantially improved by a further move to America. And thirdly, the language difficulties were minimised by the unskilled nature of the work being done by the Lithuanians in the blast furnaces and the coal mines.

Source C by Murdoch Rodgers in *History Today*

Source C

For the vast majority of them America was the ultimate destination and Scotland was regarded, at least in the early part of this period, as only a temporary stop on that journey. There were sound financial reasons for having such a break. Firstly, there were ample opportunities to earn money in the expanding coal, iron and steel industries in Lanarkshire and Ayrshire. Secondly, employment with some of the larger companies included provision of company-owned housing. And thirdly, for a time it was cheaper to travel to America via the ports of Leith and Glasgow rather than go direct. Given the impoverished conditions of most Lithuanian immigrants, these financial considerations must have had an important bearing on the development of a community in Scotland. Once it began to get itself established it was primarily through the immigrants' continuing correspondence with Lithuania that growth was sustained.

Source D from ed. Billy Kay, *Odyssey: Voices From Scotland's Recent Past* (1980)

Source D

Although seasonal migration continued throughout the nineteenth and twentieth centuries, thousands of Irish folk decided to make Scotland their permanent home. By 1851 there was already a settled Irish community in the Gorbals in Glasgow which numbered well over 200,000. At this time there was a marked Irish presence in the textile industry, where they became skilled spinners, weavers and dyers. For many of the single men the pull of road was strong and generations of Irish men helped to build the railways in the nineteenth century and roads, dams and tunnels in the twentieth century. Eventually the great public work projects of the 1920s and 1930s were completed and there was no longer a demand for an army of travelling workers. The Gorbals with its settled Irish community and job prospects was a magnet to the men of the road.

> Attempt all of the following questions.

10 Evaluate the usefulness of **Source A** as evidence of the reasons for Scottish emigration.

In making a judgement you should refer to:
- *the origin and possible purpose of the source*
- *the content of the source*
- *your own knowledge.*

6

11 Compare the views of **Sources B** and **C** about the experience of immigrants to Scotland.

Compare the sources overall and in detail.

5

12 How fully does **Source D** explain the effects of migration and empire on Scotland, to 1939?

Use the source and your own knowledge.

9

[Now go on to Section 2]

Section 1 – Scottish – 20 marks

Part E – The Impact of the Great War, 1914–1928

Source A from an account by Captain Wyllie of the Royal Scots Fusiliers written in 1952 about the Battle of Loos

Source A

We were in the reserves and went forward after the attack some hours later. We moved forward to our front line trenches and from there we launched a gas attack before the brigades went over; the wind was light and variable and got half way towards the German line and the gas came back on to us. The attacking lines were through it too quickly for it to do any harm except in a few cases. One battalion was so badly gassed that only one platoon attacked the German line; it was here that Piper Laidlaw won his VC by marching up and down on top of the parapet while the entire German Army shot at him. His bag was punctured in several places. The trench we were in had a number of dead and wounded lying in the bottom.

Source B from Ewen A. Cameron, *Impaled Upon A Thistle* (2010)

Source B

Even demobilisation was no guarantee of safety as was demonstrated in the tragic death of 200 soldiers who died on the *Iolaire* in sight of Stornoway harbour in 1919. The end of the war brought a flu epidemic, possibly killing as many as 34,000, including returning soldiers. The loss of a relative in battle was not a common experience for most Scottish families, but mounting losses from the volunteer army brought this to the forefront of Scottish life. The Scottish landscape is littered with war memorials in towns and villages where the number of names on the memorial outnumbered the current population. The Scottish National War Memorial at Edinburgh Castle opened in 1927. This recorded the names of all the Scottish war dead and was an attempt to express a sense of indebtedness rather than an aggressive proclamation of victory.

Source C from Trevor Royle, *The Flowers of the Forest* (2006)

Source C

The dying also continued at home. In 1918 there was a flu epidemic against which there was no medical defence. Unknown numbers of young men came home safely from the war, only to fall victim to the disease. Another group of servicemen encountered unexpected death within sight of their own homes when the *Iolaire* foundered on rocks at Stornoway in 1919. Sport too paid a price. Rugby players were commemorated by a simple stone arch at Murrayfield stadium in Edinburgh. All over Scotland, similar memorials were erected, some of them included the figure of a kilted Scottish soldier or symbolic figure of peace or a plain Celtic cross. There were also moves to commemorate the names of the dead nationally. In 1918, the Scottish National War Memorial committee was set up to memorialise Scotland's contribution to the war.

Source D from I.G.C. Hutchison, *Scottish Politics in the Twentieth Century* (2000)

> **Source D**
>
> After the First World War, the Conservatives were helped by a significant shift in the politics of four key national organisations, namely, the Church of Scotland, the legal and educational systems and the press. These represented official Scotland and spoke for the nation. By the mid-1920s, Liberal papers had all gone. In Dundee and Aberdeen, they were each taken over by the Tory rival. In Glasgow, the Daily Record, switched its politics when bought over by Conservative owners. The Church of Scotland was conservative, showing little interest in issues of social reform. There was overwhelming and continuing church support for involvement in the First World War. The Scottish legal system also became linked to the Tories through the number of advocates who became MPs. In the education sector, the Tories were dominant, firmly controlling the return of MPs for the university seats.

> Attempt all of the following questions.

13 Evaluate the usefulness of **Source A** as evidence of the experience of Scots on the Western Front.

    In making a judgement you should refer to:
    - *the origin and possible purpose of the source*
    - *the content of the source*
    - *your own knowledge.*

6

14 Compare the views of **Sources B** and **C** about the impact of military losses on Scottish society.

    Compare the sources overall and in detail.

5

15 How fully does **Source D** explain the impact of the war on Scottish politics?

    Use the source and your own knowledge.

9

[Now go to Section 2]

Section 2 – British – 20 marks

Attempt ONE question from the part you have chosen.

Part A – Church, State and Feudal Society, 1066–1406

16 *The landed classes were the most important part of feudal society.*
How valid is this view?

20

17 To what extent was David I successful in his attempts to increase royal power in Scotland?

20

18 *King John's attempts to increase royal authority were successful in England.*
How valid is this view?

20

Part B – The Century of Revolutions, 1603–1702

19 How important were political issues as a reason for the problems faced by King James after the Union of the Crowns in 1603?

20

20 To what extent was the character of Charles I the main reason for the outbreak of civil war in England?

20

21 *The role of Charles II was the main reason for the Revolution Settlement of 1688–1689.*
How valid is this view?

20

Part C – The Atlantic Slave Trade

22 How important were racist attitudes in the reasons for the development of the slave trade?

20

23 *Racism and prejudice were the most important factors governing relations between slaves and their owners.*
How valid is this view?

20

24 How important were vested interests as an obstacle to abolition?

20

Part D – Britain, 1851–1951

25 To what extent were pressure groups the main reason why Britain became more democratic, 1851–1928?

20

26 *The Suffragettes did little to help achieve votes for some women in 1918.*
How valid is this view?

20

27 To what extent did the social reforms of the Liberal Government, 1906–1914, meet the needs of the British people?

20

Part E – Britain and Ireland, 1900–1985

MARKS

28 How important were the Irish cultural revival and the re-emergence of Irish Republicanism as reasons for the growth of tension in Ireland to 1914?

20

29 To what extent were IRA tactics and policies the main obstacle to peace in Ireland, 1918–1921?

20

30 *The issue of civil rights was the most important reason for the developing crisis in Northern Ireland by 1968.*

How valid is this view?

20

[Now go to Section 3]

Section 3 – European and World – 20 marks

MARKS

Attempt ONE question from the part you have chosen.

Part A – The Crusades, 1071–1204

31 To what extent was the emergence of a knightly class the main reason for the calling of the First Crusade? — 20

32 How important was the military power of the Crusader knights as a reason for the success of the First Crusade? — 20

33 To what extent was Richard more successful than Saladin, both as a military leader and as a diplomat during the Third Crusade? — 20

Part B – The American Revolution, 1763–1787

34 How important was the role of George III as a reason for colonial resentment towards Britain by 1763? — 20

35 To what extent did the views of Edmund Burke represent British opinion towards the conflict in the colonies? — 20

36 *French entry into the war explains why the colonists won the War of Independence.* How valid is this view? — 20

Part C – The French Revolution, to 1799

37 How important were the grievances of the bourgeoisie in the developing threat to the security of the Ancien Regime in the years before 1789? — 20

38 To what extent were the attitude and actions of Louis XVI the main reason for the failure of constitutional monarchy, 1789–1792? — 20

39 *The role of Napoleon was the most important reason for the establishment of the Consulate.* How valid is this view? — 20

Part D – Germany, 1815–1939

40 How important were economic factors as a reason for the growth of nationalism in Germany, 1815–1850? — 20

41 *Resentment against Prussia was the most significant obstacle to German unification, 1815–1850.* How valid is this view? — 20

42 To what extent was the role of Hitler the main reason why the Nazis achieved power in 1933? — 20

Part E – Italy, 1815–1939

MARKS

43 To what extent was resentment of Austria the main reason for the growth of nationalism in Italy, 1815–1850?

20

44 *The attitude of the Papacy was the main obstacle to Italian unification, 1815–1850.*
How valid is this view?

20

45 How important were the weaknesses of Italian governments as a reason why the Fascists achieved power in Italy, 1919–1925?

20

Part F – Russia, 1881–1921

46 *The security of the Tsarist state was never seriously challenged in the years before 1905.*
How valid is this view?

20

47 *The work of Pytor Stolypin was central to the successful strengthening of Tsarist authority between 1905 and 1914.*
How valid is this view?

20

48 To what extent was the appeal of the Bolsheviks the main reason for the success of the October Revolution, 1917?

20

Part G – USA, 1918–1968

49 To what extent was isolationism the main reason for changing attitudes towards immigration in the 1920s?

20

50 *The impact of the Republican government policies in the 1920s was the main reason for the economic crisis of 1929–1933.*
How valid is this view?

20

51 How important was the role of Martin Luther King in the development of the Civil Rights campaign, after 1945?

20

Part H – Appeasement and the Road to War, to 1939

52 How important was the Peace Settlement of 1919 as a reason for the aggressive nature of the foreign policies of Germany and Italy in the 1930s?

20

53 To what extent were economic difficulties the main reason for the British policy of appeasement, 1936–1938?

20

54 *The Munich Agreement was a success.*
How valid is this view?

20

Part I – The Cold War, 1945–1989

MARKS

55 How important was the crisis over Korea as a reason for the emergence of the Cold War, up to 1955?

20

56 *The arms race was the main reason for the Cuban Missile Crisis of 1962.*

How valid is this view?

20

57 To what extent were the developing policies of co-existence and détente the main reason why the superpowers attempted to manage the Cold War, 1962–1979?

20

[End of Practice Paper A]

Higher
History

HODDER
GIBSON
LEARN MORE

Duration: 2 hours and 20 minutes

Total marks: 60

Section 1 – Scottish – 20 marks

Attempt ONE part.

Section 2 – British – 20 marks

Attempt ONE question from the part you have chosen.

Section 3 – European and World – 20 marks

Attempt ONE question from the part you have chosen.

In the exam, you must write your answers clearly in the answer booklet provided and clearly identify the question number you are attempting.

Use **blue** or **black** ink.

Section 1 – Scottish

Attempt ONE part.

Parts

Section 2 – British

Attempt ONE part.

Parts

Section 3 – European and World

Attempt ONE part.

Parts

Section 1 – Scottish – 20 marks

Part A – The Wars of Independence, 1249–1328

Study the sources below and attempt the questions which follow.

Source A from the Chronicle of John of Fourdon, circa 1350

Source A

Macduff managed to get John, king of Scotland, summoned to the English king's parliament held in London. John accordingly appeared in person and he resolved after discussing the matter with his council, that he would answer the English king by proxy [another person would speak on his behalf]. When therefore the king was called and appeared in court the king of England, sitting upon the judgement seat, would not in any way listen to the king's proxy until the king of Scotland should rise from his place and standing in front of him convey his answers to his proxy with his own lips. John fulfilled these commands and having experienced innumerable insults and slights from all, contrary to his kingly rank and dignity, he eventually conveyed his answers to his proxy; and after taking leave, returned home greatly crestfallen.

Source B letter from Hugh de Cressingham to Edward, 24 July 1297

Source B

Sire, at the time when this letter was made not a penny could be raised in your realm of Scotland by any means. You order me that if any Scotsmen have paid to your enemies rents which ought to have been paid to you, I should tax them again and pay the money to you. I will do so, sire, as speedily as I shall be able. But, sire, by far the greater part of your counties of the realm of Scotland still do not have officers to do your work, owing to death, sieges, or imprisonment; and some have given up their districts, and others dare not return; and in some counties the Scots have appointed and established bailiffs and ministers, so that no county is in proper order, except Berwick and Roxburgh, and this only recently.

Source C from Colm McNamee, *The Wars of the Bruces* (1997)

Source C

This first Scottish raid into England after Bannockburn appears to mark a new departure in the evolution of a broader Scottish strategy. The strategy is characterised by increasingly long-distance raids deep into northern England; secondly by concentrated pressure on two strategic points, Carlisle and Berwick; and thirdly by involvement in Ireland. The strategy was only partially successful. The raids ravaged wide areas of northern England, but without forcing the English to make peace, though they were spectacularly successful in demoralising the northern communities and in breaking their will to resist and most especially in the extraction of cash in return for truce; of the strategic towns, only Berwick fell to the Scots and not until 1318, whereas Carlisle survived assault in 1315 and 1316; and intervention in Ireland ended in catastrophe in 1318.

Source D from Geoffrey W.S. Barrow, *Robert Bruce and the Community of the Realm of Scotland* (1988)

Source D

After Bannockburn the Scottish raids south of the Border became so regular and frequent that they amounted to the virtual subjection of England north of the Tees and involved the selective devastation of a still larger area. Northumberland suffered heavy depopulation and was reduced to a miserable anarchy. The Scottish leaders had three chief objects in view: revenue in blackmail; the recovery of Berwick, now the only Scottish town and castle left in enemy hands; and plain terrorization. All three objectives were achieved, though it took time. A conservative estimate would put Bruce's total income in blackmail at £20,000, Berwick fell in 1318. And throughout northern England the mere rumour of a Scottish raid sent peasants fleeing to the woods and moors while clergy and gentry made joint efforts, as best they could, to buy immunity.

Attempt all of the following questions.

1 How fully does **Source A** explain the relationship between John Balliol and Edward I?

   Use the source and your own knowledge.

   9

2 Evaluate the usefulness of **Source B** as evidence of Scottish resistance.

   In making a judgement you should refer to:
   - *the origin and possible purpose of the source*
   - *the content of the source*
   - *your own knowledge.*

   6

3 Compare the views of **Sources C** and **D** about the ambitions of Robert Bruce.

   Compare the content overall and in detail.

   5

[Now go to Section 2]

Section 1 – Scottish – 20 marks

Part B – The Age of the Reformation, 1542–1603

Study the sources below and attempt the questions which follow.

Source A from eds. W. Croft Dickinson, G. Donaldson, I.A. Milne, *A Source Book of Scottish History, Volume 2, 1424 to 1567* (1958)

Source A

In the latter part of 1566 Mary's increasing contempt for her husband was clear. Before the end of the year there was talk of divorce (which, however, would make the prince illegitimate) or of dissolving the marriage by more violent means; the archbishop of St Andrews was restored which would enable him to annul Bothwell's recent marriage to Lady Jane Gordon; pardons were granted to the murderers of Riccio, now Darnley's enemies; and substantial financial concessions were made to the reformed church. Darnley was murdered on the night of 9–10 February 1567. Bothwell, widely regarded as the murderer, obtained his divorce on 7 May, and on the 15th married Mary, to the scandal of even her warmest supporters (including the pope). The queen had formally taken the reformed church under her protection in April, and the marriage ceremony was protestant.

Source B from the Act establishing Presbyterian government of the Kirk (the 'Golden Act'), 1592

Source B

Our sovereign lord declares that it shall be lawful for the kirk every year to hold and keep general assemblies, if the king's majesty, or his commissioner, be present at the general assembly before the dissolving thereof, and appoint the time and place when and where the next general assembly shall be held. In case neither his majesty nor his said commissioner is present for the time, where the general assembly is being held, it shall be left to the general assembly to nominate and appoint time and place where the next general assembly shall be kept and held, as they have done in times past. Our lord also approves the synodal and provincial assemblies to be held by the kirk and ministry twice each year as they are presently done within every province of this realm.

Source C from eds. B. Harris, A. MacDonald, *Scotland: The Making and Unmaking of the Nation c.1100–1707, Volume 2: Early Modern Scotland c.1500–1707* (2007)

Source C

At some point in their lives, nearly all parishioners would have appeared before the kirk session, which was made up of elected elders and deacons. The elders did not just discipline those who misbehaved. Couples had to appear before the kirk session to ask that their marriage banns be proclaimed, and for their children to be baptised. Parish elders were a remarkably intrusive group of men. They snooped into the most personal aspects of people's lives. Scotland alone among Reformed nations abolished not just saints' days, but also celebrations, including Christmas and Easter. Only in Scotland was punishment by humiliation – the public 'performing' of repentance – carried out with a special piece of furniture, known as the penitents' seat, installed in every parish church with the express intention of making offenders more visible, more humiliated before their neighbours.

B

Source D from ed. I.B. Cowan, *Blast and Counterblast: Contemporary Writings on the Scottish Reformation* (1960)

Source D

The reformed church possessed a rudimentary organisation at congregational level. This body, known as the Kirk Session, consisted of elders and deacons, who were elected annually. Marriage was always celebrated in church and stern measures were taken against any who attempted to perform the ceremony privately. Banns were published three times in the parish church of both parties. Scotland also introduced the sinners' chair into church for the public humiliation of those parishioners who had offended the elders in some way. In their violent reaction against all innovations which they felt had little scriptural authority, the Reformers banned the observance of Festivals and Saint Days. In this matter, however, the opinion of the people was not in step with that of the church and many of the old festivals continued to be observed, although not necessarily from religious motives.

Attempt all of the following questions.

4   How fully does **Source A** explain the reign of Mary, 1561–1567?

    Use the source and your own knowledge.

    9

5   Evaluate the usefulness of **Source B** as evidence of the relationship between the Kirk and King James VI.

    In making a judgement you should refer to:

    • *the origin and possible purpose of the source*
    • *the content of the source*
    • *your own knowledge.*

    6

6   Compare the views of **Sources C** and **D** about the impact of the Reformation on Scotland, to 1603.

    Compare the content overall and in detail.

    5

[Now go to Section 2]

Section 1 – Scottish – 20 marks

Part C – The Treaty of Union, 1689–1740

> Study the sources below and attempt the questions which follow.

Source A from T.M. Devine, *Scotland's Empire, 1600–1815* (2004)

Source A

Initially, the proposed treaty alienated whole sections of Scottish opinion. The Kirk's alarm came from a real fear that by closer association with England, bishops would once again be imposed on the church. The Kirk became the most formidable opponent of the project. The treaty was also anathema to the Jacobites who rightly saw it as a major obstacle to their hope of one day restoring the Stuarts to the throne. Rampant Anglophobia continued well into 1706. Indeed, as the Scottish Parliament met in October 1706 at the start of the historic session to debate the draft articles of union, opposition had not subsided. Not all burghs and counties sent in petitions, but those that did were virtually all vehemently anti-union in content. Presbyterian ministers remained loud in their denunciations, vigorously condemning the proposed union as a profane threat to Scotland's historic reformed tradition.

Source B from a letter by James Ogilvy, 1st Earl of Seafield, to Godolphin, on the progress of the Articles of Union in the Scottish Parliament, 7 November 1706

Source B

My lord, since my last letter, we have carried by a majority of 32 votes the first article of the Union in the terms I formerly mentioned. However, we have had to make some alterations, which my Lord Commissioner and her majesties servants have found to be necessary so that the Union may be passed. I hope that we will be allowed to make these alterations. There have been several addresses against the Union presented to the Parliament, but what troubles me most is that from the Kirk, which declares the Union inconsistent with their principles, it being contrary to the Covenant that the bishops sit in the Parliament, but I have not seen it. I hear it is to be presented tomorrow. A copy of it shall be transmitted.

Source C from William Ferguson, *Scotland 1689 to the Present* (1965)

Source C

In spite of the optimistic forecasts of the unionist pamphleteers there was no sudden burst of prosperity after 1707. Sundry acts of parliament, indeed, were hostile to Scottish economic interests. Thus a bill intended to promote the Scottish linen interest was wrecked by the Irish linen lobby. And in 1712 it was proposed, in defiance of the Treaty of Union, to apply the malt tax to Scotland. By the end of that year Scottish parliamentary representatives of all parties agreed that the only solution to these ills was the repeal of the Union. The motion moving to dissolve the union was only narrowly defeated by four proxy votes; and this episode was not merely a shift in the endless manoeuvrings of interests and groups to exert pressure on the ministry. The Union was decidedly unpopular and not only in Scotland.

B

MARKS

Source D

Tax increases in Scotland were likely to bite deeply because the Scottish economy was still in the doldrums in the first decade after union, and those pamphleteers who had optimistically predicted an economic miracle were now proven wrong. In 1713 the House of Commons voted to apply the malt tax to Scotland in direct defiance of the provisions of the treaty itself. The fury was such that the tax was never properly enforced. To the Scots this was the climax of a whole stream of provocative actions which threatened to break the union. Scottish peers and members of the Commons came together and agreed that the only solution was repeal of the treaty. The motion was put by the Earl of Findlater in the House of Lords in June 1713 and was only narrowly defeated by four proxy votes.

Attempt all of the following questions.

7 How fully does **Source A** explain the arguments for and against union with England?   9
   Use the source and your own knowledge.

8 Evaluate the usefulness of **Source B** as evidence of the passing of the Act of Union.   6
   In making a judgement you should refer to:
   • *the origin and possible purpose of the source*
   • *the content of the source*
   • *your own knowledge.*

9 Compare the views of **Sources C** and **D** about the effects of the Union, to 1740.   5
   Compare the content overall and in detail.

[Now go to Section 2]

Higher History

Section 1 – Scottish – 20 marks

Part D – Migration and Empire, 1830–1939

Study the sources below and attempt the questions which follow.

Source A from Murdoch Rodgers in *Odyssey: Voices From Scotland's Recent Past* (1980), ed. Billy Kay

Source A

By 1914 the 'Ice-cream Parlour' had become a common feature in most towns and villages in Scotland. However, some of the local population looked upon the growth of ice-cream and Italian associations with considerable misgivings. The most vocal complaints came from the United Free Church who condemned the Italians for keeping their shops open on Sundays. Furthermore, it was alleged that moral as well as spiritual values were under threat. In evidence to the Parliamentary Committee on Sunday Trading in 1906, it was suggested that ice-cream parlours might be 'morally contaminating' as 'young people of both sexes congregate there after legitimate hours and sometimes misbehave themselves.' The police also added their weight to the opposition. Standards of behaviour, it was claimed, were low and were 'acceptable only to their alien owners and to people of loose moral habits'.

Source B from a letter by James Mouat Garriock in Vancouver, Canada to his mother in Lerwick, Scotland in 1891

Source B

This letter is different from what is normally published at home, but it is the truth. The journey over from Scotland was long, but uneventful. After my arrival I tried hard for work, but without success. After about six weeks, I found a job for only two days surveying the harbour and bay but this made me ill because of the sewage on the shore. I have had a little work in checking goods from ships but this occurs only once a month. Many who have the means are leaving as fast as they can and going to the States, where there is more employment.

Source C from Esther Breitenbach, *Empire and Scottish Society* (2009)

Source C

Personal connections, press coverage and the missionary movement in churches all combined to impress on Scots that they were part of an imperial enterprise. Empire had a significant impact on Scots at home. Over time, the numbers of people choosing active engagement with empire grew. This engagement was seen in two main ways – firstly in religious and charitable concerns and secondly, in an enthusiasm for imperialism itself. Among the many Scots for whom Empire provided jobs or professions, missionaries formed an important group. This shaped perceptions of the Empire and of the colonial peoples, and of the role of Scots in the 'civilising mission'. Through the development of a Scottish missionary tradition and creation of national heroes amongst missionary figures – representations which were also used in the secular sphere – a claim of specific Scots contribution to Empire was generated and widely endorsed.

Source D from T.M. Devine, *To the Ends of the Earth: Scotland's Global Diaspora* (2011)

Source D

So intense was the Scottish engagement with empire that it had an impact on almost every nook and cranny of Scottish life. Scottish society had strong ties to empire. In the nineteenth century, Scottish professionals penetrated every corner of the Empire, so that in virtually every area of employment, Scots had a high profile. The British Empire also had a potent influence on Scottish national identity. Before 1914, Scottish patriotism was not in conflict with the Union, but integrated with it. It was commonly asserted that imperial expansion only occurred after Union, hence it was a partnership with England in which the Scots had played their full part. The link between empire and the national churches also seemed strong. The cult of David Livingstone reached its height in the 1920s when small donations by ordinary Scots financed a memorial centre in Blantyre.

Attempt all of the following questions.

10 How fully does **Source A** explain the experience of immigrants in Scotland?

Use the source and your own knowledge.

9

11 Evaluate the usefulness of **Source B** as evidence of the impact of Scots on the Empire.

In making a judgement you should refer to:

- *the origin and possible purpose of the source*
- *the content of the source*
- *your own knowledge.*

6

12 Compare the views of **Sources C** and **D** on the impact of empire on Scotland, up to 1939.

Compare the sources overall and in detail.

5

[Now go to Section 2]

Section 1 – Scottish – 20 marks

Part E – The Impact of the Great War, 1914–1928

Study the sources below and attempt the questions which follow.

Source A from Trevor Royle, *The Flowers of the Forest* (2006)

Source A

By the summer of 1915 it was not uncommon to see women in highly visible roles at bank or post office counters, or working as ticket collectors. Edinburgh reported a sharp increase in women's employment in the capital. The process of putting women into jobs vacated by men was known as 'substitution' and by 1917 it was estimated that one in three working women were substituting male workers' jobs. However, their efforts did not mean that they received equal pay: a male postman received 35 shillings a week while his female counterpart received 10 shillings less. However, as many parts of commercial and industrial life would have ground to a halt without women, the employment of women was a bonus for the war effort.

Source B from an account by Dorothy Wiltshire, a young Scottish woman during the First World War, in the 1970s

Source B

I do remember shortages of food because my mother wasn't well and couldn't go out to the shops. We weren't rationed in those days and you had to be out quite early. When you got to the top of the queue very often the door was shut and that was all for the day. So it meant that many a time I came home and there was very little for a meal. But she would get a sheep's head from the butcher, and make soup with the bone and a lovely pie with vegetables with the meat. During my lunch hour I used to go to try and get some shopping for mother but at that time nearly all the food was finished – even butter and marge. It was a very difficult time as far as food was concerned.

Source C from I.G.C. Hutchison, *Scottish Politics in the Twentieth Century* (2000)

Source C

'Red Clydeside' is at best only a partial explanation of the rise of Labour after 1918. It is uncertain how many of those involved were socialist revolutionaries. Another element sees the rents question, rather than factory unrest as vital as it mobilised a wider spectrum of occupations and also propelled women to prominence. The ILP lay behind the rents campaign, and the electoral breakthrough in Scotland can be related to the housing issue. Influences other than war-time tensions on the Clyde helped Labour in the early 1920s. Low numbers of military men voted in 1918 so the victory in 1922 may owe more to the higher turnout. A major bonus for Labour was the support of the Irish Catholic community. In 1918, 10 Catholics stood as candidates for Labour in Glasgow and the community's newspaper, the Glasgow Observer, was strongly pro-Labour.

Source D from Ewen A. Cameron, *Impaled Upon A Thistle* (2010)

Source D

The dominant image of Labour comes from the 'Red Clydesiders' elected in 1922. But even the 1922 election was not all it seemed: there was a strong strand of social conservatism in those elected, traditional attitudes to women for example. Greater stress can be placed on the role of Labour during the Great War rather than the 1918 'fourth Reform Act'. It is not certain that all voters got to vote in 1918, residence requirements acted against many younger middle class men getting the vote. The politics of housing played a more important role in Labour's breakthrough: the wartime rent strikes raised the profile of Labour's distinctive message. Irish support was also relevant to Labour's rise. By 1922, there was a resolution to the 'Irish question' and the ILP's support for state funded education for Catholics was important.

Attempt all of the following questions.

13 How fully does **Source A** explain the on Scottish society?

Use the source and your own knowledge.

9

14 Evaluate the usefulness of **Source B** as evidence of the impact of the war on food and rationing.

In making a judgement you should refer to:
- *the origin and possible purpose of the source*
- *the content of the source*
- *your own knowledge.*

6

15 Compare the views of **Sources C** and **D** about the reasons for the rise of the Labour Party in Scotland after 1918.

Compare the sources overall and in detail.

5

[Now go to Section 2]

Section 2 – British – 20 marks

Attempt ONE question from the part you have chosen.

Part A – Church, State and Feudal Society, 1066–1406

16 To what extent was the most important role of the Church in medieval society political?

20

17 How important was the impact of the Civil War in the increase of central royal power in the reign of Henry II of England?

20

18 *Changing social attitudes were the most important reason for the decline of feudal society.*
How valid is this view?

20

Part B – The Century of Revolutions, 1603–1702

19 To what extent were the policies of Charles I in Scotland successful?

20

20 How important was Cromwell's dominance as a reason for the failure to find an alternative form of government, 1649–1658?

20

21 *The Revolution Settlement of 1688–1702 successfully altered the balance of power between the monarchy and parliament.*
How valid is this view?

20

Part C – The Atlantic Slave Trade

22 How important was the slave trade to the British economy?

20

23 *The slave trade had a negative impact on African societies.*
How valid is this view?

20

24 To what extent was the decline in the economic importance of slavery the main reason for the success of the abolitionist campaign in 1807?

20

Part D – Britain, 1851–1951

25 *By 1928, Britain had successfully become a democratic country.*
How valid is this view?

20

26 How important were the social surveys of Booth and Rowntree as a reason why the Liberals introduced social welfare reforms, 1906–1914?

20

27 To what extent were the Labour social welfare reforms, 1945–1951, effective in meeting the needs of the British people?

20

B

Part E – Britain and Ireland, 1900–1985

28 To what extent did the First World War have an impact on Ireland?

20

29 How important were divisions in the Republican movement as a reason for the outbreak of the Irish Civil War?

20

30 *The role of the British Army was the most important obstacle to peace between 1968 and 1985.*

How valid is this view?

20

[Now go to Section 3]

Section 3 – European and World – 20 marks

Attempt ONE question from the part you have chosen.

Part A – The Crusades, 1071–1204

31 How important were overpopulation and famine as motives for Christians from different classes to take the cross?

20

32 *The Christian defeat at Hattin was the main reason for the fall of Jerusalem in 1187.* How valid is this view?

20

33 *The crusading ideal declined in the years up to the Fourth Crusade in 1204.* How valid this view?

20

Part B – The American Revolution, 1763–1787

34 How important was the Boston Massacre as a reason for the colonists' moves towards independence?

20

35 To what extent did the League of Armed Neutrality change the global nature of the war?

20

36 *The political impact of the American Revolution was significant.* How valid is this view?

20

Part C – The French Revolution, to 1799

37 *The effects of the American Revolution were the main reason for the French Revolution in 1789.*
How valid is this view?

20

38 How important was the role of Robespierre as a reason for the Terror, 1792–1795?

20

39 To what extent did the urban workers gain most from the French Revolution?

20

Part D – Germany, 1815–1939

40 *By 1850 supporters of nationalism had made significant progress in their aims.* How valid is this view?

20

41 How important were the actions of Napoleon III in the unification of Germany, by 1871?

20

42 To what extent was the crushing of opposition the main reason why the Nazis were able to stay in power, 1933–1939?

20

B

Part E – Italy, 1815–1939

43 *Nationalism in Italy had significantly grown by 1850.*
How valid is this view?

20

44 To what extent was the unification of Italy achieved by 1870 due to the role of Cavour?

20

45 How important were social controls as a reason why the Fascists were able to stay in power, 1922–1939?

20

Part F – Russia, 1881–1921

46 How important was discontent with repressive government and its policies as a cause of the 1905 revolution?

20

47 To what extent was the February Revolution in 1917 caused by the role of Tsar Nicholas II?

20

48 *The role of Trotsky was the main reason for the victory of the Reds in the Civil War.*
How valid is this view?

20

Part G – USA, 1918–1968

49 How important were the activities of the Ku Klux Klan as an obstacle to the achievement of civil rights for black people up to 1941?

20

50 *The New Deal was a success for America in the 1930s.*
How valid is this view?

20

51 To what extent was the Civil Rights movement effective in meeting the needs of black Americans, up to 1968?

20

Part H – Appeasement and the Road to War, to 1939

52 How important were pacts and alliances in the methods used by Germany and Italy to pursue their foreign policies from 1933?

20

53 To what extent was British foreign policy successful in containing Fascist aggression, 1935 to March 1938?

20

54 *Changing attitudes to Appeasement were the main reason for the outbreak of war in 1939.*
How valid is this view?

20

Part I – The Cold War, 1945–1989

55 *Soviet policy that was used to control Eastern Europe was successful.*
How valid is this view?

20

56 To what extent did the USA lose the war in Vietnam due to the strengths of North Vietnam?

20

57 How important was Western economic strength as a reason for the end of the Cold War?

20

[End of Practice Paper B]

Higher
History

Duration: 2 hours and 20 minutes

Total marks: 60

Section 1 – Scottish – 20 marks

Attempt ONE part.

Section 2 – British – 20 marks

Attempt ONE question from the part you have chosen.

Section 3 – European and World – 20 marks

Attempt ONE question from the part you have chosen.

In the exam, you must write your answers clearly in the answer booklet provided and clearly identify the question number you are attempting.

Use **blue** or **black** ink.

Section 1 – Scottish

Attempt ONE part.

Parts

Section 2 – British

Attempt ONE part.

Parts

C

Section 1 – Scottish – 20 marks

Part A – The Wars of Independence, 1249–1328

Study the sources below and attempt the questions which follow.

Source A from Geoffrey W.S. Barrow, *Robert Bruce and the Community of the Realm of Scotland* (1988)

Source A

The bad news from the north reached the Scottish government early in October. Queen Margaret had died in Orkney on her way to Scotland. There was no obvious successor and the news of her death set in train a struggle for the throne between a number of claimants of whom two were of outstanding importance: Robert Bruce the elder and John Balliol. The important lords were gathering at Perth. Robert Bruce, in his seventieth year or thereabouts, had arrived unexpectedly with a strong body of armed men, and it was rumoured that his friends the earls of Mar and Atholl were raising their forces. At the same time John Balliol was styling himself 'heir of Scotland'. It looked as though the guardianship would collapse and the question of succession be settled by open war between the claimants.

Source B letter from Bishop William Fraser to Edward I of England, 7 November 1290

Source B

Your ambassadors and the Scottish ambassadors and also some nobles of the kingdom of Scotland met at Perth. But a sad rumour spread among the people that our lady was dead and because of this the kingdom of Scotland is troubled and the community perplexed. When the rumour was heard Sir Robert Bruce came to the meeting with a large number of followers to consult with some who were there. We do not yet know what he intends to do or how he intends to act. But the earls of Mar and Atholl are collecting their army and some other nobles of the land have been persuaded to join their party. Because of that there is a fear of a general war and a large-scale slaughter unless the Most High, through your active involvement and good offices, administer a quick cure.

Source C from Michael Lynch, *Scotland: A New History* (1991)

Source C

Details of the origins of the revolt of 1297 have long been known to historians. The decisive move was the linking up of opposition in Moray with a rising in the shires to the east of the Spey and in the important burgh of Aberdeen. The leader of the northern rising was Andrew Murray, the son and heir of a leading baron. Murray died in November 1297, probably of wounds sustained at the battle of Stirling Bridge. It was the first and the last pitched battle which William Wallace won. Neither a general nor a guerrilla by instinct, Wallace deserves to be remembered as a patriot and a charismatic warlord. That was why the community entrusted him with sole guardianship of the realm in the spring of 1298.

C

Source D

In the year 1308, John Comyn and Philip Mowbray with a great many Scots and English, were again gathered together at Inverurie. When king Robert heard of this he commanded his men to arm him and set him on horseback. When this had been done he advanced with his army against the enemy to the battle ground. When the opposing party saw him they were all afraid and fled. When the rout was over and the enemy was overthrown and scattered, King Robert ravaged the earldom of Buchan with fire; and of the people, he killed whom he would, and to those whom he would have live, he granted life and peace. And from that day the king gained ground and became ever more strong himself; while the opposition was daily losing confidence.

Attempt all of the following questions.

1 Compare **Sources A** and **B** about the succession problem in Scotland.

Compare the content overall and in detail.

5

2 How fully does **Source C** explain the role of William Wallace and Scottish resistance?

Use the source and your own knowledge.

9

3 Evaluate the usefulness of **Source D** as evidence of the reasons for the rise and triumph of Robert the Bruce.

In making a judgement you should refer to:

* *the origin and possible purpose of the source*
* *the content of the source*
* *your own knowledge.*

6

[Now go on to Section 2]

Section 1 – Scottish – 20 marks

Part B – The Age of the Reformation, 1542–1603

Source A from Gordon Donaldson, *Scotland: James V–James VII* (1994)

Source A

In St John's Church at Perth, on Thursday 11 May, Knox preached a sermon which led to a riot in which church ornaments and furnishings were destroyed. The houses of the Black and Grey Friars and the Carthusian monks were also destroyed. The Lords of the Congregation were able to occupy Perth on 25 June and to advance by Stirling, to Edinburgh, where they arrived at the end of the month. At Edinburgh, the town council, hired sixty men to protect the church of St Giles, but their concern was more for the preservation of the fabric than for the retention of the old ceremonies, and John Knox was appointed minister of the capital on 7 July. English troops under Lord Grey entered Scotland in support of the Congregation, at the end of March.

Source B from Michael Lynch, *Scotland: A New History* (1991)

Source B

The Reformation crisis of 1559 was sparked off by a riot in Perth. The town's religious houses were sacked within nine days of Knox's return to Scotland from France and Geneva on 2 May. By July the Congregation, now comprising a cross section of society from nobles to lairds and burgesses, had 'purged' a series of towns in central Scotland, including St Andrews and Dundee, and entered the capital, where Knox was installed as its first Protestant minister on the seventh of the month. Mary of Guise was deposed as Regent in October 1559 and a provisional government established which turned to England for military aid while still protesting its loyalty to Mary and Francis as its sovereigns. The arrival of an English fleet in January 1560 and an army two months later proved to be the decisive factor.

Source C from A.R. MacDonald, *The Jacobean Kirk, 1567–1625* (1998)

Source C

By the middle of 1592, the fragile relationship between the Crown and the Kirk was once again clear. Although there had been episodes of co-operation, the period between the fall of the Arran regime and the 'Golden Act' was characterised by tension. The king did not see the religious and ecclesiastical world in the terms in which most of the Kirk saw it. James could talk of the necessity to root out Catholicism and to promote the Protestant religion, however, he did not share the fervour which most of the Kirk appears to have borne against Catholicism. This factor unified the Kirk, and their belief that it was the ministers' job to ensure the godly conduct of government, created an atmosphere of conflict with the Crown rooted in the king's disinclination, as far as the Kirk saw it, to purify the nation.

C

Source D from *The First Book of Discipline* (1560)

Source D

Seeing that God has determined that his Kirk here on earth shall be taught not by Angels, but by men; and seeing that men are borne ignorant of God, and of all godliness. Of necessity it is that you be most careful for the education, and godly up-bringing of the youth of this realm. We ought to be careful that they have knowledge to profit from that which ought to be most dear to us, the kirk and our Lord Jesus. Of necessity therefore we judge it, that in the towns every kirk have one Schoolmaster appointed, such a one at least as is able to teach Grammar, and the Latin tongue. In the countryside, either the reader or the minister there appointed, must take care over the children and youth of the parish, to instruct them.

Attempt all of the following questions.

4   Compare the views of **Sources A** and **B** about the Reformation of 1560.   5
    Compare the sources overall and in detail.

5   How fully does **Source C** explain the relationship between the monarch and Kirk
    in the reign of James VI?   9
    Use the source and your own knowledge.

6   Evaluate the usefulness of **Source D** as evidence of the impact of the Reformation
    on Scotland, to 1603.   6
    In making a judgement you should refer to:
    - *the origin and possible purpose of the source*
    - *the content of the source*
    - *your own knowledge.*

[Now go on to Section 2]

Section 1 – Scottish – 20 marks

Part C – The Treaty of Union, 1689–1740

Study the sources below and attempt the questions which follow.

Source A from Christopher A. Whatley, *The Union of 1707* (1998)

Source A

Riding on a rising tide of national anti-English fervour, and recognising that the regal union was no longer working, the parliament of 1703 was less compliant than its predecessor and against the wishes of the pro-Hanovarian Court, passed an Act of Security, which meant that Scotland would not be bound to support England's nomination for a successor to Queen Anne. This was followed by a second declaration of Scottish freedom from the dictates of the Court, the Act anent (concerning) Peace and War, which reserved to the Scottish parliament the right after Anne's death to declare war and conclude peace. Economic warfare was opened with the Wine act. This was followed in 1704 with the passage of an act which forbade the import but allowed the export of wool, steps which were judged by English woollen merchants to be hostile.

Source B from T.M. Devine, *Scotland's Empire, 1600–1815* (2004)

Source B

An Act of Security, passed in open defiance of the Court party, stated that the Scots Parliament had the right to decide on Queen Anne's successor and that England and Scotland could not have the same sovereign in the future unless the London parliament granted the Scots 'free communication of trade and the liberty of the plantations'. The governing ministry was then forced to accept the equally contentious Act anent (concerning) Peace and War, which gave the Scots Parliament the right to declare war and make peace if the two nations continued to share a sovereign after Anne's death. A third measure, the Wine Act, formally permitted trade with France during the war. The Wool Act passed during the session the following year, was regarded as openly hostile by England in allowing the export and prohibiting the import of wool.

Source C from Michael Lynch, *Scotland: A New History* (1991)

Source C

The Scottish parliament opened on 3 October 1706, but the opposition, which embarked on delaying tactics from the outset, succeeded in postponing serious consideration of the first of the Articles for a month. Article 1 (on the principle of incorporating union) was passed on 4 November by 116 votes to 83. It was as near as the opposition ever came to opposing a major clause. The majority had been less than the court had expected, and the ministry on the same day brought before the House a bill guaranteeing the Presbyterian settlement of the Church. The Kirk was bought off which was a sign that it still had a powerful voice in Scottish life, but that its role in politics was now to sit on the sidelines. On 16 January 1707, the Treaty was ratified with a majority of 43.

Source D from a letter by George Lockhart of Carnwath to the Old Pretender, 18 December 1725

Source D

Arms, ammunition, saddles, money, are all needed here. It is also very necessary to send a good number of officers. I have mentioned this because your friends are not so numerous as they were in 1715. However, the opposition to the Union daily increases and that is the way in which Scotsmen will be roused to help your cause. Now I am fully persuaded the better part of the English are far from thinking the union beneficial to either country. It will be helpful for the King to gratify his friends in Scotland, and thereby advance your interest. In order to do this, as soon as your army lands, a manifesto should be published with respect to religion and containing an assurance of your design to maintain the two kingdoms in their ancient independent state by dissolving the union.

Attempt all of the following questions.

7 Compare the views of **Sources A** and **B** about worsening relations between Scotland and England.

Use the sources and your own knowledge.

5

8 How fully does **Source C** explain the passing of the Act of Union?

Compare the content overall and in detail.

9

9 Evaluate the usefulness of **Source D** as evidence of the effects of the Union, to 1740.

In making a judgement you should refer to:

- *the origin and possible purpose of the source*
- *the content of the source*
- *your own knowledge.*

6

[Now go on to Section 2]

Section 1 – Scottish – 20 marks

Part D – Migration and Empire, 1830–1939

Study the sources below and attempt the questions which follow.

Source A from Marjory Harper, *Adventurers & Exiles: The Great Scottish Exodus* (2003)

Source A

Scots were lured overseas by a variety of economic, social and cultural incentives. The recurring promise of independence through landownership was a powerful attraction, particularly to those whose security and prospects had been eroded by the commercialisation of farming in Scotland. For those with money to spare, foreign fields offered an attractive opportunity for the investment of both financial and human resources. The skilled working class sought higher wages and better working conditions overseas, especially in the United States. Throughout the nineteenth century guidebooks and newspapers poured forth a torrent of advice and encouragement, generally trying to steer emigrants in the direction of Canada. The most effective encouragement came from the satisfied emigrant's letter home, particularly if it came with money or a prepaid ticket. But for emigrants lacking overseas contacts, professional emigration agents were instrumental in deciding on destinations.

Source B from T.M. Devine, *To the Ends of the Earth: Scotland's Global Diaspora* (2011)

Source B

Emigration was not caused so much by poverty – as by the lure of opportunity. Throughout the nineteenth and twentieth centuries, Canada and Australasia were magnets for those who wished to work the land, but rural tradesmen and industrial workers tended to opt more for the USA. A primary incentive was the possibility of owning land that was cheap to acquire and plentiful whereas in Scotland even wealthy farmers were dependent on their landlords. This can be seen in the weekly *People's Journal*, Scotland's most popular periodical. It was specially designed to promote the interests of the working classes and virtually every issue had articles on emigration worldwide, providing advice on changing employment conditions and opportunities available overseas for people from both town and country. Most of those who left may have had few resources but they had some modest means.

Source C from T.M. Devine, *To the Ends of the Earth: Scotland's Global Diaspora* (2011)

Source C

There is also the issue of Scottish impact on new lands. Many Scots emigrants like those from England had a decided advantage over the peasant masses that flocked across the Atlantic in their millions from Ireland, Central and Eastern Europe and the Mediterranean in the course of the nineteenth century. The economic, social and religious development of Scotland ensured that its emigrants spoke mainly Scots–English, were usually Protestant, literate and often highly or semi-skilled in the practices of an advanced industrial and agrarian economy. They were also drawn abroad for the most part, not by crisis or disaster, but by a desire to exploit opportunities and achieve aspirations not easily satisfied at home. Moreover, unlike many other nationalities, Scots rarely experienced systematic prejudice or discrimination in the new lands and offered them skills which were much in demand there.

Source D from an account by J. Tobias in 1976, who grew up in the Gorbals, Glasgow

Source D

My parents had a hard life at the beginning. Father told us that he used to get up at maybe three to work. They'd no clock, nothing! The poverty was absolutely diabolical. He was a blacksmith and then worked for twelve years for a company and the boss was a real slave driver! Well he went to a Jewish company of merchants and they supplied him with an anvil, bellows and equipment to start up on his own. They supplied him with steel to do the work and some of the merchants gave him a little credit. He started his own business in 1900 in MacFarlane Street in the Gallowgate and many a week he'd come home with hardly a penny in his pocket after he'd paid one or two bills. It wasn't easy going.

Attempt all of the following questions.

10 Compare **Sources A** and **B** about the reasons for emigration of Scots.
Compare the sources overall and in detail.

5

11 How fully does **Source C** explain the impact of Scots emigrants on the Empire?
Use the source and your own knowledge.

9

12 Evaluate the usefulness of **Source D** as evidence of the contribution of Jewish immigrants to Scotland, to 1939.
In making a judgement you should refer to:
* *the origin and possible purpose of the source*
* *the content of the source*
* *your own knowledge.*

6

[Now go on to Section 2]

Section 1 – Scottish – 20 marks

Part E – The Impact of the Great War, 1914–1928

Study the sources below and attempt the questions which follow.

Source A from Derek Young, *Scottish Voices From the Great War* (2001)

Source A

As war was declared, men rushed to enlist. Their reasons were as complex and varied as their backgrounds. Nowhere was this more evident than in Scotland, which although small in size, provided a higher proportion of volunteers than any other home country. Some enlisted out of a sense of enthusiastic patriotism or duty. Others saw it as an opportunity for adventure, with memories of the short-term service in the Boer war still fresh in their mind. Others saw it as relief from unemployment or the chance of escape, however temporary, from a life of drudgery. Whatever the reason, men came forward in unprecedented numbers. The demand for manpower was immediate, with Lord Kitchener making a direct appeal to the patriotism of the people of Scotland. This call for manpower was responded to enthusiastically, with crowds of volunteers filling the recruiting offices.

Source B from Ewen A. Cameron, *Impaled Upon A Thistle* (2010)

Source B

At the outbreak of the war there was a consensus that the crisis had to be faced with a volunteer army. An appeal was made by Lord Kitchener, for new recruits to be organised into new battalions of existing regiments. Recruitment was a mixture of individual decisions, information and opportunity. The first few weeks of the war saw large numbers of recruits, but this was not sustained. 54% of all the Scottish volunteers of 1914–1915 had enlisted by the end of 1914. This was the period in which influential institutions and social groups were most enthusiastic about the war. It has been suggested that the initial surge of recruits in 1914 can be explained by the negative impact of the war on certain parts of the economy. There was a pool of recruits from these industries because of the threat or reality of unemployment.

Source C from Clive H. Lee, *Scotland and the Great War* (1999)

Source C

The West of Scotland played an important part in military production. The Clyde contained 90% of Scottish shipbuilding and marine engineering in 1914 and proved an ideal location, secure from the threat of the German navy. The three main naval dockyards came under Admiralty control and this was extended to the rest of the industry under the Munitions of War Act 1915. The Great War created considerable activity in Scotland's heavy industries, especially in the Glasgow and Lanarkshire areas. Apart from the increases in production and employment, there were technological gains, for example, in shipbuilding where production processes were simplified by the Ministry of Shipping. In addition, wartime pressure to increase the speed of production led to the introduction of pneumatic and electrical tools. There were similar advances in the munitions industry, again under central control.

C

Source D from an oral account by Robert Irvine, a Scottish soldier from Glasgow, remembering his service during the First World War in 1963

Source D

Some time after I was in France news of the activities of the union shop stewards were filtering through to the soldiers in the trenches. The married men in particular were a wee bit resentful, because they were getting letters from their womenfolk that the landlords were putting up rents and so forth. Gradually this resentment spread to the young unmarried members of the Forces. I believe it was confirmed later that General Haig had written to Lloyd George: 'For heaven's sake, resolve your war there in Glasgow and Scotland or you'll lose the battle here.' The resentment was growing to such a pitch. There is no doubt that Clyde Worker's Committee and shop stewards did have some impact on the troops fighting because the more we experienced the folly of war, the more we appreciated the work that our comrades at home were doing at home. We realised that we were fighting for the capitalists while the shop stewards at home were fighting for the workers.

Answer all of the following questions.

13 Compare the views of **Sources A** and **B** about voluntary recruitment in Scotland at the beginning of the war.

   Compare the sources overall and in detail.

   5

14 How fully does **Source C** explain the wartime effects of the First World War on Scottish industry and the economy?

   Use the source and your own knowledge.

   9

15 Evaluate the usefulness of **Source D** as evidence of the impact of the war on Scottish politics.

   In making a judgement you should refer to:
   - *the origin and possible purpose of the source*
   - *the content of the source*
   - *your own knowledge.*

   6

[Now go to Section 2]

Section 2 – British – 20 marks

Attempt ONE question from the part you have chosen.

Part A – Church, State and Feudal Society, 1066–1406

16 *David I was successful in his attempts to increase royal power in Scotland.*
How valid is this view?

20

17 To what extent were King John's attempts to increase royal authority successful in England?

20

18 How important was the growth of towns as a reason for the decline of feudal society?

20

Part B – The Century of Revolutions, 1603–1702

19 *Religious issues were the main reason for the outbreak of civil war in England.*
How valid is this view?

20

20 How important was the role of parliament as a reason for the Revolution Settlement of 1688–1689?

20

21 To what extent were the changes brought about by the Revolution Settlement, 1688–1702, significant?

20

Part C – The Atlantic Slave Trade

22 *Financial considerations were the most important factor governing relations between slaves and their owners.*
How valid is this view?

20

23 How important was the slave rebellion in Saint-Domingue as an obstacle to abolition?

20

24 To what extent was the effect of slave resistance the main reason for the success of the abolitionist campaign in 1807?

20

Part D – Britain, 1851–1951

25 *Changing attitudes to women did more than any other reason to achieve votes for women in 1918.*
How valid is this view?

20

26 To what extent were the social reforms of the Liberal Government effective in solving the main causes of poverty?

20

27 To what extent were the Labour social welfare reforms, 1945–1951, successful in creating a welfare state 'from the cradle to the grave'?

20

Part E – Britain and Ireland, 1900–1985

28 *The position of Unionists in the North was the most important obstacle to peace, up to the Anglo-Irish Treaty, 1918–1921.*

How valid is this view?

20

29 How important was the role of the IRA as a reason for the developing crisis in Northern Ireland by 1968?

20

30 To what extent was the role of the Irish government the main obstacle to peace, 1968–1985?

20

Section 3 – European and World – 20 marks

> Attempt ONE question from the part you have chosen.

Part A – The Crusades, 1071–1204

31 How important was aid from Byzantium as a reason for the success of the First Crusade?

20

32 *Richard and Saladin were both great diplomatic and military leaders during the Third Crusade.*

How valid is this view?

20

33 To what extent did the crusading ideal decline in the years up to the Fourth Crusade in 1204?

20

Part B – The American Revolution, 1763–1787

34 To what extent did the views of George III represent British opinion towards the conflict in the colonies?

20

35 How important was British military inefficiency in explaining why the colonists won the American War of Independence?

20

36 *The American Revolution made little political impact.*
How valid is this view?

20

Part C – The French Revolution, to 1799

37 How important was the character of Louis XVI as a reason for the failure of constitutional monarchy, 1789–1792?

20

38 *Political instability was the most important reason for the establishment of the Consulate.*

How valid is this view?

20

39 *The peasantry was most affected by the French Revolution.*
How valid is this view?

20

Part D – Germany, 1815–1939

40 *Austrian strength was the most important obstacle to German unification, 1815–1850.*
How valid is this view?

20

41 To what extent were the weaknesses of the Weimar Republic the main reason why the Nazis achieved power in 1933?

20

42 How important was propaganda as a reason why the Nazis were able to stay in power, 1933–1939?

20

C

Part E – Italy, 1815–1939

43 How important were social, economic and cultural divisions as an obstacle to Italian unification, 1815–1850?

20

44 *The role of Mussolini was the most important reason why the Fascists achieved power in Italy, 1919–1925.*
How valid is this view?

20

45 To what extent was foreign policy the main reason why the Fascists were able to stay in power, 1922–1939?

20

Part F – Russia, 1881–1921

46 *Between 1905 and 1914, the Tsarist government successfully regained its authority.*
How valid is this view?

20

47 To what extent were the weaknesses of the Provisional Government the main reason for the success of the October Revolution, 1917?

20

48 *Disunity among the Whites was the main reason for the victory of the Reds in the Civil War.*
How valid is this view?

20

Part G – USA, 1918–1968

49 *Weaknesses in the US banking system were the main reason for the economic crisis of 1929–1933.*
How valid is this view?

20

50 How important was the experience of black servicemen in the Second World War in the development of the Civil Rights campaign, after 1945?

20

51 *The Civil Rights movement was effective in meeting the needs of black Americans, up to 1968.*
How valid is this view?

20

Part H – Appeasement and the Road to War, to 1939

52 To what extent were attitudes to the Paris Peace Settlement the main reason for the British policy of appeasement, 1936–1938?

20

53 To what extent can it be argued that the Munich Agreement was a success?

20

54 *The occupation of Bohemia and the collapse of Czechoslovakia were the main reason for the outbreak of war in 1939.*
How valid is this view?

20

Part I – The Cold War, 1945–1989

55 To what extent was Khrushchev's domestic position the main reason for the Cuban Missile Crisis of 1962?

20

56 *The economic cost of the arms race was why the superpowers attempted to manage the Cold War, 1962–1979.*

How valid is this view?

20

57 How important was the defeat of the Soviet Union in Afghanistan as a reason for the end of the Cold War?

20

[End of Practice Paper C]

Higher
History

Practice Paper A

Section 1 – Scottish – 20 marks

Part A – The Wars of Independence, 1249–1328

1   **Evaluate the usefulness of** Source A **as evidence of the succession problem, 1286–1292. (6)**

In making a judgement you should refer to:

- *the origin and possible purpose of the source*
- *the content of the source*
- *your own knowledge.*

Candidates can be credited in a number of ways up to a maximum of 6 marks.

Examples of aspects of the source and relevant comments:

Aspect of the source	Possible comment
Author: Roger Brabazon	Useful as Brabazon was Edward's official spokesman so we can assume he was accurately delivering Edward's will.
Type of source: speech	Useful as a speech is designed for broad consumption. Less useful as speeches are designed for effect and may have added emotive language.
Purpose: to convey Edward's views	Useful as Edward had been called in to deal with the issue of succession and this was a statement of his desire to solve the problem.
Timing: May 1291	Useful as the speech is a contemporary source that amply demonstrates the issues surrounding the succession problem in Scotland that followed the death of Alexander III.

Content	Possible comment
Our king, seeing that the peace of the kingdom of Scotland has been disturbed by the deaths of the king Alexander and of his children who were relatives of our king. He is greatly distressed by their deaths	Useful as Edward defines the problem that led to his being called to help the Scots. The deaths of Alexander III and his granddaughter had led to no ruler in Scotland.
wishing to do justice to all who can lay any claim to the inheritance of the kingdom of Scotland and to keep the peace among the people	Useful as Edward is indicating that there are a number of people who may have claims to the throne of Scotland and that he is seeking to behave justly.
our lord king asks for your agreement and for recognition of his overlordship	Useful as Edward sought to use the opportunity of the succession problem to further the English desire to dominate the British Isles.

Possible points of significant omission may include:

- Edward had previously claimed overlordship of Scotland, but Alexander III had pointedly refused to do homage for this, instead just acknowledging Edward's overlordship for lands Alexander held in England.
- The deaths of Alexander III and his granddaughter, the Maid of Norway, led to a crisis in leadership in Scotland.
- Differing groups emerged around the Bruce and Balliol families, with competing claims to the Scottish throne.
- Bishop Fraser of St Andrews called on Edward to intervene as he feared civil war because the Bruce faction were gathering their forces.
- The Scots appointed Guardians to run Scotland on the death of Alexander III.
- Edward used the succession crisis to further English claims on Scotland by refusing to recognise the Treaty of Birgham and putting pressure on the Scots by demanding they meet him at Norham. He threatened the Scots by mobilising the northern English armies.
- All nine serious claimants to the Scottish throne swore an oath of fealty to Edward as did the Guardians and other leading Scots nobles.

- The Great Cause eventually led Edward to decide on John Balliol as king in November 1292. Balliol was left in no doubt as to who was in charge as Edward demanded he do homage.

Any other valid points that meet the criteria described in the general marking instructions for this kind of question.

2 **Compare the views of** Sources B **and** C **about the relationship between King John of Scotland and Edward I of England. (5)**

Compare the content overall and in detail.

Candidates can be credited in a number of ways up to a maximum of 5 marks.

Possible points of comparison may include:

Overall: Sources B and C agree about the circumstances that led to a breakdown in relations between King John and Edward I of England in that both see the context being the English going to war with France. This led to demands for military service which in turn led to the creation of a Guardianship and alliance with France.

Source B	Source C
The international crisis which engulfed Edward in 1293–4 brought about the actual split between England and Scotland. War with France coincided with the outbreak of a rising in Wales in September 1294.	The breakdown of Anglo-French relations provided exactly the catalyst the Scots needed in order to make their bid for freedom.
A similar demand, framed in terms of personal service, had been sent in June 1294 to the King of Scots, ten of his earls and sixteen barons.	The demand for military service in France was a powerful reminder, not just to the Scots, but also to the recently conquered Welsh of Edward's success in extending and formalising English authority throughout the British Isles.
It was the reluctance of the Scots to become involved in the English war effort which drove them into an alliance with France.	The Scots did not rush to follow, partly because they wisely intended to play a card denied to the Welsh: an alliance with France. Also because Balliol was reluctant to commit himself to an all-out war with England.
This may have provoked the decision made at a parliament held in Stirling in July 1295 to give control to a council of twelve, made up equally of bishops, earls and barons.	In order to get round this reluctance, the political community adopted an extraordinary policy: they sidelined the king and installed a caretaker government of twelve guardians.

3 **How fully does** Source D **explain the reasons for the rise and triumph of Robert Bruce? (9)**

Use the source and your own knowledge.

Candidates can be credited in a number of ways up to a maximum of 9 marks.

A maximum of 2 marks may be given for answers which refer only to the source.

Possible points which may be identified in the source include:

- The Scots entered Northumberland at Norham and marched the length of the county to Newburn on the Tyne, where they stayed three days, devastating, burning and intimidating Newcastle.
- The Lanercost Chronicle goes on to say that they crossed into Durham, but there they did not burn much because the inhabitants bought them off.
- At Stainmore they carried off yet more cattle.
- At the Reycross they met with resistance organised by Andrew Harclay of the Carlisle garrison.

Possible points of significant omission may include:

- There were other raids into the North of England by Bruce or his lieutenants in 1315, 1316, 1318, 1322, 1323 and 1328.
- Raids may have brought wealth and exercised Bruce's soldiers, but they were less successful in bringing Edward II to the negotiating table. The south of England was where the main English magnates and wealth lay, and the north of England was a long way away for many of them.
- Bruce dealt with his internal enemies, the Comyn–Balliol faction, with decisive victory in the Battle of Inverurie and the subsequent destruction of the Comyn lands in Buchan.
- The death of Edward I in 1307 meant he was succeeded by Edward II, who was less interested in Scotland and was not the military leader that his father had been.
- Bruce was supported by key groups in Scotland such as the Church.
- The Scots defeated the English at Bannockburn and at the Battle of Old Byland where the English king was almost captured.

- The Scots undertook a campaign in Ireland under Edward Bruce and Thomas Randolph.
- There was diplomatic recognition of Bruce's kinship from France in 1310.
- The English government of Isabella and Mortimer was weakened after the removal of Edward II.
- The Treaty of Edinburgh recognised Robert the Bruce as King of Scotland in his own right.

Any other valid points that meet the criteria described in the general marking instructions for this kind of question.

Part B – The Age of the Reformation, 1542–1603

4   **Evaluate the usefulness of** Source A **as evidence of the reasons for the Reformation of 1560. (6)**

In making a judgement you should refer to:

- *the origin and possible purpose of the source*
- *the content of the source*
- *your own knowledge.*

Candidates can be credited in a number of ways up to a maximum of 6 marks.

Examples of aspects of the source and relevant comments:

Aspect of the source	Possible comment
Author: Archbishop Hamilton	Useful as he was a senior churchman, the Archbishop of St Andrews, as well as active in attempts to suppress Protestantism.
Type of source: address	Useful as it is a formal communication of concerns within the Roman Catholic Church about the condition of the church. Possibly less useful as Hamilton was an active opponent of Protestantism.
Purpose: to describe the condition of the church in the Merse (Scottish Borders)	Useful as it shows the condition of a church in the borders of Scotland.
Timing: primary source/contemporary	Useful as source is contemporary to the time when the Church in Scotland was coming under criticism over its decay.

Content	Possible comment
We discovered and saw with our own eyes, that a great many of the parish churches – their choirs as well as their naves – were wholly collapsed and, as it were, levelled to the ground. Others were partly ruined or threatened collapse with weak walls or missing roofs.	Useful as it describes the disrepair of many churches in Scotland.
Many of the churches did not even have a baptismal font, suitable clothing for the priests and instructions for the celebration of mass.	Useful as this indicates the impact of disrepair on the act of worship for parishioners.
This meant that their parishioners could not hear the divine services or masses as a good Christian should.	Useful as it shows that important religious acts of service were not happening.

Possible points of significant omission may include:

- There were weaknesses in the Catholic Church of Scotland: decline and corruption; pluralism had not been addressed. Minors were given top positions in the Church. The Crown and nobility took much of the Church revenues. Monarchs placed their offspring in important positions in the Church.
- Useful as further evidence of decline of the Catholic Church in terms of the act of worship.
- Useful as illustrates the impact of the decline on parishioners.
- There was a growth in Protestant belief between 1547 and 1559, especially in urban centres, such as Perth and Dundee.
- Leadership and preaching developed with the arrival of Knox from the continent in 1559. His preaching led to rioting in Perth, for example.
- There was growing dislike of Mary of Guise's pro-French policies.
- There were concerns from Protestants over Mary's marriage to the Dauphin of France.
- There was support for Protestantism from England on Elizabeth I's accession to the throne in 1558, in terms of Bibles in English and practical military help in the end.

- There was growth in support for Protestantism among important noble families.
- There was development of the Lords of the Congregation who were encourged by support from England.
- There were attacks on Catholic religious houses, such as in Perth in 1559.

Any other valid points of explanation that meet the criteria described in the general marking instructions for this kind of question.

5 Compare the views of Sources B **and** C **about the reign of Mary, 1561–1567. (5)**

Compare the sources overall and in detail.

Candidates can be credited in a number of ways up to a maximum of 5 marks.

Possible points of comparison may include:

Overall: Sources B and C agree that Mary returned to Scotland on the death of her husband, but that there was opposition from the likes of John Knox. They also agree that she was advised to tread carefully and could take mass privately. However, there is a little more detail in Source C, which points out that the mass was objected to by Protestants.

Source B	Source C
On 5 December 1560, however, Francis II died, and it was soon evident that Mary would return to Scotland to rule in person.	Within a month, it was clear to more astute diplomats amongst the Congregation, such as Maitland of Lethington, that she would return to Scotland.
There were those, including Knox and the Hamiltons, to whom a Catholic princess could not be acceptable ...	Knox preached a sermon on the following Sunday that one mass was more dangerous than the landing of ten thousand armed enemies and Mary's rule was not acceptable.
... while a more moderate group, headed by Lord James Stewart and Maitland of Lethington, sought compromise.	A climate of compromise established itself and Lord James's advice to Mary was to act carefully.
Mary was allowed to accept the Catholic Mass, but it must be done in private.	Mary and her household attended mass in her private chapel at Holyrood and Lord James barred the door against Protestant protesters.

6 How fully does Source D **explain the impact of the Reformation on Scotland, to 1603? (9)**

Use the source and your own knowledge.

Candidates can be credited in a number of ways up to a maximum of 9 marks.

A maximum of 2 marks may be given for answers which refer only to the source.

Possible points which may be identified in the source include:

- Protestants laid great stress upon education and insisted that all Ministers should be examined as to their qualifications.
- Emphasis was laid upon literacy and the use of books.
- Medieval Scotland possessed three universities; there was much room for improvement in the provision of schools, while university education urgently required an overhaul.
- Lack of finance proved to be an insurmountable obstacle to the realisation of these ambitious plans.

Possible points of significant omission may include:

- The aim of a school in every parish in Scotland was not achieved, but literacy of the population did improve.
- Clergy or readers were encouraged to educate the young in the word of God.
- The treatment of Catholic clergy was relatively lenient. They could keep two-thirds of their revenues for life.
- The Kirk Session sought to police the morals of their congregations, through the introduction of the sinning stool, for example. It was also concerned with control of events such as weddings.
- The observation of Catholic festivals was actively discouraged; for example, Easter and Christmas were abolished as festivals.
- There were changes to the act of worship as Protestant practices were introduced.
- English rather than Latin was used for services. The Bible was translated and was available in English, which made it accessible to those who spoke English.
- Changes to church buildings, such as the removal of statues, etc. were made. They were replaced with plain parish kirks.
- Scotland changed from being a Catholic country to being a Protestant one, albeit with a small Catholic minority.
- Trade with Europe continued throughout this period, for example with the Dutch.

Any other valid points that meet the criteria described in the general marking instructions for this kind of question.

Part C – The Treaty of Union, 1689–1740

7 **Evaluate the usefulness of** Source A **as evidence of worsening relations between Scotland and England. (6)**

In making a judgement you should refer to:
- *the origin and possible purpose of the source*
- *the content of the source*
- *your own knowledge.*

Candidates can be credited in a number of ways up to a maximum of 6 marks.

Examples of aspects of the source and relevant comments:

Aspect of the source	Possible comment
Author: Scottish Parliament	Useful as the Scottish Parliament represented the will of an albeit relatively select but significant group of the rich and well connected in Scotland.
Type of source: Act of Parliament	Useful as an official government Act of Parliament.
Purpose: to assert Scottish independence in the matter of the declaring of war	Useful as showed the general feeling of the politically powerful in Scotland at that time.
Timing: 1703	Useful as a contemporary Act of Parliament from the time when relations between England and Scotland were worsening.

Content	Possible comment
After her majesty's death, and failing heirs of her body, no person being king or queen of Scotland and England shall have the sole power of making war with any prince or state without the consent of parliament.	Useful as this statement shows the will of the Scottish Parliament that no future monarch of Scotland and England could take Scotland to war without the explicit consent of the parliament.
No declaration of war without consent shall be binding on the subjects of this kingdom ...	Useful as further reinforces the previous point that the people of Scotland will not go to war without the agreement of the Scottish Parliament.
Everything which relates to treaties of peace, alliance and commerce is left to the wisdom of the sovereign, with consent of the estates of parliament who shall declare the war.	Useful as it extends the point of the need for the consent of the Scottish Parliament from control over the declaration of war to the broader foreign policy of treaties, alliances and even commerce.

Possible points of significant omission may include:

- The Act anent (concerning) Peace and War was a response to the English Act of Settlement which had made members of the House of Hanover heirs to the throne of England.
- The Scots were concerned that rule by Hanoverians would lead to unwelcome Scottish involvement in German and continental wars.
- The Act of Security passed in 1704 asserted the right of the Scottish Parliament to appoint their own successor to Queen Anne who had died without an heir.
- The English Parliament retaliated with the Alien Act, removing Scottish trading privileges in England.
- Anti-English sentiment was seen in an incident in Worcester when an English ship was seized and its captain and two crew were executed.
- Illegal Scots trade with the colonies was affected by English enforcement of the Navigation Acts.
- The Wool Act allowed the export and prohibited the import of wool and was seen as an aggressive act against English trade.
- The Wine Act permitted trade with France during the War of the Spanish Succession and was not liked by the English.
- Effect of English wars: Scots were unhappy with the War of the Spanish Succession and its knock-on disruption to Scottish trade with the continent.
- Many Scots blamed the English for the failure of the Darien Scheme following instruction from William that no English assistance be given to the Scots after pressure from English trading groups.

Any other valid points that meet the criteria described in the general marking instructions for this kind of question.

8 **Compare the views of** Sources B **and** C **about the arguments against union between Scotland and England. (5)**

Compare the content overall and in detail.

Candidates can be credited in a number of ways up to a maximum of 5 marks.

Possible points of comparison may include:

Overall: Sources B and C agree in their arguments against the Union. They agree that the Union will bring increased taxation and have an effect on Scottish manufacturing. They also agree that union will influence Scotland, though there is disagreement here as Source B talks about religion, etc. while Source C talks in more abstract terms. There is agreement that union will have a bad effect on the Ancient Kingdom of Scotland.

Source B	Source C
… we judge going into this Treaty will bring an insupportable burden of taxation upon this land	I think I see the Honest Industrious Trades-man loaded with new Taxes and Impositions …
That it will prove ruining to our manufactures.	Petitioning for Encouragement to his Manufactures, and Answered by counter-petitions.
… it will expose our Religion, Laws and Liberties and consequently all that's valuable in our country, to be overthrown by England.	But above all, My Lord, I think I see our ancient country of Scotland, looking round about Her, seeing Her religious and legal freedoms treatened by England.
… one of the most ancient nations so long and gloriously defended by our worthy patriots will be ended and with fatal consequences of which we tremble to think about.	That in this our day, we should not mind the things that concern the very existence and well-being of our Ancient Kingdom, before they be hid from our Eyes.

9 **How fully does** Source D **explain the effects of the Union to 1740? (9)**

Use the source and your own knowledge.

Candidates can be credited in a number of ways up to a maximum of 9 marks.

A maximum of 2 marks may be given for answers which refer only to the source.

Possible points which may be identified in the source include:

- The free trade area which opened up after 1707 brought prosperity only to a few Scots.
- The most obvious symbol of economic success in post-Union Britain were the Glasgow tobacco lords, who by the 1750s controlled almost half of all Scotland's imports.
- The worst forecasts of the swamping of Scottish manufactures after 1707 did not happen, but such industries found at best only sluggish demand for their produce in the new English market, both domestic and colonial.
- In the most important sector of the Scottish economy, in which eight or nine out of every ten Scots were still employed – in agriculture – the effects of Union were marginal.

Possible points of significant omission may include:

- Numerous Scottish weights and measures were replaced with new imperial or 'Union' ones.
- There was an verall increase in taxation. Duties rose five-fold, for example.
- More efficient tax collection systems were introduced which led to resentment.
- There was a loss of toll revenue from old cross-border trade.
- Darien investors were fairly quickly reimbursed with money from the Equivalent.
- The introduction of the new malt tax was fiercely opposed and there were even riots.
- Smuggling increased massively as a result of the increases in taxation.
- Higher taxes had a huge impact on some Scottish industries, such as paper production, shoe-making, candle-making and the important linen and wool industries.
- There was a significant rise in Scottish merchant trade; huge expansion in mercantile trade in coal, salt and grain and an increase in vessels needed to facilitate this trade.
- There was an increase in land improvement, such as enclosures.
- There was an increase in transatlantic trade as previous restrictions were removed.
- Fast growing west-coast ports, such as Port Glasgow and Greenock, were testament to improved access to the plantations in the Caribbean.
- Scottish tobacco merchants increased their trade, though real growth happened after 1740.
- There were fewer Scottish mercantile losses as they benefited from the protection of the Royal Navy.
- Many ex-Jacobites became bond servants in the colonies.

- There was an expansion of jobs for Scots in the 1720s, especially as a result of Walpole's policies, which reflected a more conciliatory approach to Scotland from British politicians; for example, in the British armed forces and as doctors.
- The reintroduction of patronage in 1712 led to resentment among the Presbyterian community who had assumed that the Union would entrench their view of religion. They welcomed George I, however, when he succeeded Anne as a protector of Protestantism.
- There was immediate widespread opposition to union across Scotland, not just in the Highlands.
- Initially there was much political opposition and there was a motion to repeal union in 1713, though it did, just, fail.
- The Whig party were dominant in Scotland.
- The office of Secretary of State was abolished from 1725.
- The Scots Privy Council was abolished in 1708.
- There was a desire for restoration of the Stuart dynasty.
- There were invasion scares in 1708 and 1719 in support of the Jacobites.
- There was resentment towards George I after 1714.
- The Jacobites rose in strength in 1715, but were poorly led and ultimately failed.

Any other valid points that meet the criteria described in the general marking instructions for this kind of question.

Part D – Migration and Empire, 1830–1939

10 Evaluate the usefulness of Source A **as evidence of the reasons for Scottish emigration. (6)**

In making a judgement you should refer to:

- *the origin and possible purpose of the source*
- *the content of the source*
- *your own knowledge.*

Candidates can be credited in a number of ways up to a maximum of 6 marks.

Examples of aspects of the source and relevant comments:

Aspect of the source	Possible comment
Author: John Will, a Scottish émigré after the First World War	Useful as it is from a first-hand account of someone who left Scotland with his family so would be well-informed about the reasons why Scots left at this time.
Type of source: interview with John Will	Useful as oral history from someone who was personally involved in emigration, so would have insight into the different reasons why people left Scotland.
Purpose: to record the reasons why John Will's family left Scotland	Useful as it shows the impact of the First World War on Scottish emigration.
Timing: 1994	Useful as it is from the account of someone who directly experienced emigrating from Scotland, reflecting on their experience with the benefit of hindsight – had time to think about their experience with more perspective. Less useful as hindsight may have changed the detail and significance of the events in the family's decision to emigrate.

Content	Possible comment
Scots people are traditionally very educational minded and it didn't look like much opportunity for his kids.	Useful as it shows that Scots left because they wanted better opportunities for their children than those offered at home.
He had read a lot about California, the orange groves, the climate, land of opportunity – he decided we should emigrate to Southern California.	Useful as it shows that emigrant Scots went to America because of its attractions and opportunities.
The primary reason for emigrating was better economic conditions abroad.	Useful as it shows some Scots emigrated after the First World War because the the economies of other countries meant more money could be made.

Possible points of significant omission may include:

- Many soldiers returned from the First World War to cramped and unsanitary housing conditions; some chose to emigrate rather than return to their old life.

- Low wages and economic depression also caused many to emigrate.

- Scottish emigrants made up 58 per cent of British emigration in the 1920s.

- Most emigration took place in the early 1920s in a bid to beat new USA immigration quotas in 1923.

- Government assistance in the shape of the 1922 Empire Settlement Act encouraged emigration to Canada rather than the USA.

- Worldwide economic problems reduced the attraction of emigration for those who had been looking for a higher standard of living.

- Return emigration, of those for whom emigration had not worked out, broke up the networks of communities which had encouraged many Scots to continue to emigrate.

- In the 1930s, emigration was reduced because there was not as much financial assistance and destination countries were unenthusiastic about supporting very poor emigrants.

Any other valid points that meet the criteria described in the general marking instructions for this kind of question.

11 Compare the views of Sources B **and** C **about the experience of immigrants to Scotland. (5)**

Compare the sources overall and in detail.

Candidates can be credited in a number of ways up to a maximum of 5 marks.

Possible points of comparison may include:

Overall: The sources agree that the Scotland was attractive to Lithuanians because of its cheap transport links, better housing and wages, but that for many Lithuanians, Scotland was a temporary stop on the way to the Americas.

Source B suggests that most Lithuanians regarded Scotland as a stepping stone to the USA with Scotland being desirable as language, housing and money issues were catered for. However, although Source C also describes similar experiences for the Lithuanian community, it mentions that immigration continued to Scotland because of positive ongoing letters home.

Source B	Source C
The ultimate destination of most of the emigrants was the United States and Scotland, initially, was probably no more than a stepping stone.	For the vast majority of them America was the ultimate destination and Scotland was regarded, at least in the early part of this period, as only a temporary stop on that journey.
With cheap shipping routes between, for example, Hamburg or Bremen and Leith and Dundee, Scotland was easily accessible from the continent.	For a time it was cheaper to travel to America via the ports of Leith and Glasgow rather than go direct.
Employment with the large companies in the Lanarkshire area such as Baird, Merry and Cuninghame included provision of company owned housing.	Employment with some of the larger companies included provision of company-owned housing.
Wages in Scotland were high by Lithuanian standards and could only be substantially improved by a further move to America.	There were ample opportunities to earn money in the expanding coal, iron and steel industries in Lanarkshire and Ayrshire.

12 How fully does Source D **explain the effects of migration and empire on Scotland, to 1939? (9)**

Use the source and your own knowledge.

Candidates can be credited in a number of ways up to a maximum of 9 marks.

A maximum of 2 marks may be given for answers which refer only to the source.

Possible points which may be identified in the source include:

- Although seasonal migration continued throughout the nineteenth and twentieth centuries, thousands of Irish folk decided to make Scotland their permanent home.

- By 1851 there was already a settled Irish community in the Gorbals in Glasgow which numbered well over 200,000.

- There was a marked Irish presence in the textile industry, where they became skilled spinners, weavers and dyers.

- Generations of Irish men helped to build the railways in the nineteenth century and roads, dams and tunnels in the twentieth century.

Possible points of significant omission may include:

- Irish settlement was concentrated in Glasgow and the west of Scotland. Significant numbers also settled in Dundee and Edinburgh.

- The Irish were employed in coal mines and factories.

- Irish workers were strongly represented in the textile industry and also in the building of the canals and railways.
- Initially, Irish workers pushed down wages and had a reputation as strike breakers in the coal and iron industries.
- Irish people experienced poor living conditions and wages, mainly living in the poorer parts of towns and cities.
- Some Scots blamed Irish immigration for problems in the areas where they lived; for example, the spread of diseases and drunkenness.
- Irish immigrants gained a reputation for heavy drinking among some Scots.
- Some Scots regarded Catholic Irish immigration as a threat to their way of life because of their religion.
- Separate religious and social organisations helped create a distinct and separate identity for Irish Catholic immigrants; for example, the St Vincent de Paul Society for helping the poor, and Celtic and Hibernian football clubs.
- Separate Catholic schools were initially funded by the local Catholic community.
- The 1918 Education (Scotland) Act created state funded schools in Catholic communities.
- In 1923, the Church of Scotland published a pamphlet called 'The Menace of the Irish Race to our Scottish Nationality'.
- There were some anti-Irish Protestant societies in the 1920s and 1930s, and race riots in Morningside, Edinburgh.
- The Irish contribution to the growth of the Scottish trades union movement was significant.
- The Irish contribution to the economic growth of Scotland was significant albeit in mainly unskilled jobs.
- A negative impact of Irish immigration was the sectarian rivalry between the Irish Catholics and Protestants.
- Irish immigrants also contributed to the culture of Scotland through the Protestant Orange Lodge Order.
- Some Protestant Irish were recruited from Ireland for their skills in engineering and shipbuilding.
- Irish Catholic support helped boost the rise of the Labour Party in Scotland after the creation of the independent Ireland in 1922.
- Other immigrant groups such as the Italians, Jews and Lithuanians also had an impact.

Any other valid points that meet the criteria described in the general marking instructions for this kind of question.

Part E – The Impact of the Great War, 1914–1928

13 Evaluate the usefulness of Source A **as evidence of the experience of Scots on the Western Front. (6)**

In making a judgement you should refer to:

- *the origin and possible purpose of the source*
- *the content of the source*
- *your own knowledge.*

Candidates can be credited in a number of ways up to a maximum of 6 marks.

Examples of aspects of the source and relevant comments:

Aspect of the source	Possible comment
Author: Captain in the Royal Scots Fusiliers	Useful as the author was a serving field army officer during the First World War. It is the view of someone who had first-hand experience of the war and will be well-informed about the role of Scots on the Western Front.
	Less useful as this extract only reflects the experience of one soldier who was in the reserve section at Loos.
Type of source: Account by Captain Wyllie, Royal Scots Fusiliers	Useful as oral history from a soldier who personally commanded other soldiers at the Battle of Loos, so would be well-informed about what happened at the battle. It is the eyewitness account of an officer who would have a broad understanding of the war. It is a personal recollection so the source may be more useful because it is intended to be an honest account of what happened.
Purpose: To record a personal experience of the Battle of Loos	Useful as it is a record of a Scottish soldier's experience of a key battle for Scottish soldiers on the Western Front.
Timing: 1952	Useful as it is from the account of someone who experienced the Battle of Loos, reflecting on their experience with the benefit of hindsight – had time to think about their experience with better perspective.
	Less useful as hindsight may have changed the detail and emotions about the event.

Content	Possible comment
We moved forward … and … launched a gas attack before the brigades went over; the wind was light and variable … and the gas came back on to us.	Useful as it tells us that the British launched their attack with gas and the attacking soldier were caught in the gas attack.
The attacking lines were through it too quickly for it to do any harm except in a few cases. One battalion was so badly gassed that only one platoon attacked the German lines.	Useful as it shows the impact of the gas attack on some of the attacking solders.
It was here that Piper Laidlaw won his VC by marching up and down on top of the parapet while the entire German Army shot at hm. His bag was punctured in several places.	Useful as it shows one of the many acts of individual heroism by Scottish soldiers during the Battle of Loos as evidenced by the many battle honours awarded to Scottish regiments including a VC to Piper Laidlaw.

Possible points of significant omission may include:

- The Battle of Loos 1915 was the first time that gas was used by the British.

- Douglas Haig, the battle commander, intended that gas would be a breakthrough weapon to make up for inadequate artillery.

- Haig's battle plan did not take into account the length of the attacking line when using gas – the wind needs to be blowing away from the troops for them to be protected/unaffected by the use of gas. With such a long attacking line, the wind would have had to be blowing in several different directions at once to be away from all troops. Haig was warned of this before the battle.

- Haig has subsequently been criticised for trying to achieve a breakthrough battle on terrain he knew to be unsuitable for such an attack.

- In the remainder of the war, gas cylinders were replaced by gas-filled shells.

- Different types of gas (chlorine, phosgene, mustard) were used. They had differing effects; phosgene was most feared as it was colourless and odourless.

- Many of Scotland's early war volunteers had their first experience of fighting at Loos in September 1915.

- The 9th and 15th Scottish Divisions were involved in the attack – the 15th was a completely new and inexperienced division. The 15th was given the task of acquiring Loos itself and capturing Hill 70. The 15th was given such a difficult task by their commander, General Rawlinson, because he considered them to be one of the finest divisions he had ever met, even without battle experience.

- The 9th Division lost almost 3,000 men, killed and missing, from 25 to 28 September and the 15th lost over 3,000 in one day.

- The 15th attacked bravely and achieved their objectives, but in the confusion most headed south instead of east, which meant that those who had captured Hill 70 got caught in machine-gun fire from the sides, in front of uncut German barbed wire and the rest of the division was too far south to support a successful attack.

- Loos had been preceded by a series of battles: Neuve Chapelle, Aubers Ridge and Festubert. All of these battles involved Scottish soldiers. Neuve Chapelle had been successful, in no small part due to the role of Scottish soldiers.

- The Scottish losses were huge and were devastating for some communities because men had volunteered together.

- Approximately one-third of the 20,598 names of the missing at Loos are Scottish.

- The bravery and fighting spirit of the Scottish units is evidenced in the battle honours awarded: five Victoria crosses were given to Scots after the battle.

- Recipients of battle honours included Piper Daniel Laidlaw of the KOSB (King's Own Scottish Borderers) who continued to play his pipes to encourage the Scottish attack despite his pipes being partly shot to bits – he was given a VC.

- Although Loos was unsuccessful in achieving a breakthrough, Scots solders felt proud of the unbelievable courage demonstrated.

- Three Scottish divisions, 9th, 15th (Scottish) and 51st (Highland), took part in the Battle of the Somme.

- 51 Scottish infantry battalions took part in the Somme over the course of the battle, July–November.

- There were huge Scottish casualties on the first day. Examples include 15th (Cranston's) Royal Scots lost 18 officers and 610 soldiers wounded, killed or missing; 16th (McCrae's) Royal Scots lost 12 officers and 573 soldiers; 16th HLI (Highland Light Infantry) lost 20 officers and 534 men.

- The 9th (Scottish) Division performed well during the five months of fighting. They were known for their innovative battle tactics, including the use of artillery.

- As a fighting division, casualties of the 15th were high: 314 officers and 7,203 other ranks.

- Trenches often did not provide adequate shelter. Trench conditions were often poor and damp. They attracted rats and led to problems such as trench foot.

- There were changes to medical care and improvements to medical treatments, for example, field stations close to the front, blood transfusions etc.

- There were changes to battle tactics; the use of artillery became more important.

Any other valid points that meet the criteria described in the general marking instructions for this kind of question.

14 **Compare the views of** Sources B **and** C **about the impact of military losses on Scottish society. (5)**

Compare the sources overall and in detail.

Candidates can be credited in a number of ways up to a maximum of 5 marks.

Possible points of comparison may include:

Overall: The sources agree that Scotland felt the impact of military losses not only on the battlefield but through disease or accidents, which can be seen in the scale and range of commemoration across Scotland.

Source B suggests that demobilisation, the flu epidemic and losses from the volunteer army made the biggest impact on commemoration. However, Source C suggests that disaster and military losses among Scotland's sporting heroes had a big impact.

Source B	Source C
Even demobilisation was no guarantee of safety as was demonstrated in the tragic death of 200 soldiers who died on the Iolaire in sight of Stornoway harbour.	Another group of servicemen encountered unexpected death within sight of their own homes when the Iolaire foundered on rocks at Stornoway.
The end of the war brought a flu epidemic, possibly killing as many as 34,000, including returning soldiers.	In 1918 there was a flu epidemic against which there was no medical defence. Unknown numbers of young men came home safely from the war, only to fall victim to the disease.
The Scottish landscape is littered with war memorials in towns and villages where the number of names on the memorial outnumbered the current population.	All over Scotland, similar memorials were erected, some of them included the figure of a kilted Scottish soldier or symbolic figure of peace or a plain Celtic cross.
The Scottish National War Memorial at Edinburgh Castle opened in 1927. This recorded the names of all the Scottish war dead and was an attempt to express a sense of indebtedness.	In 1918, the Scottish National War Memorial committee was set up to memorialise Scotland's contribution to the war.

15 **How fully does** Source D **explain the impact of the war on Scottish politics? (9)**

Use the source and your own knowledge.

Candidates can be credited in a number of ways up to a maximum of 9 marks.

A maximum of 2 marks may be given for answers which refer only to the source.

Possible points which may be identified in the source include:

- The Conservatives were helped by a significant shift in the politics of four key national organisations, namely, the Church of Scotland, the legal and educational systems and the press.
- By the mid-1920s, Liberal papers had all gone. In Dundee and Aberdeen, they were each taken over by the Tory rival.
- The Scottish legal system also became linked to the Tories through the number of advocates who became MPs.
- In the education sector, the Tories were dominant, firmly controlling the return of MPs for the university seats.

Possible points of significant omission may include:

- The Liberal party was split by attitudes to war. Some Scottish Liberals never reconciled themselves to supporting the war effort and became involved in the anti-war movement.
- Lloyd George took advantage of war issues to take over the leadership of the party and the job of Prime Minister in 1916. This split the party and led to its decline post war as Coalition Liberals supported Lloyd George. Supporters of Herbert Asquith, the former Prime Minister, also stood as Liberals.
- The split in Liberals had a catastrophic effect on the Scottish Liberal Party as there were many Asquithian Liberals in Scotland. Local party organisations such as that in Stirling were riven by disagreements with the result that previously vibrant associations barely campaigned in the post-war elections. The split became formal in 1920.
- Some Scottish Liberals turned away from the party in disgust after Lloyd George had been slow to rule out challenging Asquith at the Paisley by-election in 1920.
- Conservatives were the main beneficiaries of the war, winning most of the MPs and 30 per cent of the popular vote.
- Labour also did well from the war, winning as many votes as the Conservatives, but losing out on the number of MPs owing to the first-past-the-post system.

- Despite the 1918 Representation of the People Act, issues with voter registration meant that turnout was only 60 per cent of those eligible to vote.
- The war had an impact on women and politics. Some women, such as Mary Barbour and Helen Crawfurd, continued to play prominent roles in local politics.
- The pattern of political support changed: the middle class increasingly supported Conservatives whereas Labour picked up support from the industrial working class and more moderate and liberal thinkers.
- Immediately after the war, home rule was a live political issue; there were two attempts to introduce home rule bills in 1924 and 1927.
- Longer term, home rule waned as a significant political concern.
- The Battle of George Square in Glasgow in January 1919 was arguably the height of 'Red Clydeside'.
- The influence of John Maclean waned.
- The Labour Party grew in the 1922 elections, with 142 MPs, 29 MPs in Scotland and 10 MPs in Glasgow alone.
- There was a short-lived Labour Government in 1924.
- The failure of the Land Settlement Act, 1919, to resolve demands for land quickly led to land raids on islands like Lewis.
- There was a General Strike in 1926.

Any other valid points that meet the criteria described in the general marking instructions for this kind of question.

Section 2 – British – 20 marks

Part A – Church, State and Feudal Society, 1066–1406

16 *The landed classes were the most important part of feudal society.*

How valid is this view? (20)

Context: Feudal society developed in medieval Britain based around the relationship between land ownership and service to the land owner. The most important parts of medieval society are generally agreed to be the king, nobility, knights and the peasantry, as well as the medieval Church.

The landed classes

- In general, the landed classes refers to the barons and other significant members of the nobility. They owned significant estates across Britain. Many could hold lands in very different parts of the country; such as the Bruce family, who had extensive estates in both Scotland and England.

- As part of their relationship with their tenants, the barons could demand service from peasants in the form of military service and work on the lord's manor in return for the land they tilled.

- Many barons were very wealthy and could serve as members of the king's retinue as well as being a potential source of opposition.

Other factors

Peasants

- The work of the feudal peasant was vital for the feudal system. Their work and service was essential for the system to work.

- Peasants would serve as men-at-arms in feudal levies.

- They became more important within the system as their ability to negotiate for their service improved; for example, when the Black Plague decimated the population.

- They could be politically important as well, as demonstrated by the Peasants' Revolt of 1381.

The king

- The king was at the top of the feudal system and could use his powers through giving land and positions to men of influence.

- The king sought to bind powerful magnates to him with personal loyalty and patronage. In return he received military service and taxation (feudal dues).

- The king could raise revenue in a wide range of ways: scutage (money paid in lieu of military service), shield tax, etc.

- A king was also important in giving judicial powers to the main magnates.

Knights

- A knight could be created by the king in return for military or some other service.

- During the High Middle Ages, knighthood was considered a class of lower nobility.

- By the Late Middle Ages, the rank had become associated with the ideals of chivalry, a code of conduct for the perfect courtly Christian warrior.

- Often, a knight was a vassal who served as a fighter for a lord, with payment in the form of land holdings.

- The lords trusted the knights, who were skilled in battle on horseback.

Any other relevant factors.

17 To what extent was David I successful in his attempts to increase royal power in Scotland? (20)

Context: David I succeeded to the throne of Scotland in 1124. He brought feudal ideas with him from his time in England and Normandy. These were introduced with varying success in parts of Scotland.

Introduction of feudal land-holding

- Military feudalism was introduced in the south-west, Lothians and across North-East Scotland.

- David brought allies with him in the form of French and English knights who were used to the idea of feudalism. They were often given difficult areas to police for David.

- There were some clashes with those following the traditional Celtic system of mormaers of Scotland. They were used to their own power and operated in an independent way, for example the earls of Moray.

- It was more difficult to penetrate the west and north of Scotland in terms of introducing feudalism, though David did have positive relations with many of the traditional earls in places like Fife.

Development of independent military forces

- The introduction of feudal land-holding allowed David to develop an effective military force. For example, it helped him subdue Moray and dominate the north of England, though it performed poorly at the Battle of the Standard and did not merge well with the more unruly Celtic elements of his army.

Developing the economy

- Burghs with preferential trading rights were introduced, in order to generate income. Burghs produced important revenue from their system of taxes, rents and fines. Examples include Stirling and Perth.
- Silver coinage and moneyers (people who mint coins) were introduced.

Law and order

- Royal power was practically expanded or reinforced with the development of existing royal castles such as Roxburgh, particularly around the burghs, as well as grants of lands to allies, for example, in Moray, to a Flemish knight.
- David also extended his power through intermediaries such as alliances with the powerful earls of Orkney.
- Royal justice expanded as King David granted Scottish magnates the right to hold their own court in his name.
- Judicial officers such as the Justiciar (supreme judges) were appointed.

Development of government

- The rudimentary development of government aimed such as sheriffs, as well as offices like Chamberlain and Chancellor to secure revenues and expand royal justice. Howevere, there is also evidence of the retention of old systems with Gaelic terms and officials.

Church development

- David is associated with Church developments, especially the introduction of the Roman form of religion as compared to the existing Celtic one.
- Lands were granted to several monastic orders, such as the Cistercians.
- There was sensitivity to local needs as well. Local saints, such as St Mungo were praised.

Any other relevant factors.

18 *King John's attempts to increase royal authority were successful in England.*

How valid is this view? (20)

Context: John succeeded to the English throne on the death of his brother Richard. In a controversial reign, he struggled to hold the Angevin Empire together as well as face the challenges of his own magnates.

Loss of Normandy

- The loss of Normandy to Philip II of France by 1204 led to the collapse of much of the Angevin Empire. Much of John's foreign policy was geared to recovery of the lands north of the Loire.
- The only sizeable land mass controlled by John in France was the Duchy of Aquitaine.
- John found it difficult to secure the assistance of English barons in his attempts to regain his French lands.

Military power

- John was a reasonable military commander. For example, he was victorious at the Battle of Mirabeau.
- John made use of mercenaries in his armies.
- The Royal Navy was established during john's reign.
- John built up alliances with other groups who were suspicious of the growth of Capetian power, such as the counts of Boulogne and Flanders.
- However, John's allies were eventually defeated at the Battle of Bouvines in 1214.

Royal administration

- Record keeping and tax gathering improved during John's reign.
- John was very active in the administration of England and was involved in every aspect of government.
- Many roles in government were filled by new men, which did cause resentment among the English barons.

The economy and taxation

- Relentless conflict led to a demand for revenue and John was active in raising taxation.
- 'Scutage' was implemented eleven times in seventeen years far more frequently than under Richard or Henry.

- John created a new tax on income and movable goods in 1207, which produced £60,000.
- He also created a new set of import and export duties, payable directly to the Crown.
- John implemented the confiscation of the lands of barons who could not pay or refused to pay.
- There were improvements in the quality of silver coinage.

Relationship with the barons

- There was much resentment at the increases in taxation.
- There was also resentment at the expectation of service in France, especially from northern barons.
- The failure of military campaigns led to open revolt in 1215.
- Magna Carta was negotiated to end the revolt. This attempted to define rights, etc., but was never actually implemented by either side.

Relationship with the Church

- John fell out with Pope Innocent III on the appointment of a new archbishop of Canterbury.
- This led to John's excommunication, which actually helped him seize Church revenue.
- Reconciliation occurred when John made England a fief of the Papacy, which led to ecclesiastical support for John.

John's personality

- John could be petty and vindictive; there are many examples of his poor treatment of allies and enemies.
- John's harsh treatment of prisoners after the Battle of Mirabeau offended the sensibilities of many of his allies, particularly William de Roches of Anjou, who eventually sided with Philip of France.
- There is debate over what John did with his nephew Arthur, though most think John murdered him.

Any other relevant factors.

Part B – The Century of Revolutions, 1603–1702

19 How important were political issues as a reason for the problems faced by King James after the Union of the Crowns in 1603? (20)

Context: James VI of Scotland became King of England in 1603. A firm believer in the divine right of kings to rule, he would come up against resistance in several areas during his reign in England.

Politics

- The English Parliament was used to criticising the monarchy. James's belief in the divine right of kings opposed this and led to clashes between the king and parliament.
- Examples of James's bad behaviour include his attempt to influence parliamentary freedom by locking up some MPs. He was also inconsistent, giving in to parliament in the Goodwin case.
- Goodwin had been elected to parliament, but as an outlaw was not allowed to sit in parliament according to royal proclamation. James was challenged by parliament and he backed down, but not before the damage to relations had been done.

Economic issues

- James's desire to be financially independent of parliament led to a series of measures designed to raise revenue that alienated groups. For example, cash was raised by selling earldoms and other titles created by James.
- The Great Contract, whereby parliament would pay off James's debts and give him an annual income, ended as James lost patience.

Religious issues – Presbyterianism

- James believed in hierarchical religion and thus came into conflict with parliament, where a lot of Puritans sat as MPs.
- James did not want to see the Presbyterian form of religion develop and thus supported the Episcopal Church.
- Puritan demands for Church reform did not find favour with James.

Religious issues – Roman Catholicism

- There was an increasing feeling that James was sympathetic to Roman Catholicism, evidenced by his allowing his son to marry a Roman Catholic princess. Allowing her to worship mass privately seemed to confirm these suspicions.
- The development of anti-Catholic sentiment across the country owing to the discovery of Guy Fawkes' gunpowder plot as well as events on the Continent such as the beginnings of the Thirty Years' War.
- James's failure to agree the marriage of the Prince of Wales to the Spanish infanta did not please the Spanish faction at court, but pleased the British people.

Legal issues

- As with other areas, James sought to behave as he wished in legal matters. He sought to influence the courts by appointing judges favourable to the Crown, as well as moving to legally protect allies among the magnates.
- Parliament did not like his moves to control and influence the judiciary, thinking it an abuse of power.
- Difficulties of practical rule in both England and Scotland.
- James had not enjoyed ruling Scotland and stayed in England for the vast bulk of his time as the ruler of two countries. However, he still sought to influence events in Scotland with the use of sympathetic clans to collect revenue, for example.
- His ideas for more incorporating union between Scotland and England were opposed and did not progress.

Any other relevant factors.

20 To what extent was the character of Charles I the main reason for the outbreak of civil war in England? (20)

Context: Charles I was the son of James I. He believed in the divine right of kings and this led to confrontation with parliament over issues such as finance. However, other issues also contributed to the outbreak of civil war.

Character of Charles I

- In his youth, Charles suffered from poor health and a lack of parental affection. He had a fierce temper.
- Charles acceded to the throne in 1625 and, in many ways, cut a regal figure.
- His strong beliefs over his role as King, religion and the role of parliament brought him into conflict with parliament.
- There is debate about the extent to which he was dominated by favourites like Buckingham and his wife Henrietta.
- Charles tended to surround himself with people who agreed with him. This led to a lack of awareness and alienation from the developing opposition to his rule.

Other factors

Economic issues

- Charles' desire to be financially independent of parliament led to conflict as he used a variety of methods to raise revenue.
- During the 1630s, Charles continued to collect tonnage and poundage, impositions and, in addition, revived ancient royal levies. All these violated the principle of no taxation without consent.
- An ancient custom, not enforced for 100 years, required that all men with landed income worth more than £40 p.a. should present themselves for knighthood at the King's coronation. In 1630, Charles fined those who failed to do so. This 'Distraint of Knighthood' was based on an Act of 1278.
- He levied fines for those encroaching on royal forests.

Religious matters

- England was a predominantly Protestant country with a significant number of Puritans. Puritans were well represented in parliament.
- It was felt that Charles favoured Catholicism, as his marriage to Catholic Henrietta Maria and her observance of mass seemed to confirm.
- Charles' Bishop of Canterbury, Archbishop William Laud, was widely considered to be a crypto-Catholic.

Political issues

- Charles sought to rule without parliament; from 1629 to 1640 he did so during the Eleven Years' Tyranny.
- Charles came into conflict with parliament as he did not really listen to them and did what he wished.
- His reliance on ministers, such as the Duke of Buckingham and the Earl of Stafford, reinforced his desire to rule in an absolute manner.
- Parliament sought to re-establish its authority on being recalled in 1640. This led to confrontation and the eventual Civil War.

Legal issues

- Charles used courts to enforce royal policy. This extended to the use of courts by his ministers to favour the government of Charles.

Legacy of James I

- It can be argued that Charles' belief in the divine right of kings and religion were a continuation of policy started under his father.

Scottish issues

- There was fierce opposition to the imposition of Laud's prayer book in Presbyterian Scotland. This led to the National Covenant and subsequent military failure in the Bishops' Wars, which further weakened Charles' authority.

Other relevant factors.

21 *The role of Charles II was the main reason for the Revolution Settlement of 1688–1689.*

How valid is this view? (20)

Context: The monarchy was restored in 1660. By 1688 the increasingly absolute rule of James II, among other factors, led parliament to ask his Protestant daughter, Mary, and her husband, William of Orange, to become joint monarchs.

Charles II

- Charles theoretically agreed limitations on his power but, in reality, he was able to get round any restrictions.
- Charles was suspected of being sympathetic to Catholicism, which alarmed many MPs and subjects.
- Charles ruled alone for four years, dissolving parliament in March 1681 and ignoring the Triennial Act in 1684.
- In 1683, he imposed a new Charter for the City of London which said that all appointments to civil office, including Lord Mayor, should be subject to royal approval.

Other factors

Religious issues

- The Declarations of Indulgence, 1687 and 1688, were two proclamations issued by the King, which gave greater religious freedom to those who did not conform to Anglicanism. It was feared that this was to encourage Catholicism and was opposed by many Anglicans. Presbyterians were suspicious of this.
- Charles declared himself to be a Catholic on his deathbed and had had a controversial religious policy during his life. He allied with his cousin, the Catholic King of France, during the Third Dutch War, for example.
- Charles was succeeded by his brother, James II, who was Catholic. James promoted Roman Catholics to key posts in government and the army.
- The birth of a Catholic heir for James directly precipitated the Protestant political elite of England to approach James's daughter, Mary, and her husband, William of Orange, who were Protestants, to be joint monarchs instead of James.

James II

- The leading Protestant nobility of England suspected James of trying to form an absolute government in England. He dismissed parliament.
- On his succession to the throne, James was faced by rebellion from Argyll and Monmouth. James increased his army's size as a result, which increased suspicion in England.
- James used his dispensing power to allow Roman Catholics to command several regiments without having to take the oath required by the Test Act; this further increased suspicion.
- James suspended laws against Roman Catholics and promoted Catholics to important positions, such as Sir Roger Strickland to be Admiral of the Royal Navy.

Political issues

- There was political conflict between parliament and both James and Charles during their reigns.
- Both rulers were frequently accused of misusing royal privilege. For example, James II's use of the Suspending and Dispensing Powers in 1687.
- Both kings supported the divine right of kings and had absolutist tendencies, ruling on their own without parliament.

The role of parliament

- Parliament resented James II's abuses of power but took comfort from the thought that he would be succeeded by his Protestant daughter Mary, but when James's wife gave birth to a Catholic son, parliament acted.
- Parliament wrote to Mary, by now married to the Dutch Prince William of Orange, offering her the Crown.
- In March 1689, parliament drew up a Declaration of Right, which legalised a new relationship between Crown and parliament in matters such as finance, law, the succession and religion. William and Mary agreed to this.

Any other relevant factors.

Part C – The Atlantic Slave Trade

22 How important were racist attitudes in the reasons for the development of the slave trade? (20)

Context: By the eighteenth century, Britain had developed an enviable Empire, including the fertile Caribbean islands. The successful cultivation of the crops on these islands depended on the plentiful supply of cheap labour.

Racist attitudes

- The enslavement of Africans was justified by the ideology of racism – the mistaken belief that Africans were inferior to Europeans. The unequal relationship between slaves and owners only served to confirm this prejudice in the minds of slave owners.
- Colonists took on and accepted the endemic racism against African natives among members of the merchant and landowning classes.
- Europeans claimed that African captives would suffer if the slave trade was abolished; for example, criminals and prisoners of war would be harmed or executed at home.
- Colonists claimed that slaves were better off provided with homes, protection and employment by enlightened Europeans rather than African despots.

Other factors

Military factors

- The Seven Years' War was a decisive war fought between Britain, France and Spain. Many of the most important battles of the Seven Years' War were fought at sea. Britain's victory and naval supremacy meant that other European countries were unable to challenge Britain for control of desirable lands, so Britain was free to develop and exploit their resources.
- Britain emerged from the war as the leading European imperial power, having made large territorial gains in North America and the Caribbean, as well as India. Slave labour was necessary to exploit these gains.

Importance of West Indian colonies

- The Caribbean islands were rich in spices and had an ideal climate for growing sugar and tobacco. Europe quickly became addicted to these products and demand soared.
- The slave trade was an important source of tax revenue for the government. The sugar, tobacco and rum from the West Indies were a valuable source of exports and status with the rest of Europe.
- The development of commercial finance, insurance and legal sectors was symbiotic with the slave trade. Profits from the slave trade financed the development of many new businesses.
- West Indies colonies provided an important source of income for the younger sons of wealthy families. The profits from the islands allowed new fortunes to be made and enabled middle- and upper-class families to maintain their social status and lifestyles.
- Profits from the slave trade funded many political careers, built numerous grand houses and endowed universities and other educational and cultural institutions.

Shortage of labour

- Profits made from the trade in sugar and tobacco created more demand for labour to work on plantations in the colonies.
- Crops such as sugar cane were labour intensive and required a large labour force to plant, look after, harvest and process the crop in harsh conditions. In order to keep profits high, labour costs had to be kept low, hence the development of slavery.
- Native islanders were virtually wiped out by the diseases brought by Europeans. Indentured servants proved less than capable of coping with the harsh conditions of working on the plantations.
- Before slaves were used, plantation workers were treated badly, which created a labour shortage in the West Indies.

Failure of alternative sources

- A limited number of native islanders were available for work on the plantations, especially after the high death rate from disease. Few colonists were willing to work on plantations as manual labour.
- Criminals would often be transported to the colonies, as an alternative to hanging. There were also political prisoners such as Jacobites who were transported. However, after 1745, there was a more settled political situation and there was an insufficiently constant supply.
- Some Britons, particularly Scots, sold themselves as indentured servants, on 3–7 years fixed contracts. However, numbers were limited as was shown by the numbers of indentured servants who found themselves transported to the West Indies after being plied with drink and kidnapped.

Religious factors

- The Church of England had links to slavery through the United Society for the Propagation of the Gospel, missionary organisations which had plantations and owned slaves. The Church of England was also sometimes a slave owner through being the beneficiary of wills.
- The Church of England supported laws preventing the education of enslaved Africans.

- Some Christians quoted the Bible to support slavery; for example, selective passages such as the Curse of Ham from Genesis. Other Bible passages, such as Exodus, telling the story of the escape of Israel from slavery in Egypt, were banned in British colonies because they could be interpreted as being anti-slavery.

Any other relevant factors.

23 *Racism and prejudice were the most important factors governing relations between slaves and their owners.*

How valid is this view? (20)

Context: As the Atlantic slave trade grew and became ever more profitable, the justifications for maintaining the trade became ever more self-interested. The keeping of slaves was supported by racist attitudes and prejudice which emphasised the supposed inadequacies of black people.

Racism and prejudice

- There was widespread ignorance of African society and culture and a general assumption that if African societies were organised differently from European ones, they were inferior.
- There was virtually no awareness of Africa's rich history and an assumption that Africans were primitive in comparison to Europeans, which meant that Europeans widely assumed they were bringing enlightenment to the 'dark continent' through effective government.
- Africans were not regarded by Europeans as fellow human beings owing to the colour of their skin. This was used as an excuse for extreme brutality.
- A strong pro-slavery West Indies lobby produced books and newspaper articles justifying the slave trade by using racial stereotypes.

Other factors

Financial considerations

- The debate over conditions on board ship for transporting slaves, that is 'tight pack' or 'loose pack', was not based on humanitarian concerns, but what was the most effective way to successfully transport the most slaves to auction in the West Indies in order to make the biggest profit.
- The motivation of most people in the slave trade was financial; it was the quickest way to make big profits.
- There were many absentee plantation owners in the British Caribbean islands, which meant estates were managed by overseers. Their primary concern was often to amass as much profit as possible so they too could become property owners. As a result, the treatment of slaves was harsh.
- Although slaves were valuable as property, their replacement cost was not prohibitive. This meant slaves were cheap enough to be treated badly or worked to death. Slave owners referred to the human cost as 'wastage'.
- The health risks associated with long stays in the West Indies were well known: tropical diseases. White plantation owners sought to keep their stay on the islands as short as possible in order to minimise these risks and return to Britain to enjoy their money.

Fear of revolt

- White owners and overseers were heavily outnumbered by black people. There was a constant fear of slave revolt both on ships and on plantations. The need for security of the ship's crew meant that slaves were kept under deck for long periods of time and usually shackled for the whole passage.
- Well-publicised revolts in islands like Haiti (Saint-Domingue), Antigua and Jamaica fuelled fear of rebellion.
- Day-to-day life on plantations was dominated by vigilance over the possibility of rebellion. Even minor 'offences' were harshly punished by draconian legal codes.

Humanitarian concerns

- Conditions varied on West Indian plantations. Where a planter's family lived with him, often small communities developed, with affectionate relationships between slaves and the free population. However, there was often little moderation of the realities of slavery.
- In Africa and on board ship, there was little personal contact between slaves and sailors. Slaves were treated as cargo, with little concern other than to keep them alive.

Religious concerns

- The existence of slavery in the Bible was used as a justification for the slave trade by traders and owners.
- Many prominent church goers were slave owners or traders. Their social status meant religious arguments were used to give slave trading respectability.
- Participants in the slave trade claimed that slaves were being exposed to the 'civilising influence' of Christianity. They also argued that slavery benefited slaves because through Christianity they had the chance to get salvation before God.
- The religious faith of some participants moderated their treatment of slaves.

Any other relevant factors.

24 How important were vested interests as an obstacle to abolition? (20)

Context: The early progress of the abolitionist campaign was slow owing to a range of vested interests. However, by the 1790s, the abolitionists were winning the moral argument.

The power of vested interests

- Merchants from London, Liverpool and Bristol ensured that their MPs influenced successive governments to help maintain/ protect the slave trade. They either bought votes or put pressure on others.

- The nature of politics at this time meant that there weren't distinct political parties but various interest groups. The House of Commons was dominated by the West India lobby, which for a long time was the most powerful. The Duke of Clarence, one of George III's sons, was a member of the West India interest group.

- Governments were often coalitions of different interest groups, often pro slavery. This ensured that opposition to the slave trade did not gather government support.

- Many absentee plantation owners or merchants held high political office or were MPs themselves. For example, William Beckford, owner of an estate in Jamaica, was twice Mayor of London. In the later eighteenth century, over 50 MPs represented the slave plantations.

- MPs who supported the slave trade vigorously opposed attempts to introduce laws banning the trade. They made powerful speeches arguing that the livelihoods of thousands of British people and the millions made by the slave trade necessitated its continuation.

- MPs used delaying tactics to slow down or prevent legislation to abolish slavery. For example, Henry Dundas, the unofficial 'King of Scotland', Secretary of State for War and First Lord of the Admiralty used his position to protect the interests of slave owners and merchants. In 1792, he effectively 'killed' Wilberforce's Bill banning the slave trade by proposing a compromise that any abolition would take place over several years, which Dundas knew Wilberforce could not accept.

- Slave merchants would exert direct pressure on the government, for example, in 1775, a petition was sent from Bristol urging support for the slave trade.

Other factors

Slave rebellion in Saint-Domingue

- Pro-slavery groups pointed to this rebellion as an example of what would happen if slaves were freed. The revolt began in 1791 and continued until 1804. An independent country, calling itself Haiti, was set up under the leadership of Toussaint L'Ouverture. It is estimated that as many as 200,000 people died due to this rebellion. The general fear of slave revolt was increased as a result.

- Unsuccessful attempts by colonial French troops to regain control of Haiti shocked the British Government. There were fears that the rebellion could spread to neighbouring British islands such as Jamaica. Any attempts to abolish the slave trade were banned because it was claimed that the West Indies could become unsafe and unstable.

- The British were humiliated when their attempts to regain control of Haiti were also unsuccessful.

- However, attitudes changed after the French Revolution when the Revolutionary Government attempted to regain control; once war was declared between Britain and France it was seen as a way of striking at the French.

The effect of the French Revolution

- Sympathy for the French Revolution disappeared with the execution of Louis XVI. Wealthy people reacted with horror to the idea that similar society upheaval could happen in Britain. Many wealthy people associated abolitionism with the dangerous radicalism in France.

- The abolitionist cause was associated with revolutionary ideas; for example, Clarkson openly supported the French Revolution.

- General fears about law and order led to laws limiting the right of assembly and protest. Even abolition campaigners like William Wilberforce supported these laws. The laws limited the growth of abolition societies.

- After Napoleon came to power in France, Britain became involved in the French Revolutionary Wars, leading to a decrease in support for abolition.

- Supporters of the slave trade argued that it was necessary to pay for Britain's involvement in the French Revolutionary Wars; it seemed unpatriotic not to support the slave trade.

- Radicals used similar tactics as abolitionists to win public support – associations, petitions, cheap publications, public lectures, public meetings, pressure on parliament, etc. This linked abolitionism with political radicalism in people's minds, which during the French Revolutionary Wars, they felt pressure to oppose.

Importance of the trade to the British economy

- The slave trade generated money – West Indian colonies were an important source of valuable exports to European neighbours.

- British people had become addicted to cheaper sugar and tobacco from the plantations and British cotton mills depended on the cotton crops raised by slaves.

- British shipbuilding benefited from the slave trade, as did associated industries.
- British industry received a boost from trading with Africa.
- Alternative funds would have to be raised in order to compensate for the loss of trade and revenue; taxes would have to be raised to compensate for the loss of trade and revenue.
- Britain's finance and insurance industry prospered on the back of the slave trade. Many individual fortunes were made.
- Abolition would help foreign rivals such as France as other nations would fill the gap left by Britain.

Fears over national security

- Abolition would decrease the number of jobs for sailors and the maritime industry – and so reduce the number of experienced sailors for the Royal Navy. Pro-slavery campaigners pointed out that Britain's global dominance was based on the strength of its navy; there was a possibility that Britain would lose its advantage over rivals.

Anti-abolition propaganda

- Lobbyists like the East Indies group conducted a powerful propaganda campaign to counter that of the abolitionists, producing countless letters and articles for newspapers.
- Pro-slavery campaigners produced books and plays supporting the slave trade. For example, in 1785, William Beckford wrote a book *Remarks Upon the Situation of Negroes in Jamaica*; Thomas Bellamy wrote a play in 1788 called *The Benevolent Planters*, telling the story of black slaves separated in Africa, but reunited by their owners.
- Slave owners and their supporters argued that the abolition of the slave trade was not legal because it would undermine a central tenet of British law: the right to private property. They successfully discouraged the Government from contemplating abolition without compensation because of the massive legal battle that would ensue.

Attitude of British governments

- Successive governments were more concerned with maintaining revenue and the rights of property of their wealthiest citizens rather than the rights of black slaves who had no political stake or influence in Britain.

Any other relevant factors.

Part D – Britain, 1851–1951

25 To what extent were pressure groups the main reason why Britain became more democratic, 1851–1928? (20)

Context: Due to Britain's industrial revolution, there were significant economic and social changes by 1851. These helped to spark political changes and introduce a different view of what government should be for and what it should do.

Role of pressure groups

- The Reform League and the Reform Union played significant roles in the popular pressure for reform leading up to the 1867 Reform Act.
- Large-scale demonstrations, like Hyde Park in 1867, were influential; such demonstrations seemed to indicate the unrest that might follow if reasonable concessions were not made.
- Trades unions were also important; they gave many people their first experience of involvement in politics, increasing the desire for national political influence; unfavourable strike legislation led unions to help set up the Labour Party to directly represent their views.
- Suffragists and Suffragettes had a monumental influence on the campaign for votes for women.
- Groups like the Fabian Society and Social Democratic Federation played a significant role in spreading socialist ideas leading to the growth of the Labour Party.

Other factors

The effects of industrialisation and urbanisation

- Industrialisation led to the growth of the towns and two significant classes: the skilled working class and the middle class. Both had the education and the means to put across their demands for political influence.
- Development of 'white collar' workers and their growing economic wealth led to demands for reform.
- Urbanisation helped the spread of new political ideas like socialism, leading to the setting up of a third political party, Labour, by 1906, directly representing the interests of the working class, the largest social group in Britain.
- Urbanisation and growing class identity within an industrial workforce plus the spread of socialist ideas led to demands for a greater voice for the working class. Also, the growth of the Labour Party offered a greater choice.
- The 1870 (1872) Education Act gave everyone a basic education, increasing literacy, and leading to more people having access to the political debate through popular newspapers, which helped increase the demand for reform.
- Development of the railway network helped improve communication and gave political parties the means to develop national organisations.

Changing political attitudes

- During the American Civil War, cotton workers had supported the anti-slavery North against the pro-slavery South, which could have provided the cotton mills with cotton to keep workers in jobs. This impressed politicians like Gladstone and decreased 'the fear of the mob'.
- Former Prime Minister Palmerston died; this was an important symbol of changing ideas in politics where new ideas rather than reaction were welcomed.
- Growth of the Liberal Party, which was reform orientated, forced the Conservatives to consider reform too or see votes go to the party most willing to see change.
- New Liberalism gradually took over in the Liberal Party. New Liberals like Lloyd George believed in bigger government; direct involvement of government in helping people's lives get better.
- Development of national political party organisations, Liberals and Conservatives, helped increase the number of people directly involved in politics and accelerated the process of parties changing their policies to appeal to voters.

Party advantage

- Political parties needed to win hearts and minds – Gladstone was the first to use a single-issue campaign to get the attention of the electorate (1880, Midlothian campaign). Gladstone was a believer in reform. His governments were responsible for reforms in the 1880s and they proposed the eventual 1867 reform.
- Conservatives were also sympathetic to reform, hoping to attract the support of the middle classes. The development of party organisations, for example, in 1870 the Conservative Central Office and in 1867 the National Conservative and Unionist Association, plus local political clubs such as the Scottish Conservative Club and the Primrose League in 1881 brought many more people into politics, especially women.
- In the 1860s there was a race for reform as the Liberals and Conservatives competed to be the party that extended the franchise, hoping to gain the gratitude of the voters. Gladstone was defeated in 1866 and the Government fell. Reform came in 1867, passed by Disraeli, who went further than anyone wanted as he humiliated Gladstone by passing any amendment as long as it didn't come from Gladstone.

Impact of the First World War

- The personal sacrifice of men and women during the war changed attitudes about who deserved the vote. Many men who were conscripted in 1916 did not have the vote. The role of women in filling the jobs vacated by men decreased opposition to votes for women.
- Fears of a revival of a militant women's campaign helped lead to the 1918 Representation of the People Act, giving the vote to all men and some women.
- The debate continued over whether women were being rewarded for their war effort; only middle-class women over the age of 30 got the vote. These were not the women who had undertaken hazardous or gruelling roles in industry during the war.
- The coalition government in 1918 made it easier to give women the vote; no one party could claim credit.

The effects of examples of developments abroad

- Votes for women in places like New Zealand and Scandinavian countries had not led to political meltdown, so reform worked.
- As the 'mother of all democracies', it was difficult for Britain not to reform. Also, once reform had occurred, it created a snowball effect.

Any other relevant factors.

26 *The Suffragettes did little to help achieve votes for some women in 1918.*

How valid is this view? (20)

Context: Like men, women's social and economic status was changed by the industrial revolution. This led to increasing demands for political rights, but progress for many women was frustratingly slow.

Militant Suffragette campaign up to 1914

- Emmeline Pankhurst formed the Women's Social and Political Union (WSPU) in 1903. The WSPU adopted the motto 'Deeds Not Words'.
- The new strategy gained publicity. Newspapers immediately took notice, which meant the Suffragettes had achieved their first aim – to make votes for women an issue that couldn't be ignored.
- Violent protest escalated from 1907 and especially after 1911, for example the window smashing campaign and arson attacks. The Suffragettes aimed to put pressure on the government by provoking insurance companies.
- The prisons filled with Suffragettes, whom the government refused to treat like political prisoners.
- In retaliation, the women used starvation as a political weapon to embarrass the government. The government reacted by introducing the Prisoner's Temporary Discharge for Ill Health Act (the Cat and Mouse Act).

- Suffragettes divided public opinion for and against. On the one hand, it is unlikely the Liberal Government would have looked at the issue of votes for women before the First World War without the Suffragettes. On the other, the militant campaign provided an excellent example for those who argued that women could not be trusted with the vote.

Other factors

The women's suffrage campaign

- The National Union of Women's Suffrage Societies (NUWSS) believed in moderate, 'peaceful' tactics to win the vote, such as meetings, pamphlets, petitions and parliamentary bills.
- The largely middle-class members of the NUWSS made good use of family and social connections to lobby for their campaign.
- Membership remained relatively low at about 6,000 until around 1909 but grew to 53,000 by 1914 as women, angered by the Suffragettes, distanced themselves from their campaign.

Changing attitudes to women in society

- By 1868, women had advanced their legal status significantly; they could, in theory, divorce their husbands and keep custody of their children after divorce. They had also won the right to keep legal title over their property after marriage.
- By the beginning of the twentieth century, women had won the right to stand and take part in local elections, for example Poor Law Guardians and local council elections. Winning the vote in national elections was the next logical step.
- Millicent Fawcett, a leader of the NUWSS, argued that wider social changes were vital factors in the winning of the right to vote.

Part played by women in the war effort

- At the outbreak of war, the suffrage organisations suspended their campaign for the vote. A WSPU pro-war propaganda campaign, funded by the government, encouraged men to join the armed forces and women to demand 'the right to serve'. This patriotism helped balance the negative publicity from the WSPU's pre-war campaign and convinced public opinion that women were 'doing their bit'.
- Women's war work was important to Britain's eventual victory. Over 700,000 women were employed in the vital role of making munitions.
- The creation of a wartime coalition after 1916 made it more likely for change to happen; no one party could claim the credit.
- Politicians were anxious to enfranchise more men who had been conscripted to fight, but who were not eligible to vote. Women could be 'added on' to legislation that was happening anyway.
- Debates over the significance of the war in giving women the vote continue, however; those enfranchised were not the women who had worked long hours and risked their health and lives in the munitions factories.
- The war certainly acted as a catalyst but significant progress had been made towards female franchise before it started.

Example of other countries

- Women were already able to vote in other countries such as New Zealand, and in some American states. It made Britain look less progressive in comparison if former parts of the Empire had achieved votes for women before the 'mother democracy'.

Any other relevant factors.

27 To what extent did the social reforms of the Liberal Government, 1906–1914, meet the needs of the British people? (20)

Context: Industrialisation had led to significant social and economic changes including a growing population and urbanisation. By the late nineteenth century, these had created social needs which were too big for the old local schemes, such as poor relief, to solve and there were increasing demands for government action.

The young

- The Provision of School Meals Act, 1906, allowed local authorities to raise money to pay for school meals but did not force local authorities to provide school meals.
- After 1907, medical inspections for children were made compulsory but no treatment of the illnesses or infections found was provided until 1911.
- The Children's Charter of 1908 banned children under sixteen from smoking, drinking alcohol or begging. Special courts were set up for children accused of committing crimes. Young offenders' prisons – borstals – were set up for children convicted of breaking the law. Probation officers were employed to help former offenders in an attempt to avoid re-offending.
- It took some time to implement the Children's Charter reforms; it is debatable how much impact the reforms had on many children.

The old

- Rowntree had identified old age as the time when most people dropped unavoidably below his poverty line.
- The Old Age Pensions Act (1908) gave people over 70 up to 5 shillings a week. Once a person over 70 had income above 12 shillings a week, their entitlement to a pension stopped. Married couples were given 7 shillings and 6 pence.

- The level of benefits was low. Few elderly poor lived until their seventieth birthday. Many of the old were excluded from claiming pensions because they failed to meet the qualification rules.

The sick

- Illness was identified by Booth and Rowntree as a major cause and consequence of poverty.
- The National Insurance Scheme of 1911 applied to workers earning less than £160 a year. Each insured worker got 9 pence in benefits from an outlay of 4 pence – 'ninepence for fourpence'.
- Only the insured worker got free medical treatment from a doctor. Other family members did not benefit from the scheme. The weekly contribution was in effect a wage cut which may have made poverty worse in many families.

The unemployed

- Unemployment or irregular work was a major cause of poverty.
- The National Insurance Act (Part 2) only covered unemployment for some workers in some industries and, like Part 1 of the Act, required contributions from workers, employers and the government.
- For most workers, no unemployment insurance scheme existed.

Other reforms

- The 1906 Workman's Compensation Act covered 6 million workers who could now claim compensation for injuries and diseases which were the result of their working conditions.
- In 1909, the Trade Boards Act tried to protect workers in the sweated trades, like tailoring and lace making, by setting up trade boards to fix minimum wages.
- In 1908, the Mines Act and the Shop Act improved conditions by limiting working hours and allowing time off.
- In 1911, parliament broke the power of the unelected House of Lords, stopping them from vetoing finance bills and giving them power only to delay legislation from the elected House of Commons. Not only did this improve democracy, it gave future governments the ability to raise the money as well as the power to enact more social legislation.

Any other relevant factors.

Part E – Britain and Ireland, 1900–1985

28 How important were the Irish cultural revival and the re-emergence of Irish Republicanism as reasons for the growth of tension in Ireland to 1914? (20)

Context: Ireland was changing by the early twentieth century. Land and local government reform had seen the emergence of politically able leaders as well as an economically independent group of farmers. Social and economic developments led to demands for political change.

Irish cultural revival and the re-emergence of Irish Republicanism

- The emergence of organisations to protect and spread Irish culture, for example the 1883 Gaelic League and 1884 Gaelic Athletic Association, although originally intended to be apolitical, encouraged Irish nationalism among many of their members.
- Sinn Féin (Ourselves Alone) was founded on 28 November 1905, when Arthur Griffith outlined the policy, 'to establish in Ireland's capital a national legislature endowed with the moral authority of the Irish nation'.
- Revival of the Irish Republican Brotherhood (IRB) – emergence of the Dungannon Clubs, for example – under new political leadership, particularly that of Sean MacDermott and Tom Clarke, encouraged young men to enlist in the IRB with the aim of creating an independent Irish Republic.

Other factors

British position in Ireland – effects of 1910 elections

- The Liberals were reliant on Irish Nationalist MP support after the elections of 1910. They offered this in return for home rule.
- Owing to a constitutional crisis, the Parliament Act was passed. This limited the 'anti-home rule' House of Lords to delaying any home rule bill that entered parliament.
- In 1912, Asquith introduced the Home Rule Bill for Ireland. It was rejected by the House of Lords, but the Commons invoked the Parliament Act in 1914 and sent it for royal assent.

Unionist response to the Home Rule Bill

- Ulster was predominantly a Protestant part of Ireland. It was more developed economically than the south and had strong political and economic links with mainland Britain. Many feared here what government from Dublin would mean.
- Unionists in Ulster were opposed to the Bill and began to set up defence groups that were termed the 'Ulster Volunteers'. There were 100,000 members by the end of 1912.
- The main figures were Irish Unionist leader Sir Edward Carson and Sir James Craig.

- Irish volunteers reorganised into the Ulster Volunteer Force in 1913.
- The ability of the British government to oppose such a force called into question the Curragh mutiny when British officers stationed in Ireland said they wouldn't use force against the Unionists.

Nationalist response to the Home Rule Bill

- The formation of the Irish Volunteers in 1913 was a reaction to the formation of the Ulster Volunteers.
- They were an amalgamation of several Irish nationalist groups and numbered 200,000 by mid-1914.
- Splits in the Irish Volunteers appeared when war broke out.

Redmond

- John Redmond, leader of the moderate Irish Parliamentary Party was a keen supporter of Irish home rule.
- Prior to 1914, there was still significant support for the limited home rule offered in the south of Ireland, though events during the First World War were to end that.
- Redmond urged support for the British war effort as a way of guaranteeing the Home Rule Bill be placed on the statute book after the war.

Any other relevant factors.

29 To what extent were IRA tactics and policies the main obstacle to peace in Ireland, 1918–1921? (20)

Context: The First World War transformed the political situation in Ireland. The moderate Irish Parliamentary Party never survived and radical Republicanism in the form of Sinn Féin emerged as the dominant political view. Limited self-government was never going to satisfy their demands.

IRA tactics and policies

- The IRA evolved out of the Irish Volunteers. It fought a guerrilla campaign against the forces of the British government between 1919 and 1921.
- The IRA used ambush tactics as well as hitting remote RIC (Royal Irish Constabulary) barracks. They also assassinated British spies and intimidated local communities if they were not supporting the IRA.
- Militarily they were pressed badly by the British forces, but their success was in lasting so long and making parts of Ireland ungovernable, except by military means.

Other factors

Legacy of the First World War – 1918 election

- The 1916 Easter Rising and the British government's reaction to it transformed politics in Ireland.
- People were disgusted by the treatment of the Easter Rising rebels and rejected the moderate policies of the Irish Parliamentary Party (Nationalists), instead turning to the more radical Sinn Féin.
- This transferred into a landslide election victory for Sinn Féin in the 1918 election. They won 73 seats. The Nationalists, in contrast, were reduced to just six seats.

Position of Ulster Unionists in the north

- In the 1918 election, the Ulster Unionists became the second largest party in Ireland.
- Irish unionists had enthusiastically supported the British war effort and had paid a blood sacrifice on the battlefield.
- They expected this sacrifice to be honoured in any post-war Irish settlement.

Declaration of Independence and the establishment of the Dáil

- After the 1918 election, the Sinn Féin representatives refused to attend parliament in Westminster.
- Sinn Féin MPs met at Mansion House in Dublin and set up the Dáil Éireann (Assembly of Ireland).
- This was not recognised by the British, but the Irish set about creating a state building.
- The Dáil met with considerable success in this period, setting up rival legal systems and winning over the bulk of the Irish.
- The British administration in Ireland effectively collapsed.

Policies and actions of the British government

- To begin with, the British used force to impose their will.
- The British government used the vicious paramilitary Black and Tans to assist the Royal Irish Constabulary (RIC) during the Irish War of Independence. They did not endear the British to the Irish population owing to their drunken and indiscriminate behaviour. There were atrocities on both sides, for example the massacre at Croke Park after the murder of British intelligence officers and the sacking of Cork city.

- There were vicious reprisals on Irish communities.
- Some attempts were made by the British to impose martial law.

Any other relevant factors.

30 *The issue of civil rights was the most important reason for the developing crisis in Northern Ireland by 1968.*

How valid is this view? (20)

Context: By the 1960s, the issue of discrimination against the Catholic minority in Northern Ireland developed into a major civil rights issue. This was due to a variety of social, economic and political reasons.

The issue of civil rights

- The civil rights movement in Northern Ireland dates from the 1960s when there were moves to campaign against injustices and inequalities.
- The most important organisation established during this period was the Northern Irish Civil Rights Association (NICRA), established in 1967 to protest against discrimination in terms of voting rights, etc.
- NICRA initially used petitions and lobbying, but these were ineffectual.
- In 1968 there were civil rights marches by the NICRA from Coalisland to Dungannon, Londonderry (Derry) and Belfast.
- Marches were opposed by the Protestant dominated police and there were Protestant counter-demonstrations.
- Rioting took place during the Derry march.
- There were concessions from Prime Minister Terence O'Neill's government over housing and an appeal to be allowed time to deliver more civil rights.

Other factors

The Unionist ascendancy in Northern Ireland and challenges to it

- Unionists dominated Northern Irish politics through the Ulster Unionist Party.
- Politics was dominated by issues like the gerrymandering of constituencies to favour Unionists. The right to vote in local elections was based on ratepayers who were more likely to be Unionists so they dominated the political process.
- The Unionist leader was Viscount Brookborough until 1963. The new Prime Minister after 1963, Terence O'Neill, was interested in building bridges with the nationalist community and with Eire but this was not popular with many Unionists, such as the followers of Reverend Ian Paisley.
- O'Neill could not automatically count on support from the British government. The Labour Party under Harold Wilson was in power and had links with the Northern Ireland Labour Party.
- British developments such as the welfare state had implications as they allowed all sections of the Northern Irish community access to benefits and all levels of education. This had implications as to rights, etc.
- The emergence of the civil rights movement by 1968 saw more forceful political campaigns against inequality.

Economic issues

- There was Protestant domination of better jobs, such as in shipbuilding, government, etc. The decline of traditional industries in the 1960s had an effect, though government protected places like the Harland and Wolff shipyard.
- There were inequalities in terms of government investment between Catholic and Protestant neighbourhoods.
- Subsidies were given to Northern Irish landowners who were mainly Protestant.
- Attempts were made to reform the economy, but these were unsuccessful due to entrenched attitudes.

Role of the IRA

- The IRA in the 1960s were heavily influenced by left-wing thinking. They split in 1969 into the Official IRA and Provisional IRA, which took a more traditional view of armed struggle and defence of Catholic areas against what they saw as the aggression of the British state.

Cultural and political differences

- A strong Catholic sense of identity emerged, encouraged by the reawakening of cultural interest and development of separate sporting culture, for example. Identity was strengthened through adversity.
- Catholic political representatives in parliament refused to recognise the partition of Ireland.
- On average, there were 10–12 Nationalists in the Northern Ireland Parliament compared to, on average, 40 Unionists. In Westminster, this was 10–12 Unionists to 2 Nationalists.
- There were splits in Unionism over O'Neill's attempts at compromise. Ultimately, this would lead to his resignation.
- There was violence in Derry when civil rights marchers were challenged by Unionists.

Any other relevant factors.

Section 3 – European and World

Part A – The Crusades, 1071–1204

31 To what extent was the emergence of a knightly class the main reason for the calling of the First Crusade? (20)

Context: Pope Urban II preached holy war to drive Muslims from Jerusalem and the Holy Land in 1095. His reasons for calling this crusade were many.

The emergence of a knightly class

- Medieval society saw the development of a knightly class.
- The Church also developed during this period and did not really approve of knights as they fought and were dedicated to acts that were against the teachings of Christ (thou shalt not kill).
- Crusade was an opportunity to use the skills of the knightly class in a productive way that would benefit Christianity and allow knights the opportunity of forgiveness of their sins. They could kill for God.

Other factors

Attempts to assert papal authority

- The Christian Church had formally split in 1054 into the Roman Catholic Church led by the Pope based in Rome and, what was to become, the Orthodox Catholic Church in the East, based in Constantinople.
- One of the important goals of the papacy was to heal this schism and unify the Christian Church.
- Pope Urban II was from the Cluniac tradition that sought to influence monarchs. Crusade was one way to do this.

The ongoing struggle between Church and state – the Investiture Contest

- The investiture controversy began as a power struggle between Pope Gregory VII (1072–1085) and Henry IV, Holy Roman Emperor (1056–1106) over who controlled the appointment of bishops and abbots.
- The calling and leading of Crusade would increase the status of the popes and reinforce their desire to be seen as having influence over princes and emperors.
- The was a counter-argument that the Investiture Contest distracted the West from Muslim attacks against Byzantium.

Fear of Islamic expansion

- Islam grew swiftly in the seventh century after its emergence in the Arabian peninsula.
- In 638, Muslim armies, under the caliphate of Umar bin al-Khattab, conquered the Holy City of Jerusalem.
- By 641, Muslims had driven the Byzantines out of Syria, Palestine and Egypt. Soon, North Africa, Spain and most of the Middle East was under Muslim control.
- This expansion led to a Christian fightback, such as the Spanish Reconquista from the early eighth century.

The threat to Byzantium

- During the eleventh century, the Byzantine Empire was suffering from major attacks by invading Muslim Seljuk Turks. The Seljuks conquered considerable land from the Byzantines in what is now Turkey and Armenia.
- The Byzantines had been defeated in 1071 at the Battle of Manzikert in eastern Anatolia. Manzikert was disastrous as it severely weakened the Byzantine Empire's ability to adequately defend its borders.
- Emperor Alexius' letter asking for help was taken very seriously in the West.

The threat to Mediterranean trade

- Constantinople was renowned for its merchants and markets.
- From the ninth century, Byzantine trade with its neighbours was at its zenith.
- Powerful Italian city states like Venice, Pisa and Genoa had preferential trade deals with Byzantium and derived great wealth from this trade. Therefore, they had no wish to see this trade disrupted.

Papal desire to channel the aggressive nature of feudal society

- Urban saw the opportunity to turn knights' behaviour into benefit for the Church and Christianity.
- Crusade also offered the opportunity to channel the aggression and disagreements between Christian states into a common cause against a common foe.

Any other relevant factors.

32 How important was the military power of the Crusader knights as a reason for the success of the First Crusade? (20)

Context: The First Crusade was a success due to a variety of reasons. It had been called to retake Jerusalem from the Muslims by Pope Urban II.

The military power of the Crusader knights

- Muslim leaders underestimated both the intentions and power of the Christian knights.
- Previous Crusades were not as militarily experienced as the First Crusade.
- A fully trained and armed knight mounted on his war-horse was a formidable opponent for anyone, let alone the more lightly armoured Muslim warriors.
- Lengthy training meant that knights were skilled and aggressive in combat as well as disciplined when needed, for example at the Battle of Dorylaeum.
- Many Crusader knights had experience of fighting the Muslims already, for example Raymond of Toulouse who had fought in Spain.

Other factors

Divisions among the Islamic states

- There were doctrinal splits in the Islamic world between Sunni and Shia. At the time of the First Crusade, Sunnis (Seljuk Turks) controlled Asia Minor and Syria, while Shia (Fatimids) controlled Egypt.
- Both sides would do deals with the Crusaders against what they saw as the greater enemy of their fellow Muslims.
- A unified Islamic response did not emerge. Divisions were even seen during battle, for example at Antioch in 1098.

The religious zeal of the Crusaders

- There was real belief that the Crusade was a result of God's will.
- While Raymond and the other leaders often quarrelled with each other over the leadership of the Crusade, The Papal Legate: Bishop Adhemar, was always recognised as the spiritual leader of the Crusade and was a crucial unifying force at times (before his death in 1098). He also led by example, for instance during the siege and Battle of Antioch.
- Religious belief was crucial at times for the success of the Crusade. For example, 'finding' the Holy Lance spurred the Crusaders on, as did the vision of Peter Desiderius urging the Crusaders to fast before the eventual taking of Jerusalem.

Misunderstanding of the Crusaders' intent

- The ideological nature of the Crusaders was not understood by the Muslim leaders. They saw the Crusade as a limited incursion, such as that practised by the Byzantines in Asia Minor. This undoubtedly helped the Crusaders as it contributed to the confused response of the Muslim leaders.

Aid from Byzantium

- The First Crusade had support from Byzantium in the form of guides and supplies. For example, as the Crusaders marched on through Anatolia, they were accompanied by some Byzantine troops under Tatikios.
- During the siege of Antioch in 1097–1098, the Byzantine navy helped keep the besieging army supplied with basic necessities.
- Alexius' army did not take part in the Crusade, but they did cause problems, diverting Muslim resources.

Any other relevant factors.

33 To what extent was Richard more successful than Saladin, both as a military leader and as a diplomat during the Third Crusade? (20)

Context: The Third Crusade is famous due to the leadership of both sides: Richard I of England and Saladin, Sultan of Egypt and Syria. In practical terms, Jerusalem was not recovered, but the Crusaders fought well and concessions were gained from the Muslims.

Richard's military strengths

- The two-year siege of Acre was ended swiftly after Richard's arrival. He gave greater purpose to the siege as well as bringing money and siege technology.
- Richard led from the front, and was also brutal, as seen by the massacre of Muslim prisoners taken at Acre.
- Richard's Crusaders showed skilled movement of troops in the Middle East from Acre to Jaffa. Military formations were skilfully placed and were supported by a fleet on their journey.
- The Battle of Arsuf saw the decisive defeat of Saladin's forces by Richard's army.
- Arsuf proved Richard's courage as a soldier and his skill as a commander.
- The taking of Jaffa and retaining it with a decisive amphibious attack showed Richard's military strengths.

- Richard realised that taking Jerusalem was not practical, though he did rebuild the fortress at Ascalon, threatening Saladin's communications with Egypt.
- Militarily, the Third Crusade transformed the chances of survival for the Crusader States.

Richard's military weaknesses

- Despite Richard's successes, the Holy Land was not totally recovered and Jerusalem remained in Muslim hands.
- Richard was fortunate at Arsuf as the Hospitallers' (a military order) indiscipline led them to attack before Richard ordered. Fortunately, Richard launched an attack in support of them.

Saladin's military strengths

- Saladin showed skill in counter-attack at Acre and Jaffa. His army destroyed the siege engines at Acre and swiftly moved to re-occupy Jaffa soon after his forces had been ejected.
- Counter-attack at the Battle of Arsuf saw many of the more enthusiastic Christian knights killed.

Saladin's military weaknesses

- Demands from his emirs meant it was difficult for Saladin to field a large army for any length of time.
- There was considerable criticism within the Muslim world that he was not able to drive the Crusaders into the sea.
- Militarily, the major actions were all defeats for Saladin, though the cohesion of his forces was maintained.

Richard's diplomatic strengths

- Richard began negotiations with Saladin, who sent his brother to meet with Richard after the taking of Jaffa.
- On 2 September 1192, following his defeat at Jaffa, Saladin was forced to finalise a treaty with Richard: Jerusalem would remain under Muslim control, unarmed Christian pilgrims and traders could visit the city.

Richard's diplomatic weaknesses

- Richard showed poor diplomacy with his allies, alienating Count Leopold of Austria, after Acre, and Philip of France, who left for home.
- He backed Guy de Lusignan as King of Jerusalem despite the fact Conrad Montferrat was more popular.

Saladin's diplomatic strengths

- Saladin and Richard engaged in diplomacy throughout much of the Third Crusade.
- Saladin recognised the need to make a truce with Richard. In 1192, the Treaty of Jaffa was agreed which partitioned Palestine in return for a three-year truce.
- Saladin held together a large and diverse Muslim force.

Saladin's diplomatic weaknesses

- Saladin faced increasing discontent from his Muslim allies.
- He negotiated a truce over Jerusalem with Richard despite his strong position overall.

Any other relevant factors.

Part B – The American Revolution, 1763–1787

34 How important was the role of George III as a reason for colonial resentment towards Britain by 1763? (20)

Context: By 1763, Britain had ruled the thirteen American colonies for over a century. Resentment towards British rule grew due to a variety of factors.

George III

- When the Seven Years' War ended, George III increased the number of British troops in the colonies. This was seen as a threat by some in the colonies.
- He used the Royal Navy to cut down on smuggling and to enforce the Navigation Acts.
- In order to pay for the war, taxes were introduced in America. This caused much resentment.

Other factors

Navigation Acts

- The Navigation Acts were a series of English laws that restricted colonial trade to the mother country, which were reinforced after the end of the Seven Years' War.

- The Navigation Acts required all of a colony's imports to be either bought from England or resold by English merchants in England, no matter what price could be obtained elsewhere.
- In reality there seems to have been minimal economic impact, but it caused resentment, as it was felt that the Act was imposed by the British parliament in which the Americans had no representation, plus it meant they could not trade with Europe as they wished.

The old colonial system

- The American colonies had traditionally been used by the British to exploit raw materials and to sell goods.
- Profits from American resources were exploited by British traders, which caused resentment.
- Plantation owners resented restrictions on their trade in sugar, cotton and molasses.
- Colonists benefited from access to the British Empire and the protection of British military forces.

The Proclamation of 1763

- The Royal Proclamation of 1763 was issued by King George III following the acquisition of French territory in North America after the end of the Seven Years' War. It prohibited all settlement beyond a line drawn along the Appalachian Mountains.
- There was resentment from a minority who wanted to push west in the search for land.

Political differences

- There was general resentment that Britain sought to govern America, but denied them representation in parliament.
- Local colonial assemblies operated efficiently and effectively.
- British governors were paid by the colonies so gave colonialists some control.

British neglect

- Colonies had operated with considerable independence from 1727 to 1760 during the Whig ascendancy.
- Colonists moved west, frequently at odds with agreements made by the British and Indians, and led to demands for change.

Any other relevant factors.

35 To what extent did the views of Edmund Burke represent British opinion towards the conflict in the colonies? (20)

Context: British opinion of the conflict in the colonies varied from support for the colonists' aims to outrage and opposition.

Edmund Burke

- Burke was a new MP in 1765. In general he was understanding of the colonists' motives and critical of British policy. For example, he spoke out against the Stamp Act. However, he did not wish the colonists to leave the British Empire.
- In 1769, he published a pamphlet that blamed the British government for creating policies that stirred the conflict.
- He understood the need for good relations with the Americans, but was criticised at home.

Thomas Paine

- Paine's pamphlets were widely read, but not necessarily supported. He attacked the monarchy and was something of a radical.
- Published in 1776, his highly popular (in America) 'Common Sense' was the first pamphlet to advocate American independence.
- His support for American independence put him at odds with prevailing thought in Britain.

George III

- George wanted to see America pay for the protection Britain had provided during the Seven Years' War. He supported taxation of American products, such as tea, and the active application of the Navigation Acts.
- He introduced the Coercive Acts in response to events such as the Boston Tea Party, causing resentment.
- He was very interested in the American Wars, and intervened politically at home as well.

Parliament

- Through the Proclamation Act in 1763, Stamp Act in 1765, Declaratory Act in 1766, Tea Act in 1773 and Coercive Acts in 1774, parliament enforced British authority over the colonies.
- The majority of lords and MPs endorsed the views of the King.
- Parliament used military enforcement as a tool to control America between 1763 and 1776.
- Prime ministers through this period supported active prosecution for the war against America.

Earl of Chatham

- William Pitt, Earl of Chatham, had effectively been Britain's leader during the Seven Years' War.
- He was sympathetic to the colonists and didn't like the Stamp Act, for example. He sought to find compromise with the colonists.
- Pitt felt that Britain could not win once war broke out.

Differing British views of the situation in the colonies

- Lord Grenville, Prime Minister 1763–1765, represented the rights of British merchants and supported their attempts to raise revenue in America.
- Lord Rockingham, Prime Minister 1765–1766, advocated British parliamentary sovereignty over America.
- The Duke of Grafton, Prime Minister 1768–1770, believed in the superiority of the British Parliament over America.
- Lord North, Prime Minster 1770–1782, believed parliament should enforce British interests and supremacy in the colonies. He believed the war could be won.
- John Wilkes was elected as an MP in 1768, was a radical and spoke out against British policy on America.
- Businessmen favoured the Navigation Acts, but wanted the war to end as it disrupted trade.
- There was some sympathy for colonists in Scotland and Ireland in terms of resentment at the power of their bigger neighbour.

Any other relevant factors.

36 *French entry into the war explains why the colonists won the War of Independence.*

How valid is this view? (20)

Context: The American War of Independence took place between 1776 and 1781, between Britain and its thirteen colonies of North America. There were a number of factors that contributed to the colonists' victory.

French entry into the war

- The French had been on the losing side in the Seven Years' War so looked for revenge on Britain during the American War of Independence by siding with the colonist rebels.
- The Franco-American Treaty was signed in 1778, recognising the United States.
- France provided valuable physical support in terms of material, troops and naval vessels.
- There was important French military contribution to the war, such as defeat of the British fleet at the Battle of Chesapeake and the supplying of siege equipment at Yorktown.

Other factors

British military inefficiency

- British military forces struggled with poor communication and operating at such a long distance from their political masters. It sometimes took months for troops to reach North America, and orders were often out of date because the military situation on the ground had changed by the time they arrived.
- There were many examples of poor military planning and operation, for example General John Burgoyne's Saratoga campaign.
- There were practical logistical problems, for example British flints could fire only six rounds before requiring re-sharpening, while American flints could fire 60 rounds before re-sharpening.
- The British suffered from a manpower shortage and could not hold ground even if it had been won in battle.

Washington's military capability

- George Washington had prestige, military experience, charisma and was known as a strong patriot when he became Commander-in-Chief of the Continental Army.
- He led, organised army training and appointed capable officers, for example, General Daniel Morgan who had fought in the American–Indian wars.
- Washington had served with the British and was aware of their systems and procedures.
- He benefited from having a very motivated army.

Washington's leadership

- Washington was a respected businessman who had entered politics and served with distinction in the Seven Years' War.
- He was a popular choice as Commander-in-Chief of the Continental Army.
- He enthused his men, listened to advice and was able to ensure logistical support for them. He trusted the men that he found to lead the army and gave them the latitude to do what was necessary.

French contribution worldwide

- The French got into massive debt owing to their participation in the American War of Independence.
- French naval forces ensured that British naval units were spread thinly as they could not now be concentrated on America, for example action in the Indian Ocean.
- The French navy made a significant contribution through action at the battles of Chesapeake Bay and Ushant.
- The French contribution encouraged others to join the war to get at the British, for example Holland and Spain.

Local knowledge

- The war was mostly fought on American soil, giving an immediate advantage to the American Continental Army.
- Most locals favoured the rebels and did not actively help the British, even burning their crops at times. The distance between Britain and the colonies already meant that supplies were slow in arriving at the front.

Any other relevant factors.

Part C – The French Revolution, to 1799

37 How important were the grievances of the bourgeoisie in the developing threat to the security of the Ancien Regime in the years before 1789? (20)

Context: The Ancien Regime in France came to an end with the Revolution of 1789. By the late eighteenth century, opposition to the monarchy and its institutions was developing for a variety of reasons.

The grievances of the bourgeoisie

- The developing bourgeoisie were members of the Third Estate. As such, they were subject to much of the taxation that the peasantry had to endure, though they could pay the taille if they did not want to do military service.
- The bourgeoisie was educated and bitterly resented the excesses of the nobility and monarchy.
- The bourgeoisie wanted access to political power, but the structures of the Ancien Regime were inflexible, leading to increased frustration as seen with the interest in the philosophs.

Other factors

Grievances held by the peasantry

- The peasantry was burdened with a mass of taxation and service by the Ancien Regime.
- They made up the mass of the population and bitterly resented the excesses of the nobility and the powers of their landlords.
- Peasants had to deal with high prices, poor harvests and bad winters in the 1780s, which added to their misery.

Role of the nobility

- Most of the nobility wished to retain the privileges they had according to their status.
- The majority supported the monarchy.
- A minority saw that the system needed to change.

Position of the clergy

- The First Estate included wealthy bishops and poor clergy. Its sympathies were therefore varied.
- The First Estate did not pay much taxation.
- Poorer priests sympathised with the lot of the peasants, but the leadership was far removed from the reality of daily life.

Financial issues

- The monarchy was in debt owing to its involvement in foreign wars like the American War of Independence, where the French had the pleasure of seeing Britain humbled, but incurred massive debt because of financing their military and naval contribution.
- Attempts to reform the system by finance ministers, like Necker and Calonne, ultimately failed owing to the opposition of the nobility and lack of support from the monarchy.

Taxation

- The tax system was unfair, with exemptions from much taxation for the wealthy First and Second Estates.
- There was a dreadful collection system, in part due to the chaotic administration system in France.
- The Third Estate paid the bulk of taxation on their income (capitation and vingtième) and indirectly on commodities like salt (the gabelle).

Corruption

- Corruption was rife, politically with lack of change, economically with the unfair tax system that was exploited at a local level and socially with the rigid estates system.

The royal family

- The French royal family lived in Versailles, in a bubble of affluence that hid the realities of life for most people.
- Louis XVI was ridiculed as a weak and indecisive monarch.
- His wife, Marie Antoinette, was hated as she was Austrian and lived an extravagant life.

Any other relevant factors.

38 To what extent were the attitude and actions of Louis XVI the main reason for the failure of constitutional monarchy, 1789–1792? (20)

Context: In the aftermath of the 1789 Revolution, the monarchy clung to a limited amount of power. This was bitterly resented by Louis, who sought to overturn the Revolution.

Attitudes and actions of Louis XVI

- Louis disliked the idea of a constitutional monarchy and was obstructive, which made him even more unpopular.
- He had vetoed key Assembly demands such as decrees against 'refractory' priests and émigrés.
- His actions on attempting to flee the Revolution in the 1791 flight to Varennes confirmed his lack of loyalty to the new government. The fact he was fleeing to join émigré nobles was also not in his favour.
- Rumours of attempts to contact émigrés and the Austrian Emperor to overturn the Revolution seemed to be confirmed.

Other factors

Character of Louis XVI

- Louis was not good at making decisions and tended to appoint 'yes' men to important positions.
- He did not support reforming ministers when he had the chance.
- He was weak and indecisive.

Weaknesses in the constitution and the government

- Louis disliked the restrictions on his power.
- The Legislative Assembly members such as the Girondins and Jacobins disliked the way Louis used his veto to block legislation. Many members were increasingly radicalised.
- Political factionalism at Assembly level increased with many groups unhappy with the political settlement after 1789.

Financial problems

- The economy was in trouble before 1789 and did not improve with the Revolution.
- Inflation spiralled out of control.
- Increases in the price of basic food stuffs like bread made workers in urban areas restless.
- There was continued heavy taxation.

Foreign affairs and the outbreak of war

- The Holy Roman Emperor, Leopold, was the brother of Marie Antoinette and increasingly viewed events in France with concern.
- He, along with the Prussian king and French émigré nobles, announced the Declaration of Pillnitz, which stated that European leaders were concerned about the well-being of Louis and his family. This was viewed with alarm by the French government, who perceived it as a threat to French sovereignty.
- The Legislative Assembly with Louis' support declared war on Austria.
- The French invasion of the Austrian Netherlands was a shambles.
- A Prussian–Austrian army, under the Duke of Brunswick, invaded and issued the Brunswick Manifesto, declaring their intention to restore Louis to the throne.
- Louis' position was now fatally undermined in the eyes of the mob.
- Louis and his family fled the mob and he was arrested on 13 August 1792. The constitutional monarchy was at an end.

Any other relevant factors.

39 *The role of Napoleon was the most important reason for the establishment of the Consulate.*

How valid is this view? (20)

Context: Political chaos characterised the Revolution, with change from the monarchy to constitutional monarchy, to radical republican terror to the Directory and eventually to the Consulate and Napoleon. The reasons for the formation of the Consulate were many.

The role of Napoleon

- Napoleon was the hero of the Revolution in many people's eyes after successfully campaigning in northern Italy against the Austrians and in Egypt against the Mamluks.
- In fact, he left his troops in Egypt after the destruction of the French fleet by Nelson, but he did return to France in October.
- It was hoped that he could bring stability to France.
- Napoleon had political aims along with Sieyès.
- Napoleon had strong support in the military and led the coup against the Directory.

Other factors

Political instability

- France had undergone a series of increasingly radical governments since the Revolution of 1789. People were tiring of the political uncertainty.
- Political factions in France viewed each other with suspicion.
- France suffered from the destruction of what had become a civil war.
- France was threatened with invasion by other European powers who did not want to see the Revolution spread to their countries.

Army involvement in politics

- As the French army improved in performance it came to be used more within France. Bonaparte, for example, as a young artillery officer had been involved in the famous 'whiff of grapeshot' incidents to put down disturbances in Paris.
- Army success in the Revolutionary Wars, such as Napoleon's conquest of Italy, made generals into heroes.
- The Directory had been protected by the army from a Royalist insurrection in 1795.

The Constitution of 1795

- The Constitution of the Year III (1795) is the constitution that founded the Directory.
- The Constitution of 1795 was intended to found a republic with a franchise based on the payment of taxes; a bicameral legislature (Council of Ancients and a Council of 500) to slow down the legislative process; and a five-man Directory. It all aimed to provide a stable system that could not be dominated by one area.
- In reality the checks and balances in the Constitution slowed down decision making and made strong and decisive government difficult to achieve.

Role of Abbé Sieyès

- Sieyès was an important theorist of the French Revolution who had been involved from its beginning. He had wanted to set up a bourgeois constitutional monarchy and was no fan of the way the Revolution had radicalised.
- He became increasingly concerned to make France stable and thought he had found the right man to support him in Bonaparte. After the overthrow of the Director, he became Second Consul, but his planned constitution never came to fruition as Bonaparte imposed his own ideas.

Any other relevant factors.

Part D – Germany, 1815–1939

40 How important were economic factors as a reason for the growth of nationalism in Germany, 1815–1850? (20)

Context: After 1815, Prussia emerged as the most powerful of the German states. However, the 39 states continued to act independently of each other. Yet, by 1850, there were growing demands for German unity.

Economic factors

- Middle-class businessmen, observing the industrial progress of rivals like Britain, envied the benefits of operating under one government and called for a more united market to enable them to compete with foreign countries.
- Businessmen complained that the numerous customs barriers were raising money for the state governments but holding back economic development because it made goods more expensive.

- The example of Prussia herself demonstrated the benefits of a free trade area within certain borders.
- After 1815, Prussia began to exploit the Rhineland's coal and iron deposits. This increase in wealth drew political power away from the conservative Austrians who were resistant to change.
- It was in Prussia's interests to develop relatively free travel along the River Rhine in order to benefit its people in its lands in the east and west.
- After 1830, the development of a rail and roads network demonstrated the benefits of closer communications and links with other states. It ended the political isolation of individual states and by facilitating economic co-operation encouraged those in favour of political union to campaign further.

Other factors

The Zollverein

- The Zollverein or customs union has been called the 'mighty lever' of German unification by Andrina Styles. By 1836, 25 of the 39 German states had joined this economic free-trade area (Austria was excluded). The economic exclusion of Austria weakened its political influence in the long term.

Cultural factors

- Language was the main unifying force; 25 million Germans spoke the same language, and shared the same culture and literature.
- Influential writers and thinkers raised the profile of Germanic art and culture abroad, thus encouraging interest at home, for example Heine, Fichte, Goethe, Brothers Grimm, Schiller, Hegel.
- Post-1815 nationalist feelings were first expressed in universities.
- There was a growth in *Burschenschaften* (fraternities), groups of students dedicated to driving the French from German soil.
- The growth of sports clubs and choral societies dedicated to the development of nationalist ideas were important in keeping these ideas alive during those years when repressive police supervision discouraged overt nationalism.
- The 1840 Rhine crisis, where the French appeared to be threatening to extend their border to the Rhine again, prompted outrage and national feeling. There was an outpouring of literature, songs and poems including the popular 'Watch on the Rhine' which called for German unity to withstand such threats.
- In 1832, the *Hambach Fest* and student demonstrations took place, but apart from some passionate flag waving, little was accomplished by the students.

Military weaknesses

- French military occupation had an impact. It made Germans realise the consequences of being politically divided, that is they were unable to withstand foreign invasion; for example, the French had humiliated Prussia at Jena and Auerstadt. Austria had also been militarily humbled by the French.
- Napoleon had operated 'divide and rule' in Germany: the North Sea coast was incorporated into France itself, and the Confederation of the Rhine was set up as a puppet state.
- Napoleon had recruited soldiers from Germany, who had fought and died for France. Only Prussia was large enough as a state to prevent this kind of scenario happening again.

Effects of the French Revolution and Napoleonic Wars

- There was a cultural impact of the French occupation; the ideas of the French Revolution – Liberté, Égalité, Fraternité – appealed to the middle classes in the German states. This was the group for whom nationalism was most likely to appeal.
- The Napoleonic Wars also had an effect; many Germans argued that they had been defeated by Napoleon because they had been divided. German princes had promoted national feeling to help raise armies to drive out the French, aiding the sense of a common German identity with common goals.

Role of the Liberals

- Liberals favoured more political influence for their class. Many Liberals were middle class and also receptive to nationalist ideas, so the cause of political progress and nationalism often went hand-in-hand.
- Even though the 1848 revolutions in Germany failed, they helped promote nationalism. For the first time, there was popular involvement in the debate over the future of Germany, however short-lived.

Any other relevant factors.

41 *Resentment against Prussia was the most significant obstacle to German unification, 1815–1850.*

   How valid is this view? (20)

Context: Although nationalism grew throughout the period there were powerful forces that opposed the integration of the Germanic states.

Resentment towards Prussia

- The economic dominance of Prussia across Germany was supported in the sense that German states joined the Zollverein, but there was resentment of that power as seen by their behaviour in the Bund, where smaller states tended to side with Austria.
- Austria resented its rejection from the Zollverein and the failure of its own customs union.
- The growth in Prussian power threatened Austrian dominance of the Bund as seen by the Treaty of Olmütz where Prussian proposals for the Erfut Union were firmly rejected.

Other factors

Divisions among the nationalists

- There were disagreements about what a united Germany should be like, especially between the *grossdeutsch* and *kleindeutsch* arguments.
- Divisions and weaknesses of the movement were seen in the 1848 risings where the Frankfurt Parliament talked much, but acted little.
- The decision of the prussian king to oppose the parliament after initially being sympathetic showed where the real power lay.

Austrian strength

- Throughout this period, Austria dominated 'Germany' politically.
- Austria was president of the Bund after the Congress of Vienna and this helped its leaders to oppose nationalism and promote the interests of the individual German states.
- There was active opposition to nationalism, through censorship and repression, as it threatened the multi-national Austrian Empire. Examples include the Karlsbad Decrees and Six Articles.
- In fact, the military power of Austria was waning, but could still be potent, as seen by their actions in Italy in the 1848 revolutions.
- The Treaty of Olmütz, 1850, signalled the political triumph of Austria over Prussia. In the short term, nationalism had been contained.

German princes

- Organisations like the Bund enhanced the power of individual rulers as decisions had to be unanimous.
- Rulers of the independent states had little interest in unification as it had implications for their rule and power.
- There were strong regional differences which were fiercely defended by the individual rulers across the Germanic states that were enhanced by long periods of independence. For example, the Kingdom of Bavaria had existed in some form since 1623.

Religious differences

- The Treaty of Westphalia that ended the devastating religious wars (termed the Thirty Years' War) across Germany left the northern Germanic states following Protestantism and the southern Germanic states following Catholicism. It also left lingering resentment.
- The religious difference exacerbated existing resentments and feelings of being different across the German states.

Economic differences

- Commercial trade developed across the Customs Union, but there were significant economic differences even within the Union.
- Prussia itself was very varied compared with the industrially more developed Rhineland given to it at the Congress of Vienna, but the eastern estates of the Junkers in the East were largely rural and bred the conservative Junker class who still had some influence at this time.

Indifference of the masses

- Through this period the mass of the population were peasants with some industrial workers. They were largely indifferent to the idea of a unified Germany, though there was some stirring of cultural pride.
- Nationalism had most effect on the middle classes. The upper classes had little interest.

Any other relevant factors.

42 To what extent was the role of Hitler the main reason why the Nazis achieved power in 1933? (20)

Context: By 1933, the Nazis had grown from a small, extremist party to the largest party in the Reichstag.

Role of Hitler

- Hitler was seen as young and dynamic when compared with the other leaders of political parties in the Weimar Republic.
- He was an excellent public speaker who used his opportunities well to advertise his beliefs, such as the trial for his part in the Munich Beer Hall Putsch.
- He gave scapegoats the blame for the condition Germany was in and had a clear message about making Germany great again.

- He knew what he wanted, power, and was willing to wait and plan for it, but to act decisively when needed, such as 'holding his nose' and going into parliament after the failure of the Munich Beer Hall Putsch, and using the opportunity of the Reichstag Fire to further his cause.

Other factors

Weaknesses of the Weimar Republic

- Initial enthusiasm for the Republic waned in the aftermath of its acceptance of the Treaty of Versailles.
- The Weimar Republic electoral system was proportional, which, though great in a democratic sense, was a disaster for such a politically polarised parliament.
- The use of Article 48 by the President could be abused and meant people got used to such a method of decision making.
- There was a lack of support from the key institutions of state, such as the judiciary, civil service and army, and an unwillingness to reform these institutions.
- The alliance between the reactionary *Freikorps* and democratic government showed the weakness of the government.

Resentment towards the Treaty of Versailles

- The key problem for the democratic politicians was their acceptance of the Treaty of Versailles.
- The German people believed they had been fighting a war of defence and the peace settlement would be based on Wilson's fourteen points.
- Germans felt betrayed by the terms of the treaty, especially the land loss.
- The right blamed the democratic politicians and created the myth of 'stab in the back' as well as the term 'November Criminals'.

Social and economic difficulties

- Reparations were bitterly resented and were blamed for the country's economic woes.
- The hyperinflation crisis of 1923 had a particularly significant impact on the country's middle classes, a group whose support the Weimar Republic needed.
- The Great Depression of 1929 transformed the political situation in Germany. It led to businesses shutting and rising unemployment. The people blamed the Republic, turning to radical alternatives as an easy answer to difficult issues.

Appeal of the Nazis after 1928

- The Nazi message had not changed, but people began to listen during the Depression.
- Its anti-communist, anti-Versailles, make-Germany-strong message had appeal among the middle classes who feared a 'Red' government.
- The Nazis also gave desperate people someone to blame: the Jews, communists, Democrats and 'November Criminals'.
- Josef Goebbels orchestrated an effective use of propaganda.

Weaknesses and mistakes of others

- There was a lack of unified opposition to Fascism within the Weimar Republic, especially between the left-wing parties of the SPD (Social Democratic Party) and KPD (German Communist Party).
- The traditional right wing, in the form of Von Papen, made mistakes, for example thinking that they could make Hitler do their will.
- The age and infirmity of Hindenburg was a weakness.

Any other relevant factors.

Part E – Italy, 1815–1939

43 To what extent was resentment of Austria the main reason for the growth of nationalism in Italy, 1815–1850? (20)

Context: Italy was a patchwork of small states in the early nineteenth century. It was dominated by the powerful Austrian Empire. However, nationalism grew for a number of reasons.

Resentment of Austria

- Austria controlled the wealthy areas of Lombardy and Venetia in the north of Italy. Austrian rulers were also in place in Parma, Modena and Tuscany.
- Austrian rule varied in Italy, for example the autocrat rulers of the Duchies were well-meaning and did their best for their subjects, but Austrian rule could also be heavy handed and the policy of promotion in the police, civil service and army only for German speakers was resented.
- Austrian military presence across the Quadrilateral fortresses (Peschiera, Mantua, Legnago and Verona) across Lombardy and Venetia, ensured the Italians were kept in their place.

Other factors

Cultural factors

- The *Risorgomento* (resurgence or re-birth) developed in this period; it was largely middle-class in its appeal.
- Artistic and literary figures turned towards nationalism; Vittorio Alfieri, Francesco Lomonaco and Niccolò Tommaseo are generally considered three great early writers who appealed to Italian nationalism. Also operas such as Verdi's 'Nabucco' and Rossini's 'William Tell'.
- Alessandro Manzoni's *I promessi sposi* (The Betrothed), was a criticism of Austrian rule.
- The development of a common Italian language further encouraged cultural unity.

Economic factors

- Italy was relatively backward economically, nevertheless there were some economic developments which encouraged nationalism.
- The new Pope, Pius IX, wished to form a customs union in Italy. He also improved the transportation system by building roads, viaducts, bridges and seaports. A series of new railway links connected the Papal States to northern Italy, which further encouraged trade.
- Such economic integration demonstrated the benefits of working together. In turn this had an impact on the desire for greater unity.

Military weakness

- Italy had been regularly invaded during the Napoleonic Wars.
- The 1815 Vienna Settlement divided Italy up into numerous states which were individually weak.

Effects of the French Revolution and Napoleonic Wars

- The French Revolution had encouraged Italian nationalists to begin with. The ideal of freedom seemed to fit well with the desire for unity and independence from foreign rule.
- However, the reality of Napoleonic rule was repressive, though it did reduce the number of Italian states and introduced common weights and measures, etc.

Role of Mazzini

- Giuseppe Mazzini brought leadership to the nationalist movement.
- He believed in Italy as a unified country with a republican government.
- He created the Young Italy movement, which had clear aims to unify Italy.

Secret societies

- These organisations were dedicated to freeing Italy from foreign rule.
- The most important was the Carbonari (charcoal burners) who had a largely middle-class support.
- They were idealistic, but did rise up in revolts in 1820, 1821 and 1831.
- Young Italy was created by Giuseppe Mazzini.

Any other relevant factors.

44 *The attitude of the Papacy was the main obstacle to Italian unification, 1815–1850.*

   How valid is this view? (20)

Context: By 1850 the forces of nationalism had grown in Italy. The revolutions of 1848 showed this. However, there were many obstacles which prevented unification from happening before 1850, such as the dominant position of Austria and her dependent duchies.

Attitude of the Papacy

- Pope Pius IX came out against nationalism in 1848; he was unwilling to fight against Austria as it was a leading Catholic power.
- In his denouncement of the war against Austria, Pius IX delivered a bitter blow to devout Catholic nationalists.
- The Roman Republic was set up in 1849 and was denounced by the Pope, who called on the Catholic powers of Europe to restore him. French forces were duly despatched and the city fell after three months of resistance. The Pope had sided with autocracy.

Other factors

Dominant position of Austria and her dependent duchies

- After the 1815 Vienna Settlement, the Austrian Emperor had direct control over Lombardy and Venetia. Fellow Habsburgs were in charge in the duchies and he had agreements with the Papacy and other states.

- Lombardy and Venetia were ruthlessly run with what was effectively a police state. Government jobs could only be gained if you spoke German.
- The Austrian army was well protected behind its defensive frontier, known as the 'Quadrilateral'.
- The Austrian Commander was the elderly Joseph Radetsky, who was a very capable military commander.
- He fell back on the Quadrilateral, waited for reinforcements and then routed the pro-unification forces of the Piedmontese monarch, Charles Albert at the Battle of Custozza.
- He besieged Venetia until the Republic of St Mark surrendered on 22 August 1849.
- The Austrian army swiftly re-established control.

Social, economic and cultural differences

- Italy was a geographically divided country.
- In particular, there were divisions between the north and south of the country in terms of economic development as well as regional dialects.

Political differences/divisions among the nationalists

- The nationalists were divided in what they wanted when the opportunity arose.
- Mazzini wanted a democratic republic, while people like Gioberti wanted a confederation of princes led by the Pope.
- Many moderate nationalists were fearful of the ideas of people like Mazzini.
- The secret societies lacked specific aims and were poorly organised.
- The 1848 Revolution was a missed opportunity, but did show divisions between leaders and states. For example, when Piedmontese soldiers 'liberated' Lombardy and Venetia they were disappointed that the people of these regions seemed to want a republic rather than to be ruled by Piedmont.

Italian princes

- The rulers of the many Italian states were going to oppose nationalism in any form as it would mean they were out of a job. For example, King Ferdinand in Naples/Sicily was threatened by rebellion in 1820. He initially promised reform, but when he had the chance he asked for Austrian help to crush the rebellion. Metternich was only too pleased to help.

Indifference of the masses

- Italy was a relatively poor European country. The mass of population were peasants who were simply not that interested in nationalism. For example, some felt that Mazzini was inspirational, but in reality he had relatively few members in his Young Italy organisation.

Any other relevant factors.

45 How important were the weaknesses of Italian governments as a reason why the Fascists achieved power in Italy, 1919–1925? (20)

Context: By 1925, Mussolini and the Fascists had gained power in Italy. Many factors contributed to the Fascist rise to power in Italy, such as the weakness of the political system and the determination of Mussolini and the Fascists.

Weaknesses of Italian governments

- Parliamentary government was weak and corrupt in Italy.
- Since unification, Italy had been governed by middle-class Liberals who formed coalitions.
- After 1919, elections were by proportional representation. This encouraged the growth of small parties and weak governing coalitions were the norm.
- The weakness of the system can be seen in the speed of its collapse.

Other factors

Role of Mussolini

- Mussolini took the Fascists on an extreme right-wing political journey, seeing parliamentary democracy as weak and degenerate. Their message proved seductive.
- He was an effective orator.
- He grasped the opportunity to seize power in the political chaos of Italy after the war.

Economic difficulties

- At the beginning of the First World War there was a boom in war-related industries.
- War was financed by extending government debt. Inflation hit the lira.
- After the war, unemployment rose to 2 million. Many unemployed were ex-soldiers who were increasingly resentful.

Resentment against the Peace Settlement

- In 1915, Italy entered the war on the side of the Entente. They had been promised land in Europe and a share of land abroad, as well as a share in any reparations after the war.
- In fact, Italy was a military liability and had to be helped by Britain and France. The war did cost 600,000 Italian lives, however. After the war, Italy was largely ignored at the Peace Conference.
- Italy got most of the European land it had been promised, but no colonies and no share of the reparations. This caused a lot of resentment.

Appeal of the Fascists

- The Fascists promised to end political chaos and oppose the 'Red menace'. There was a focus on order, reliability and power which appealed to many in the middle and upper classes.
- The Fascists were nationalistic which was popular and promised to make Italy great again.
- *Squadristi* (paramilitary militia) violence was directed against socialism so gained the support of industrialists and many of the middle class.

Role of the King

- At key moments the King gave in to the Fascists. Initially a state of emergency and imposition of martial law was agreed as the Fascists marched on Rome, but the King changed his mind.
- Mussolini demanded to be made Prime Minister. The King agreed to this.
- Even after the murder of Matteotti and the Aventine Secession, the King was unwilling to dismiss Mussolini.

Social and economic divisions

- Political divisions were exacerbated by social and economic inequalities. For example, membership of trades unions and the PSI (Italian Socialist Party) rose – strikes, demonstrations and violence occurred.
- Industrialists and the middle classes were fearful of revolution – they were concerned about a breakdown in law and order.
- In the countryside, there was seizure of common land – peasant ownership increased.
- The brutal behaviour of Fascists across the north of Italy in 1922, under Italo Balbo, was not stopped by the police.

Weaknesses and mistakes of opponents

- Political opponents were divided. Liberals were split into four factions, for example.
- There was not the political will to oppose Mussolini in the end.
- Government weakness was seen in actions like the failure to stop D'Annunzio's seizure of Fiume.

Any other relevant factors.

Part F – Russia, 1881–1921

46 *The security of the Tsarist state was never seriously challenged in the years before 1905.*

How valid is this view? (20)

Context: By the beginning of the twentieth century, the Romanov dynasty had been in power for centuries. Industrialisation and modernisation came late to Russia. The Tsar's government reluctantly began to adapt to the changed world in which they lived.

Tsarist methods of control

The Tsar maintained control by a variety of measures. Collectively these were known as the 'Pillars of Autocracy':

- **Fundamental Law:** This stated 'To the emperor of all Russia belongs the Supreme and unlimited power. God himself commands that his supreme power be obeyed out of conscience as well as out of fear'. The lack of any restrictions on Tsarist authority was the basis of its government.
- **Church:** The Church helped to ensure that the people, particularly the peasants, remained loyal to the Tsar. They preached to the peasants that the Tsar had been appointed by God and that they should therefore obey the Tsar. The Church also ensured the peasants were aware of the Fundamental Law.
- **Army:** This was controlled by the officers who were mainly upper class; some were close relatives of the Tsar. They were therefore conservative and loyal to the Tsar. They crushed any uprising and were used to enforcing order in the country and loyalty to the Tsar. Those found breaking the law could be punished by being sent for army service, where discipline was brutal.
- **Terror and exile:** The Secret Police (Okhrana) weeded out opposition to the Tsar. They did this by spying on people, irrespective of class. Any sign of opposition to the Tsar was punished by imprisonment or exile to areas like Siberia. If an individual was exiled, his whole family often went with him. Exile was a very effective way of neutralising the leaders or future leaders of opposition groups.

- **Censorship:** The civil service mainly employed middle-class people, therefore ensuring the loyalty of that class. Senior civil servants, for example Lenin's father, were given the rank of minor nobility, thus ensuring their loyalty to the system. The civil service was responsible for enforcing laws on censorship and corruption as well as meetings, which made it very difficult for the revolutionaries to communicate.

Other factors

Russification

- This policy made Russian the official language of the Empire, meaning that all official business had to be conducted in Russian. This maintained the dominance of the Russian culture over that of the minorities by ensuring that native languages were marginalised from daily life. There was also state intervention in the religion and education of national minorities. The policy treated subjects as potential enemies and inferior to Russians, antagonising groups like the Finns and the Poles who had their own language and cultural traditions.

Zubatov unions

- These were trades unions organised by the police. In the 1890s, the Tsarist government had become increasingly concerned about the rising discontent among industrial workers about their appalling pay. The Zubatov unions were used to divert workers away from political change by concentrating on wages and conditions in the factories. However, in 1903, the unions became involved in strikes and so were disbanded due to pressure from employers.

Opposition groups

- Opposition and revolutionary groups were fairly weak. There were various revolutionary groups like the Social Revolutionaries (seeking the support of peasants and land reform) and Social Democrats – Mensheviks and Bolsheviks who stressed the importance of industrial workers in overthrowing the Tsar. Most of the Bolshevik leadership was in exile before 1905, so there were very few active Bolsheviks in Russia.

- There were middle-class Liberals who wanted political change, moving from an autocracy to constitutional democracy (they wanted a British-style parliament).

- Most members of these groups came from the intelligentsia or middle classes. By definition, they were small in numbers and not likely to seriously challenge the Tsar's control over most people's lives.

- There were protests by university students in 1899. The autocracy was unwilling to believe that these protests were a genuine desire for reform and dealt with them in the usual repressive manner. Some historians think that this event marked the beginning of serious political challenges to the Tsar. Historian Alan Wood talks about the 'inflexible vessel' to describe the all-or-nothing political system that was unable to allow any safety valve of moderation and compromise.

- Some police worked as 'double agents', working to protect and undermine autocracy at the same time.

- Economic conditions had deteriorated before 1905; from 1903 there was an increase in strikes protesting about worsening working conditions in St Petersburg and elsewhere.

Any other relevant factors.

47 *The work of Pytor Stolypin was central to the successful strengthening of Tsarist authority between 1905 and 1914.*

How valid is this view? (20)

Context: The 1905–1907 Revolution seriously shook the Tsarist state. However, once the shock of revolution had worn off, the state swiftly reasserted itself with the Tsar more determined than ever to maintain his absolute autocracy. The work of Stolypin was critical to maintaining the Tsarist regime.

Stolypin

- Pytor Stolypin was appointed Prime Minister to the Tsar in 1906, replacing Sergei Witte. He aimed to restore Tsarist autocracy but also prevent further discontent by enacting limited political and economic reforms. Stolypin was assassinated in 1911 before his land reforms had begun to take full effect.

Repression

- Stolypin was given the job of restoring control after the events of 1905. He used military courts to issue death penalties. The punishment of hanging was used so frequently it was known as 'Stolypin's necktie'. Opponents of the Tsar were also sentenced to hard labour in Siberia. The Okhrana and censorship were used to silence any public criticism of the Tsar.

Land reforms

- Stolypin's main plan for restoring order and stability was through agricultural reforms. The most important reform was the cancelling of the redemption payments which had kept peasants tied to their villages for 40 years. Each peasant was given the right to sell his plot of land and leave the village. The power of the village *mir* (council) was reduced in order to boost Tsarist control.

- Stolypin also introduced reforms in education, which became compulsory, aiming to give access to more skilled jobs.

- However, the land reforms did not change agriculture as much as was hoped. In practice, the reforms did little more than reduce the number of rural disturbances.

Industrial reforms

- Stolypin introduced improvements in industrial working conditions and pay. More factories came under the control of inspectors and there were signs of improving working conditions. However, conditions actually worsened after 1906 as more peasants flooded into the city searching for work. After 1910, there was an increase in strikes and disturbances in all major cities.

- In 1912, a workers' sickness and accident insurance scheme was introduced.

Political reforms

- Stolypin wanted the support of the middle class so he tried to work with the Duma (elected legislative body) rather than against it. He changed the franchise in 1907 which prevented many national minorities, peasants and workers from voting, although they did still have a say in the Zemstvos. This allowed him to obtain a more co-operative Third Duma which passed his land reforms.

- Stolypin's work with the dumas helped to strengthen the Tsarist state as he helped secure the support of the middle class for the state. However, few urban workers had the right to vote – excluded from any political power, workers increasingly started to act on their own.

Other factors

Nature of events in 1905

- **October Manifesto:** Sergei Witte had been Finance Minister since 1893. He had been responsible for reforms which had boosted Russian industry and encouraged foreign investment from France. He had also been responsible for beginning the Trans-Siberian Railway. He was seen as the 'architect' of Russian parliamentary democracy when he became the first Prime Minister of the Council of Ministers and forced the Tsar to issue the October Manifesto, in which the Tsar made political concessions. Witte was sacked soon after as he lost support in court circles and the Duma.

- **The Duma:** Elections were allowed for a representative political body known as the State Duma. This new body could discuss matters and had minor law-making powers; however, the Tsar retained ultimate control by appointing all ministers who were solely responsible to him. Nicholas II rejected all suggestions for universal suffrage and never accepted the Duma as a legitimate political body. These political reforms may have saved the Tsarist regime in 1905, but the subsequent curbing of any political influence by the Duma merely stored up trouble.

- **Peace with Japan:** Sergei Witte's brilliant negotiations enabled the Russians to sign the Treaty of Portsmouth in 1905, ending the war with Japan. The Russians lost little from the Treaty and the ending of the war enabled the Tsarist government to return home loyal soldiers to repress rebellion at home. However, even Witte said that while the necessary political stability had been achieved, the 'peasant problem' remained.

Role of the Tsar

- The Tsar's role during 1905 had essentially been passive but, control having been restored by his ministers, he reasserted his authority with the Fundamental Laws of 1906. He also sacked ministers like Witte who had required him to make political concessions.

- The Fundamental Laws of 1906 placed further restrictions on the Duma. They reasserted Nicholas II's power to veto any legislation passed by the Duma.

Russification

- Stolypin also enforced russification and disenfranchisement to suppress the national minorities. Opposition and discontent were ruthlessly repressed and this acted as a deterrent, thereby strengthening the Tsarist state.

Opposition to the Tsar

- Revolutionary soviets (councils) had been set up in 1905; however, these were slow to pick up the mood of the people and lost the brief opportunity to topple the Tsar's regime. For example, the St Petersburg soviet was only set up in October 1905. After 1905, revolutionary parties continued to strive for mass workers' support, but their isolation from the Duma and surveillance by the Okhrana kept them underground until 1914.

- The 1914 General Strike in St Petersburg was a reflection of a vigorous trades union movement.

- Lenin's criticism of the Duma allowed the Tsar to treat it with further disdain.

- Middle-ground politicians like the Kadets and Octobrists were willing to turn a blind eye to the Tsar's use of terror in return for the limited reforms of the Duma.

Any other relevant factors.

48 To what extent was the appeal of the Bolsheviks the main reason for the success of the October Revolution, 1917? (20)

Context: The abdication of the Tsar in February 1917 had led to a largely middle- and upper-class provisional government being formed. However, the working class, isolated from political power, was represented by the revolutionary parties. Divided political power was to prove a major issue in 1917.

The appeal of the Bolsheviks

- **Leadership of Lenin**: Lenin's return in April 1917 immediately broke the initial co-operation of the Bolsheviks with the other revolutionary parties after the February revolution. He called for a second socialist revolution.

- Lenin refused to allow the Bolsheviks to work in coalition with the other revolutionary parties and insisted that the Bolsheviks work for a complete workers' revolution.

- Kerensky's announcement on 25 November of elections to the Constituent Assembly (the body that would decide the future government of Russia) prompted Lenin to return to Russia after the July Days. After a heated debate, he convinced the other Bolsheviks to seize power immediately. Without Lenin's leadership, it is doubtful that the Bolsheviks would have acted decisively. Lenin knew that they would not get a majority in the Constituent Assembly.

- **Propaganda:** Lenin's April Theses quickly became Soviet policy, with persuasive slogans such as 'Peace, Land and Bread' and 'All Power to the Soviets'.

- **Policies:** Lenin foresaw that the Bolsheviks could achieve power through the Soviets; Bolshevik power in the Soviets would be followed by Bolshevik takeover of the state. The Bolsheviks kept attending the Petrograd Soviet when most of the others stopped doing so and this gave them control of the Soviet, which they could then use against the Provisional Government.

- **Leadership of Trotsky:** In Trotsky, Lenin had found an energetic and motivational organiser who laid the plans for the October Revolution.

Other factors

The weaknesses of the Provisional Government

- The Provisional Government, as its name suggests, was never intended to be a permanent authority, which undermined its credibility.

- The Provisional Government was an unelected government; it was a self-appointed body made up from the remnants of the Tsarist Duma, which had been elected on a highly restricted franchise, thus not representative of public opinion.

- The Provisional Government decided to continue to pursue victory in the war. This was largely due to the social makeup of the Provisional Government – middle and upper classes who had supported the fall of the Tsar because they believed it was the only way to achieve victory for Russia in the war. There was also pressure from Russia's allies to continue and Russia's dependence on foreign loans which would be withdrawn if Russia did not continue to fight.

- The Provisional Government's social makeup meant that it did not see the urgency of economic and social reforms to satisfy the workers and peasants. As a result, the Provisional Government steadily lost support as public opinion backed the Soviets.

- The Provisional Government issued an eight-point programme including amnesty for all political offences, freedom of speech and elections for a Constituent Assembly. This was counter-productive as revolutionaries left jail and were able to work against the Provisional Government.

- Kornilov Revolt: In September Kerensky had to ask the Soviets and Red Guards to help defend Petrograd when the Supreme Commander of the Russian Army sent troops back to Petrograd, after falling out with Kerensky. The Bolsheviks controlled these organisations and were able to act as protectors of Petrograd. The Bolsheviks did not return their weapons to the Provisional Government after they had persuaded Kornilov's troops not to attack the city, strengthening their grab for power in October.

Dual Power – the role of the Petrograd Soviet

- The Petrograd Soviet reconvened immediately after the February Revolution. This was an organisation built up from the grass roots as each factory and soldiers' unit formed their own mini soviets and sent delegates to the city Soviet. This gave the Petrograd Soviet a popular mandate and political authority.

- The Petrograd Soviet issued Order No. 1 in March 1917 which stated that soldiers should only obey orders that were acceptable to the Petrograd Soviet.

- In September 1917, the Bolsheviks won majorities in both the Petrograd and Moscow soviets with Trotsky becoming Chairman of the Petrograd Soviet.

The decision to continue the war

- In April 1917, Paul Miliukov sent a note to Russia's allies assuring them that Russia would continue to fight. Publication of this note led to widespread protests and loss of support for the Provisional Government.

- The war continued to go badly, with failure of the July offensive and a disastrous defeat at Tarnopol.

- Mutiny and desertion increased as military failures continued. The continuation of the war caused further misery for people in Russia.

Economic problems

- With the war ongoing, food shortages and inflation had continued.

- Factory owners took advantage of the Bolshevik 'defeat' in the July Days to re-impose strict discipline in factories.

- Strikes increased again and productivity declined. Wages did not keep pace with price increases and fuel shortages continued. Pro-Bolshevik propaganda condemned the Provisional Government for extending the 'bony hand of hunger' from the winter of 1916–1917.
- The Provisional Government appointed the Land Committee in May 1917 to direct and supervise land reform but it accomplished little, leading to the peasants resorting to land seizure. This in turn increased desertion from the army as soldiers rushed home to ensure that they got their share.

Political discontent

- The Kronstadt Mutiny, July 1917: Sailors and workers attempted to set up a Soviet-style government at the naval base outside Petrograd. This event triggered the confused political uprising of the July Days.
- The July Days were strikes and demonstrations in Petrograd inspired by, but not led by, the Bolsheviks. The uprising was put down by troops loyal to the Provisional Government. Trotsky was arrested and Lenin was forced to flee to Finland in disguise. Kerensky was able to brand the Bolsheviks as traitors.
- Throughout 1917, the countryside was effectively in a state of turmoil and chaos.

Any other relevant factors.

Part G – USA, 1918–1968

49 To what extent was isolationism the main reason for changing attitudes towards immigration in the 1920s? (20)

Context: After the First World War, the USA experienced one of its episodic concerns about undesirable immigration.

Isolationism

- There were previous concerns about Irish Catholic immigration, for example prior to the American Civil War; in 1884 the Immigration Restriction League formed.
- Laws passed prior to the First World War showed evidence of concern about immigration: 1882 Chinese Exclusion Act, passed after concerns about Chinese immigration in California; 1882 Federal Immigration Act, built the framework for federal oversight of immigration and defined the criteria for undesirable immigration; 1913 Alien Land Law, California, prevented persons ineligible for American citizenship from owning or leasing land for more than three years. This law was aimed mainly at Japanese immigrants.
- At the beginning of the First World War, American public opinion had supported neutrality not intervention. The USA wanted to keep out of foreign problems and concentrate solely on American matters.
- President Wilson expressed the popular concern that America should not become involved in Europe's 'civil war'.
- When the war ended, most Americans wanted a return to isolationism. Senator Henry Cabot Lodge led a successful campaign to prevent the law allowing the USA to join the League of Nations being passed.

Other factors

Fear of revolution

- The Russian Revolution in 1917 had established the first communist state committed to spreading revolution and destroying capitalism. Many immigrants came from Russia and Eastern Europe and it was feared that they would bring communism with them, destroying the American way of life.
- 'Red Scare' of 1919: There were a series of strikes by workers, many unskilled or semi-skilled and recent immigrants from southern and Eastern Europe. Many Americans linked striking with communism and feared revolution was imminent.
- US Attorney General Mitchell Palmer's Washington DC house was blown up and letter bombs were sent to officials. During the Palmer Raids in 1920, 4,000 suspected communists in 33 cities were arrested.

Prejudice and racism

- Changing nature of immigrants: Up to about the 1880s, immigrants were WASPs (White Anglo Saxon Protestants) mainly from the north and west of Europe. After 1880, new immigrants were mainly from southern and Eastern Europe. New immigrants were often Catholic or Jewish. This worried the more established WASP American immigrants.
- New immigrants were often unfamiliar with democracy. This was viewed as a threat to the American constitution.
- New immigrants often continued to wear traditional dress. This was seen as a symbol of unwillingness to integrate into American life.

Social fears

- New immigrants mainly settled in the south-east of the USA in cities with significant communities of people from their own culture in ghettos. This was seen as anti-American.
- Working-class Americans experienced rising rents owing to increased demand for housing.

- Immigrants were blamed for high crime rates in cities – particularly those cities with high levels of immigrants. Crime was often linked to the Mafia. High-profile sons of Italians immigrants like Al Capone reinforced this stereotype.
- The trial of Nicola Sacco and Bartolomeo Vanzetti linked crime, immigration and anti-American political activity in the minds of the American public. Sacco and Vanzetti were anarchists committed to the violent overthrow of government. They were convicted of the murder of a guard and paymaster during a robbery in Massachusetts. Despite numerous appeals and doubts about their convictions, they were executed by electric chair in 1927.

Economic fears

- New production methods meant that it was possible to employ relatively unskilled immigrants on lower wages than American workers.
- Trades unions believed that anything they did to improve conditions or wages was wrecked by Italian or Polish workers who were prepared to work longer hours for lower wages.
- New immigrants were used as 'strike breakers'. This caused huge resentment and an increase in the desire to stop immigrants coming into the country.

Effects of the First World War

- Many immigrants during the First World War had sympathies for their mother country.
- Many German immigrants had supported the German side in the war and society was split when the USA joined the war against Germany.
- Irish Americans were suspected of being anti-British.

Any other relevant factors.

50 *The impact of the Republican government's policies in the 1920s was the main reason for the economic crisis of 1929–1933.*

> **How valid is this view? (20)**

Context: After the First World War, the American economy seemed to have emerged unscathed. However, economic problems slowly grew in the 1920s due, in part, to government policies.

Republican policies in the 1920s

- The USA experienced a period of prosperity after the First World War. It was believed that government should only intervene when requested to do so by business, therefore leading to the Republican administration's policy of *laissez-faire*.
- There was a failure to help farmers who did not benefit from the 1920s' boom.
- Low capital gains tax encouraged share speculation which resulted in the Wall Street Crash.
- The depression was also due to the actions – or inactions – of President Hoover. Politicians and the government were slow to realise the seriousness of the crisis. As a result, action was 'too little, too late' and focused on the needs of businessmen, not the wider American society.

Other factors

Over-production of goods

- New mass-production methods and mechanisation meant that production of consumer goods had expanded enormously.
- Cars, radios and other electrical goods had flooded the market and more was being made than people could buy, for example 1.9 million cars were made in 1920, 4.5 million in 1929.
- By 1929, those who could afford consumer goods had already bought them. Many people had bought them on credit.

Under-consumption – the saturation of the US market

- Throughout the 1920s, businesses and the better-off had benefited from low tax policies. The result of this was that the bottom 40 per cent of the population received only 12.5 per cent of the nation's wealth. In contrast, the top 5 per cent owned 33 per cent of the nation's wealth.
- Incomes did not keep up with rising productivity. For example, between 1920 and 1932, the income of farmers dropped by 70 per cent. Many Americans could not afford the new consumer goods.
- Some Americans did not benefit from the economic boom in the 1920s. For example, in 1928 an estimated 42 per cent of Americans did not earn enough money to supply their food, clothing and housing needs.
- By the end of the 1920s, demand for new consumer goods was met and the car industry was forced to lay off workers owing to falling demand.

Weaknesses of the US banking system

- A major problem was lack of regulation, specifically the lack of rules on the money reserves that banks had to keep in relation to the money lent.

- The banking system was made up of hundreds of small, state-based banks. Often, whole communities deposited their money with one bank. These banks speculated on the stock market to try to maximise profits and lending to the community it served.

- When one bank collapsed, it often led to a 'run' on other banks, resulting in a banking collapse and national financial crisis. Twenty per cent of those banks operating in 1929 had closed down by 1932.

- Bank closures led to the collapse of the finance industry which supplied credit to businesses. Without credit, businesses were unable to operate, leading to their closure, even if the business was viable.

International economic problems

- The impact of the First World War on European economies was enormous; it had turned creditor nations like Britain into debtor nations. After the First World War, Britain was unable to pull itself out of financial problems because of the loss of markets like Germany for its export-led economy. Germany's economy was experiencing real problems after its defeat. The 'loss' of two major trading partners meant demand for American goods was reduced further.

- All European states, except Britain, placed tariffs on imported goods.

- US tariff barriers meant that other countries found it difficult to pay back loans because they could not sell to America. Often these countries, for example Germany, had to refinance their loans which meant they became increasingly indebted.

Wall Street Crash

- Throughout the 1920s, share prices rose. However, this demand was fuelled by people buying 'on margin': only paying a fraction of the value in the hope that the share price would continue to rise before having to sell. Unfortunately, this meant that share prices began to outstrip the real value of the company shares being sold.

- There was an atmosphere of uncertainty in October 1929 and shareholders began to sell their stocks, believing that prices had reached their peak.

- 24 October 1929 – Black Thursday: the Wall Street Crash began as prices fell dramatically. 29 October 1929 – Black Tuesday: the stock market collapsed completely, causing panic. Many ordinary Americans were ruined, still more lost their jobs as businesses folded.

- The stock market crash did play a role in the depression but its significance was as a trigger because it caused the collapse of credit and of confidence.

Any other relevant factors.

51 How important was the role of Martin Luther King in the development of the Civil Rights campaign, after 1945? (20)

Context: The upcoming centenary of Lincoln's emancipation of slaves in 1963 highlighted the lack of progress black Americans had made in the century since they had been offered freedom and equal rights.

The role of Martin Luther King

- Martin Luther King had key skills and attributes as an inspirational speaker and was prepared to put his own life at risk for the cause of civil rights.

- Martin Luther King believed in non-violent protest to achieve civil rights goals. His belief in patient persistence to wear down the arguments of white racists was influential in enabling the American government to justify its concessions and support of civil rights.

- Martian Luther King presented a positive media image, which persuaded white Americans to join him on his campaign.

- King became President of the Southern Christian Leadership Conference in 1960, co-ordinating the work of different civil rights groups. This gave him a national platform, making him well-known.

- One of the first campaigns on which King became well-known was the 1955 Montgomery Bus Boycott. During this campaign, he motivated the black population to maintain their year-long boycott and force significant concessions from the bus company. His personal effectiveness during this campaign enhanced his reputation.

- King achieved worldwide renown with his 1964 civil rights march and 'I Have a Dream' speech, one of the modern era's most influential speeches.

- He won the Nobel Peace Prize in 1964, gaining more national and international recognition for his role.

Other factors

The continuation of prejudice and discrimination

- The experience of war emphasised freedom, democracy and human rights, yet in the USA, Jim Crow laws still existed and lynching went unpunished. Between 1896 and 1968, over 200 anti-lynching bills were introduced into Congress but none were passed owing to the opposition from southern states.

- The 1955 Emmet Till murder trial and its publicity. Till was a fourteen-year-old boy who was lynched after supposedly flirting with a white woman. None of the murderers were convicted despite strong evidence. His treatment was well publicised and outraged black Americans.

- High-profile legal cases advanced the cause of equal education for blacks: 1954 Brown Board of Education of Topeka; 1957 Little Rock Central High School. This encouraged more campaigning for wider change.
- The success of the 1955 Rosa Parks and the Montgomery Bus Boycott encouraged more campaigning.

Experience of black servicemen in the Second World War

- Black soldiers experienced freedoms from segregation in Europe and witnessed German prisoners of war receiving better treatment than they did in American military camps.
- Black soldiers were influenced by the 'Double-V-Campaign': victory in the war and victory for civil rights at home.
- Philip Randolph highlighted the problems faced by black American workers during the Second World War. He led the 'March on Washington' movement in 1941 to protest against racial discrimination. This convinced Roosevelt to issue Executive Order 8802, banning discrimination in the defence industries.
- The 'March on Washington' group also successfully pressured President Harry S. Truman to issue Executive Order 9981 in 1948, ending segregation in the armed services.
- Roosevelt also established the Fair Employment Practices Committee to investigate incidents of discrimination.
- The creation of the Congress of Racial Equality (CORE) 1942, was the beginning of a mass movement for civil rights.

Formation of effective black organisations

- In 1960, a group of black and white college students organised the Student Non-violent Co-ordinating Committee (SNCC) to help the Civil Rights movement. They started by targeting segregated lunch counters and their continued use of non-violent protest won many supporters across the country.
- They joined with young people from the SCLC (Southern Christian Leadership Conference), CORE and NAACP (National Association for the Advancement of Colored People) in staging sit-ins, boycotts, marches and Freedom Rides. Media coverage of the attacks on Freedom Riders shocked the American public and won them much support.
- Combined efforts of the civil rights groups ended discrimination in many public places including restaurants, hotels and theatres.

Emergence of effective black leaders

- Inspirational, but more confrontational, Malcolm X was the articulate voice of the Nation of Islam. He spoke against Martin Luther King's non-violent campaign and rejected the involvement of whites in the campaign for civil rights. Malcolm X was one of the first to highlight the particular problems of crime and unemployment experienced by black Americans in the ghettos.
- Stokely Carmichael drew his ideas from Marcus Garvey. He believed in black separatism and Black Power, and rejected much of Martin Luther King's non-violent approach. His ideas were very attractive to young black Americans.
- The Black Panther Party for Self-Defense was formed in 1966 by Huey P. Newton and Bobby Seale. They followed the ideas of Malcolm X and Stokely Carmichael. They were popular with young black Americans from the ghettos but membership of their group was relatively low. The Black Panthers attracted attention but lost support as a result of their confrontational tactics.
- All leaders attracted media coverage, large followings and divided opinion across the USA, but some leaders and organisations were overshadowed by the media focus on the main personalities.

Any other relevant factors.

Part H – Appeasement and the Road to War, to 1939

52 How important was the Peace Settlement of 1919 as a reason for the aggressive nature of the foreign policies of Germany and Italy in the 1930s? (20)

Context: The First World War caused not only destruction and loss of life, but significant regime changes in Italy and Germany. Both countries were dissatisfied with the outcome of the Peace Settlement of 1919 and this, combined with the rise of Fascism, prompted the two countries to seek to restore lost national honour.

The Peace Settlement, 1919

- There was considerable German resentment at the terms of the Treaty, especially the obligation to accept war guilt, disarm, lose territory and pay reparations. This created a determination to revise the Treaty of Versailles.
- One of the main aspects of Hitler's appeal in Germany was his promise to overturn Versailles and restore German honour.
- Italy had fought in the war on the side of the Allies from 1915. Italian resentment at the failure to get their land ambitions 'rewarded' at the peace negotiations had led to Italy's withdrawal from Versailles. In particular, she had hoped to gain land from Austria Hungary to gain control of the Adriatic. Italy felt that, unlike Britain and France, her suffering had not been compensated.
- When Mussolini came to power in 1922, he promised to restore Italian pride and wipe out the embarrassment of the peace treaties.

Other factors

Fascist ideology

- Nationalism was a key feature of Fascism; the belief that the people and culture of Germany and Italy were superior to those of neighbouring countries and therefore entitled to expand.
- Contempt for 'weak' democracies was also a key feature. Particular hatred was reserved for communism as a belief system likely to threaten and prevent Fascist expansion. Hitler's anti-Soviet crusade was popular with the German people.
- Italian and German Fascism incorporated racist ideas. Hitler's ideas on the Aryan race were used to justify the conquering of other lands and people for the benefit of the greater German Reich.
- Militarism – Fascists glorified war, highlighted times in history when their country had been militarily powerful, for example the Roman Empire and Prussia in the nineteenth century.
- To a large extent, foreign policies were driven by Hitler's and Mussolini's own beliefs, personalities and charismatic leaderships.
- Irredentism – the belief that 'lost' lands needed to be reincorporated, hence Hitler's commitment to include all Germans within the Reich.
- Expansionism – Mussolini's 'Roman' ambitions in the Mediterranean and Africa; Hitler's ambitions in Eastern Europe and Russia.

Economic difficulties after 1929

- Both Germany and Italy had experienced significant economic difficulties after the First World War. Hitler and Mussolini had come to power on a promise to resolve them. Aggressive foreign policies would give them the means to do so. For example, Germany used her economic and political power to make the countries of southern Europe economically dependent on Germany. Military expansion was the next logical step.
- The world economic crisis 1929–1932 impacted on the German and Italian economies and intensified international competition and protectionism, therefore necessitating, in the minds of the Germans and Italians, the need to act more aggressively to advance their interests.
- Both Germany and Italy had continuing economic problems in the 1930s, for example the needs of re-armament and domestic consumption. An aggressive foreign policy was a useful distraction and helped stimulate their economies.
- The need for additional resources led to aggressive, expansionist foreign policies; for example, Italy in Abyssinia, Germany's drive to the east.

Weaknesses of the League of Nations

- The failure of the USA to join the League of Nations and its retreat into isolationism had created a 'power vacuum' in international politics.
- The League had failed to adequately respond to Fascist aggression; for example, the success of Japan in Manchuria in defying the League, encouraging further aggression.
- Britain was more concerned with maintaining her Empire and following Appeasement than acting as the 'world's policeman'.
- France was distracted and divided by internal political divisions. Numerous government changes prevented a coherent foreign policy.
- European democracies were more concerned about the possible spread of communism rather than Fascism, for example the Spanish Civil War.
- Self-determination had created many small countries in the middle of Europe that were hard to defend.

British policy of appeasement

- Appeasement was based on serious intellectual criticisms of the Peace Settlement by the likes of John Maynard Keynes, the eminent economist of the day. Unease about the impact of Versailles became a popular sentiment.
- Hitler knew of British reservations about the Versailles Treaty and was able to play on these. With each successive crisis, he realised that the British were not willing to take action to stop him, for example re-armament, the re-occupation of the Rhineland and then the Anschluss.
- Appeasement was based on the idea of settling legitimate grievances, but to an extent it encouraged both Germany and Italy to keep increasing their demands. For example, the Abyssinian crisis where British attempts to negotiate with Mussolini resulted in the Hoare–Laval Pact, which produced a popular outcry when the terms were leaked. Mussolini saw that Britain and France were not opposed in principle to gains for Italy in East Africa and he was able to defy sanctions and keep Abyssinia.

Any other relevant factors.

53 To what extent were economic difficulties the main reason for the British policy of appeasement, 1936–1938? (20)

Context: The First World War had a profound impact on Britain. Not only did it have to cope with unprecedented military losses, but also deal with the economic impact of the war and adapt to the much changed, post-war Europe.

Economic difficulties

- The post-First World War economic slump had led to industrial problems and disputes which had culminated in the 1926 General Strike. The political and social divisions resulting from this event led to a conservative economic and political outlook, which emphasised holding on to the assets and lands Britain already possessed.
- Britain was preoccupied with dealing with domestic political problems arising from the impact of the 1929–1932 economic crisis and depression.
- Conservative economic policies dictated that budgets should be cut, which meant that it was 1936 before Britain started developing new weapons.
- Germany was a valuable trading partner and there was a reluctance to further damage international trade and commerce.

Other factors

Attitudes to the Paris Peace Settlement

- The Peace Settlement had been subject to serious intellectual criticism by the likes of John Maynard Keynes, the eminent economist of the day. It became a common assumption in government circles that parts of the Versailles Treaty needed revision.
- Britain was reluctant to act as the League of Nations 'policeman' and enforce Treaty provisions that had no direct benefit for Britain.

Public opinion

- The First World War had a continuing psychological impact on the people of Britain. Everyone knew someone who had died or come home injured from the war. Disabled ex-soldiers, either begging or selling matches, were a common sight in many towns and cities. The public did not want a repeat of the horrors of war for the next generation.
- Many political leaders shared public attitudes to another war, also having lost close relatives, for example Neville Chamberlain.
- Most people were pre-occupied with Britain's social and economic problems. This led to isolationist feelings, such as those expressed in Chamberlain's pre-Munich speech in which he deplored the idea that Britain should be facing war 'over a faraway place'.

Pacifism

- 1935 Peace Ballot. This was a five-question survey of the British public's attitudes to the League of Nations and to economic or armed foreign intervention. The results were widely interpreted by the press and the government as showing an unwillingness to take action unless in agreement with other countries.
- 1933 Oxford University Union 'King and Country' debate. The debating society overwhelmingly voted in favour of the motion that 'under no circumstances' would it vote for King and Country. This debate was well publicised and discussed.
- 1933 Fulham East by-election. The unexpected result here showed the strength of anti-war feeling when a 'safe' Conservative seat was won, instead, by a pacifist Labour candidate.

Concern over Empire

- The Empire was thought to be essential to British economic well-being and to her status as a great power.
- Fears were raised that Britain could not defend the Empire against simultaneous threats, according to a review by the Chiefs of Staff. It was thought essential to do a deal with at least one of the aggressive Fascist powers.
- There were genuine worries as to whether the Empire would assist Britain in the event of another war. The 1937 Imperial Prime Minister's Conference refused to give a firm undertaking to aid in resisting Hitler. Britain's own army was small and help would be necessary to take on Germany's army.

Lack of reliable allies

- There was a failure by most countries in the League of Nations to act in anything other than their own self-interest. Disarmament and Collective Security seemed to be empty slogans. Specific examples of self-interest include Manchuria and Abyssinia.
- The unreliability of the French, owing to its own political divisions, meant Britain was lacking one of its key allies.
- US isolationism had a similar effect.
- New democratic countries in middle and Eastern Europe seemed weak military allies. Only Czechoslovakia had a decent armaments industry, Skoda Works.

Fear of the spread of communism

- After the Russian Revolution, there was greater fear of the spread of communism than Fascism. The communists' seizure of foreign assets in Russia created suspicion of Soviet Russia.
- Nazi Germany was seen as a buffer and it was thought that destabilising the Nazi regime might lead to questions over communist revolution in Germany – as had nearly happened in 1919.

- There was fear of communism spreading into Western Europe; for example fear of the French Popular Front government and worries about a communist victory in the Spanish Civil War.

Beliefs of Chamberlain

- Chamberlain believed strongly in his own negotiating skills and that any problem had a rational, negotiable solution.
- Chamberlain dominated his government. He controlled foreign policy and in his roles as Chancellor and then Prime Minister prevented any re-armament that could not be classed as defensive spending in order not to provoke a reaction from the Germans. For example, spending on the new Spitfire and Hurricane planes was limited.

Any other relevant factors.

54 *The Munich Agreement was a success.*

How valid is this view? (20)

Context: Created after the First World War, Czechoslovakia promised to be the hallmark of success for the Paris Peace Settlement. Containing several different nationalities, it nonetheless settled down to operating as an effective democracy. However, it contained about 3 million Sudeten Germans within its borders and, in the 1930s, Hitler exploited this in his search for territorial gains. Agreement was reached in September 1939, between Germany, Britain, France and Italy to give the Sudetenland to Germany – the Czechs themselves were not consulted.

Arguments for the Settlement

- The Agreement was the pragmatic recognition that Czech defences were vulnerable to attack after the 1938 Union with Austria.
- The location of Czechoslovakia meant that neither Britain nor France would be able to prevent a German attack or provide significant support were there to be an attack.
- Public opinion showed that Britain was reluctant to risk war over mainly German-speaking Sudetenland. Chamberlain's pre-Munich speech struck a chord with many.
- The immediate British public reaction to the Munich Agreement was that of relief and rejoicing that war had been averted. Chamberlain got mobbed on his return to Downing Street and received the honour of being received on the balcony at Buckingham Palace by the King.
- Britain was not militarily ready for war, especially in her air defences – or even for offensive action.
- Failure of the League of Nations in earlier crises meant that there was a lack of alternative; there was no unified international response to Hitler.
- There was reluctance from the French to commit to intervention in Czechoslovakia, and no desire for Britain to take the lead.
- There was a lack of engagement of the USA in European affairs.
- Chamberlain's suspicion of Soviet Russia meant that he was happier to see Germany extended eastwards rather than the Russians expanding westwards.
- The unwillingness of the British Empire and Dominions to commit to supporting Britain in any war was well known.
- Poland and Hungary were willing to benefit from the dismemberment of Czechoslovakia rather than aid their neighbour.
- Munich bought Britain another year for re-armament.

Arguments against the Settlement

- Britain had been seen to surrender to Hitler's blustering and threats at an international conference, with the whole world watching.
- It was the final 'nail in the coffin' for the Paris Peace Settlement, which as co-creators and signatories, Britain and France should have been defending not tearing up.
- It could be argued it was a cynical betrayal of Czechoslovakia and democracy.
- The removal of the Sudetenland deprived the Czechs of natural border defences and left it vulnerable to further German aggression, as happened in March 1939.
- German manpower and resources were greatly enhanced by the addition of Czechoslovakia's industry and armaments factories.
- The Agreement facilitated Hitler's influence and ambitions in Eastern Europe.
- The failure to even engage the Russians in discussions about preventing German expansion created more suspicion and alienation of the Soviet Union. It convinced Stalin that the West was trying to divert Hitler's ambitions in Western Europe by encouraging him to move east. The Munich Agreement was undoubtedly part of Stalin's calculations in the signing of the Nazi–Soviet Pact in 1939, which gave Hitler the 'green light' for war.
- Poland was left very vulnerable to attack.

Differing views of the Munich Settlement

- Initially there was pro-Munich euphoria over the avoidance of war.
- A minority of opposition politicians, like Clement Atlee, and mavericks, like Winston Churchill, openly opposed the Agreement. There were some anti-Munich demonstrations in the weeks following the Munich Agreement but these were dwarfed by those in favour.
- Chamberlain was criticised for his role in the Settlement in the 1940 book, *Guilty Men*, by Michael Foot, Frank Owen and Peter Howard.
- The settlement is criticised by Winston Churchill in his post-war memoir, *The Gathering Storm* (1948) in which he accepted that Chamberlain had honourable motives but that these were mistaken; Hitler should have been resisted and more effort should have been made to work with the Soviets.

Any other relevant factors.

Part I – The Cold War, 1945–1989

55 How important was the crisis over Korea as a reason for the emergence of the Cold War, up to 1955? (20)

Context: The Cold War is the term applied to the tension and crises that emerged at the end of the Second World War between America and the Soviet Union. There were a variety of causes, ranging from long-term ideological differences to more recent issues such as differences over the future of Germany.

The crisis over Korea

- Korea was split into the communist North and capitalist South at the end of the First World War.
- The North invaded the South, encouraged by Stalin. This led to an American-led United Nations force opposing it and pushing the North back. China then invaded. The front stabilised along the 38th parallel.
- Korea was the first 'hot' war between forces broadly seen as supporting capitalism and communism.

Other factors

Ideological differences

- The Soviet Union was a communist country with a planned economy, limited political rights and a police state.
- In contrast, America was capitalist with a free market, democratic rights and freedoms. The two beliefs were polar opposites.
- America had not even recognised communist Russia until the 1930s, showing the depth of anti-communist feeling.

Tensions in the wartime alliance

- Stalin was very suspicious of the western Allies, believing them to be untrustworthy and worrying that they would do a deal with Nazi Germany against the Soviet Union. He could cite appeasement as an example of their weakness and the late opening of a second front against Nazi Germany as a sign they were willing to let the Soviets do the bulk of the fighting.
- America and Britain feared that Stalin could not be trusted as well, looking at the Nazi–Soviet Pact as an example of the kind of deals that Stalin was willing to do.
- Stalin didn't trust the Allies and spied on them during the post-war conferences.

Differences over the future of Germany

- America, Britain and France wanted Germany to play its part in the post-war world and in West Germany created a unified block with its Deutschmark. Marshall Aid was pumped in and the economy revived so it could play a full part in the post-war capitalist system.
- The Soviet Union wanted to see Germany punished for what she had done during the war. The Soviet Union stripped East Germany of its assets and put pressure on the West in Berlin, where the Allies had a presence. The Berlin Blockade and airlift was one of the first main tension points in the developing Cold War.

Dropping the atom bomb

- America dropped atom bombs on Hiroshima and Nagasaki in the last months of the Second World War. The intention was to bring Japan to the negotiating table, but Truman also wanted them used so that the Soviet Union could see the power that the USA now had. He hoped that this would keep Stalin in check.
- Stalin, on the other hand, knew about the Manhattan project, the code name for the development of the American nuclear bomb, owing to his extensive spy network. The fact it was kept secret from him confirmed his suspicions about the Allies and their untrustworthiness.

The arms race

- In the aftermath of the dropping of the atom bomb, both sides rushed to develop more powerful weapons. The intention was to show the superiority of their respective economic systems.
- First, the Soviets exploded their own atomic weapons, but soon hydrogen bombs and new delivery platforms began to be developed. Sooned there was the potential to destroy the world many times over.

Any other relevant factors.

56 *The arms race was the main reason for the Cuban Missile Crisis of 1962.*

How valid is this view? (20)

Context: The success of the Cuban Revolution was a surprise to both East and West. Castro's regime sought to reform their political and economic system, causing America to put pressure on. This and pressures on Khrushchev allowed the Cuban Missile Crisis to develop.

The arms race

- President Khrushchev of the Soviet Union was fond of showing off and saying that the Soviets were producing ICBMs (intercontinental ballistic missiles) 'like sausages'. In reality the Soviets had fallen behind the USA in the arms race, and both sides knew it.
- The Soviets did have a lot of MRBMs (medium-range ballistic missiles), however. If these could be stationed on Cuba, then just about all the major cities of the USA were within range.
- The Soviets had lived under the threat of American missiles based in Turkey and Italy, so felt that placing missiles on Cuba was fully justified.

Other reasons

The Cuban Revolution

- The removal of the pro-American Batista regime by Fidel Castro did not automatically mean Cuba would be communist.
- However, Castro's policies soon worried the Americans, especially the nationalisation of land and businesses, many of which were US owned.
- The USA refused to buy Cuba's sugar crop, but the Soviets did instead. Castro was pushed towards Khrushchev.

American foreign policy

- Under Eisenhower's administration, plans were made for an invasion of Cuba by US-trained exiles.
- Kennedy inherited the plan and doubtfully agreed to it.
- The Bay of Pigs debacle confirmed to Castro that his government was under threat.
- There were several American plots to kill Castro and remove him: Operation Mongoose, etc.

Kennedy's domestic context

- Kennedy had recently been elected on a very thin majority.
- He could not afford to be seen to be weak on communism, hence his agreement to the CIA invasion plan.

Khrushchev's domestic context

- Khrushchev was coming in for criticism from hardliners over de-Stalinisation, and from China over perceived ideological weakness.
- Khrushchev's domestic agricultural reforms had failed; a foreign policy victory would be a useful diversion.
- The possible use of missiles could be seen as a bargaining counter over the presence of French, British and US troops in Berlin.

Khrushchev's view of Kennedy

- Khrushchev met Kennedy at the Vienna conference. Kennedy was not his normal self, owing to medication. Khrushchev was bombastic and felt Kennedy was inexperienced.
- Success in building the Berlin Wall led Khrushchev to believe the USA would do nothing about the missiles.

Ideological differences

- The Cuban crisis was symbolic of the broader ideological struggle.
- Khrushchev wished to spread revolution to Central and South America from Cuba.
- America wanted to contain and roll back what it saw as the expansion of communism.

Any other relevant factors.

57 To what extent were the developing policies of co-existence and détente the main reason why the superpowers attempted to manage the Cold War, 1962–1979? (20)

Context: As the Cold War developed, the dangers of nuclear conflict soon became apparent. This and associated issues such as cost and a desire for economic development led to attempts to 'manage' the Cold War.

Policies of co-existence and détente

- The Soviet Union became embroiled in an ideological argument with China that spilled over into conflict. The desire to fight a war on two fronts focused their minds.
- East European leaders such as Erich Honecker in East Germany looked to access western economic skill to develop their economies.
- The USA was embroiled in Vietnam as well as dealing with an increasingly violent Civil Rights campaign at home. This made better relations with the Soviet Union desirable.
- West European allies in NATO sought engagement with the East to lessen tension. Willi Brandt, as Mayor of Berlin then Chancellor of Germany, sought engagement with the East for practical reasons.

Other factors

Danger of mutually assured destruction

- As the superpowers developed their nuclear arsenals, so their ability to destroy each other grew.
- The development of technologies that would allow second strike capability led to the chances of mutually assured destruction.
- There was a realisation that if war happened it could lead to the destruction of the world.

1962 Cuban Missile Crisis

- The 1962 Cuban Missile Crisis began when the Soviets attempted to place medium-range ballistic missiles on Cuba.
- This crisis saw the world come close to nuclear conflict and focused the minds of both superpowers, resulting in the introduction of the hot line between the Kremlin and White House as well as nuclear testing bans.

Cost of the Cold War

- Developing nuclear technology in terms of ever-increasing destructive power and delivery systems was expensive.
- There was a desire to diversify the Soviet economy, which was geared to heavy industry and armament production.
- The American desire to build their 'Great Society', for example, required funds that could be diverted from armaments.

Development of aerial surveillance technology

- Both sides developed far greater capability to see what the other was doing as the Cold War progressed.
- This allowed each side to verify what the other was doing and made the completion of agreements, such as SALT I, easier to police.
- An example of the good use of surveillance technology was the identification and monitoring of the Cuban missile site development.

Any other relevant factors.

[End of marking instructions for Practice Paper A]

Practice Paper B

Section 1 – Scottish – 20 marks

Part A – The Wars of Independence, 1249–1328

1   **How fully does** Source A **explain the relationship between John Balliol and Edward I? (9)**
    Use the source and your own knowledge.

Candidates can be credited in a number of ways up to a maximum of 9 marks.

A maximum of 2 marks may be given for answers which refer only to the source.

Possible points which may be identified from the source include:

* Macduff managed to get John, king of Scotland, summoned to the English king's parliament held in London.
* John … appeared in person and he resolved … that he would answer the English king by proxy.
* The King of England would not in any way listen to the king's proxy until the king of Scotland should … convey his answers to his proxy with his own lips.
* John fulfilled these commands and having experienced innumerable insults and slights from all, contrary to his kingly rank and dignity, he eventually conveyed his answers to his proxy.

Possible points of significant omission may include:

* Edward decided that the Treaty of Birgham with its guarantees of Scottish independence was no longer valid, since the marriage between Mary and Edward's son, did not happen.
* Edward exercised what he felt were his rights as feudal overlord over John.
* There were a series of legal cases where Edward over-rode decisions made by John. For example, the Burgesses of Berwick appealed to Edward over a court decision made by the Guardians, which John had upheld.
* Scottish kings were not used to being summoned to appear before an English court.
* Alexander III had refused to do homage for Scotland, though he did perform homage for lands that he held in England.
* John had to agree to some English members of his government.
* John did try to resist but he backed down in the face of threats.
* In 1294, Edward exercised his rights as feudal overlord, demanding that John bring Scottish troops to fight for him in France.
* Nobles elected a council of Guardians to help John stand up to Edward.
* John sent envoys to negotiate a treat with the French King in 1295; this was formally ratified in 1296 after Edward's invasion.
* In April 1296, John sent Edward a list of grievances with regard to Edward's handling of the issue of overlordship.
* Edward invaded Scotland and defeated the Scottish army at Dunbar.
* John decided to submit to Edward hoping for leniency: he surrendered at Kincardine.
* John was brought before Edward at Brechin and ceremoniously stripped of his royal regalia, his surcoat stripped from his body. Here John earned his nickname from the English soldiers, Toom Tabard.
* John was taken as a prisoner to London.

Any other valid points that meet the criteria described in the general marking instructions for this kind of question.

2   **Evaluate the usefulness of** Source B **as evidence of Scottish resistance. (6)**

   In making a judgement you should refer to:
   * *the origin and possible purpose of the source*
   * *the content of the source*
   * *your own knowledge.*

Candidates can be credited in a number of ways up to a maximum of 6 marks.

Examples of aspects of the source and relevant comments:

Aspect of the source	Possible comment
Author: Hugh de Cressingham	Useful as Cressingham was one of Edward's senior officials in Scotland, therefore he could speak with authority on the situation in Scotland.
Type of source: letter to Edward	Useful as a letter is a personal appeal by Cressingham to Edward. Less useful as it may be a biased response by Cressingham who had been left to control Scotland in the absence of the Earl of Warenne.
Purpose: to inform Edward of the difficulties the English administration in Scotland was having	Useful as the letter shows the extent to which the English administration was struggling to control Scotland in the face of increased active and passive resistance.
Timing: 24 July 1297	Useful as the letter is a contemporary document that was produced at the time of growing Scottish resistance to the English administration.

Content	Possible comment
at the time when this letter was made not a penny could be raised in your realm of Scotland by any means.	Useful as this provides evidence of the extent of Scottish resistance as the English cannot gather taxes in Scotland.
by far the greater part of your counties of the realm of Scotland still do not have officers to do your work, owing to death, sieges, or imprisonment; and some have given up their districts, and others dare not return	Useful as this shows how the Scots have managed to remove English officials in Scotland using a variety of means.
in some counties the Scots have appointed and established bailiffs and ministers, so that no county is in proper order, excepting Berwick and Roxburgh	Useful as this illustrates how the Scots are in effect running their own administration and English control is limited.

Possible points of significant omission may include:

- Rebellions against the English began in the spring of 1297.
- The nobles Bruce and Steward started an armed revolt against Edward at Irvine.
- Andrew Murray led the revolt in the north and took castles at Inverness, Elgin and Aberdeen.
- Murray had removed all English garrisons north of Dundee.
- William Wallace was present at the killing of Sir William Heselrig, the English Sheriff of Lanark.
- The Scottish were victorious at the Battle of Stirling Bridge, 11 September 1297.
- Wallace and Murray appointed Guardians.
- Wallace invaded the North of England, around Carlisle and Newcastle.

Any other valid points that meet the criteria described in the general marking instructions for this kind of question.

3   Compare the views of Sources C **and** D **about the ambitions of Robert Bruce. (5)**

Compare the content overall and in detail.

Candidates can be credited in a number of ways up to a maximum of 5 marks.

Possible points of comparison may include:

Overall: Sources C and D agree on the extent and success of Scottish raids into England in terms of spreading terror and extracting blackmail. However, although the sources agree on the recovery of Berwick, they do differ as to the overall success of Scottish strategy; D sees the recovery of Berwick on its own, whereas C sees it as part of a broader strategy.

Source C	Source D
The strategy is characterised by increasingly long-distance raids deep into northern England.	After Bannockburn the Scottish raids south of the Border became so regular and frequent that they amounted to the virtual subjection of England north of the Tees.
The raids ravaged wide areas of northern England.	Northumberland suffered heavy depopulation and was reduced to a miserable anarchy.
They were spectacularly successful in demoralising the northern communities and in breaking their will to resist and most especially in the extraction of cash in return for truce.	A conservative estimate would put Bruce's total income in blackmail at £20,000
of the strategic towns, only Berwick fell to the Scots and not until 1318, whereas Carlisle survived assaults in 1315 and 1316.	Berwick fell in 1318.

Part B – The Age of the Reformation, 1542–1603

4 How fully does Source A **explain the reign of Mary, 1561–1567? (9)**

Use the source and your own knowledge.

Candidates can be credited in a number of ways up to a maximum of 9 marks.

A maximum of 2 marks may be given for answers which refer only to the source.

Possible points which may be identified from the source include:

- Before the end of the year there was talk of divorce (which, however, would make the prince illegitimate) or of dissolving the marriage by more violent means.
- Pardons were granted to the murderers of Riccio, now Darnley's enemies.
- Darnley was murdered on the night of 9–10 February 1567.
- Bothwell ... married Mary, to the scandal of even her warmest supporters (including the pope).

Possible points of significant omission may include:

- There was criticism of Mary from Knox who objected to her religion as well as the fact she was able to privately worship.
- After her marriage, the Protestant nobles gathered an army. Mary and Bothwell fled from Borthwick to gather an army in the Borders.
- On 15 June 1566, the two sides faced each other at Carberry. Talks lasted throughout the day, ending with Protestant lords agreeing to obey Mary if she sent Bothwell away.
- During the talks, Mary waited until Bothwell had a chance to escape before she agreed to join the Protestant lords.
- Far from welcoming her, the troops cried 'Burn the whore!' She had the same reception in Edinburgh before being sent to Loch Leven Castle.
- Following Darnley's murder, posters appeared accusing Bothwell of the crime. They also showed Mary as a mermaid – the symbol for a prostitute. Stories about Mary re-marrying spread across Scotland, England and Europe.
- Mary and Bothwell married in a Protestant service, which ruined her reputation as she had married her husband's murderer and abandoned the Catholic Church.
- After Mary was imprisoned in Loch Leven Castle, some nobles seized power for themselves. On 24 July 1567, Mary was forced to abdicate in favour of her son James, and Moray was declared regent. This angered many people. The Scots divided into two parties, the King's Party and the Queen's Party. Both groups looked to Queen Elizabeth for support.
- Moray struggled to control the divided kingdom; Mary escaped. Her supporters were defeated at Langside. Mary then fled to England to seek help from her cousin, Elizabeth I.
- Mary was kept as a prisoner in England for the rest of her life.
- While captive, Mary became the centre of many Catholic plots against Elizabeth, with the Babington Plot leading to her execution in 1587.

Any other valid points that meet the criteria described in the general marking instructions for this kind of question.

5 Evaluate the usefulness of Source B **as evidence of the relationship between the Kirk and King James VI. (6)**

In making a judgement you should refer to:

- *the origin and possible purpose of the source*
- *the content of the source*
- *your own knowledge.*

Candidates can be credited in a number of ways up to a maximum of 6 marks.

Examples of aspects of the source and relevant comments:

Aspect of the source	Possible comment
Author: James VI's government	Useful as illustrated James's view of the power relationship between monarch and kirk.
Type of source: Act of Parliament	Useful as parliamentary Act was law of the land.
Purpose: to give parliamentary approval to Presbyterian courts	Useful as recognised the recovery of Presbyterian influence within the Kirk but it did not reduce the power of the monarch.
Timing: 1592	Useful as contemporary source from the middle of James's reign when he was asserting monarchical control over the Kirk.

Content	Possible comment
Our sovereign lord declares that it shall be lawful for the kirk every year to hold and keep general assemblies, if the king's majesty, or his commissioner, be present at the general assembly before the dissolving thereof.	Useful as shows the desire of the King to control the Kirk and when it holds its assemblies.
In case neither his majesty nor his said commissioner is present for the time, where the general assembly is being held, it shall be left to the general assembly to nominate and appoint time and place where the next general assembly shall be kept and held.	Useful as recognition that the Kirk used to determine as and when they could hold their assemblies.
Our lord also approves the synodal and provincial assemblies to be held by the kirk and ministry twice each year as they are presently done within every province of this realm.	Useful as, again, sees the desire for secular control of the Kirk, albeit at a lower level.

Points of significant omission may include:

- James believed in his divine right to rule, which put him at odds with the Kirk. There were opposing views of people like Andrew Melville that the King should be accountable to the authority of the Kirk.
- In Trew Law, James appears frustrated by the lack of respect he receives from his subjects; while in Basilikon Doron, James is determined to bring Scotland's remote localities under more direct royal control.
- Relations with the Kirk deteriorated after 1592, leading to conflict in 1596.
- Andrew Melville, the influential protestant reformer believed government should not have control over the Church and was moderator of the General Assembly in 1578 when the *Second Book of Discipline* was published.
- The *Second Book of Discipline* (1578) established a vision of a Presbyterian Kirk but the 'Black Acts' (1584) subsequently stated the supremacy of the monarch in all matters.
- The establishment of Presbyteries in 1581 meant there was a possible challenge to royal authority.
- In 1584 Black Acts were introduced, which asserted royal authority over the Kirk.
- James sought to extend the power of the monarch and bishops over the Kirk by: having bishops recognised as moderators of Presbyteries; allowing bishops to hear cases of excommunication/deposition of ministers; visiting parishes; appointing schoolmasters; giving the monarch the power to determine the time and place of the General Assembly.
- James also faced challenge to his authority from Catholics. In 1594, James ordered the suppression of a rebellion by the Catholic earls of Huntly and Errol.
- Due to the rebellion in December 1596, James fled from Edinburgh, but this made him more determined to control the Kirk.
- In 1597, Andrew Melville was deposed as Rector of St Andrews.

Any other valid points that meet the criteria described in the general marking instructions for this kind of question.

6   **Compare the views of** Sources C **and** D **about the impact of the Reformation on Scotland, to 1603.** (5)

Compare the content overall and in detail.

Candidates can be credited in a number of ways up to a maximum of 5 marks.

Possible points of comparison may include:

Overall: Sources C and D agree about creation of the kirk session and its role in terms of celebrations like marriage. They also agree on the banning of festivals and the role of the Kirk in humiliating people who had sinned in some way. However, there is a slight difference in that Source D goes on to explain that many old festivals continued to be celebrated.

Source C	Source D
At some point in their lives, nearly all parishioners would have appeared before the kirk session, which was made up of elected elders and deacons.	The reformed church possessed a rudimentary organisation at congregational level. This body, known as the Kirk Session, consisted of elders and deacons, who were elected annually.
Couples had to appear before the kirk session to ask that their marriage banns be proclaimed, and for their children to be baptised.	Marriage was always celebrated in church and stern measures were taken against any who attempted to perform the ceremony privately. Banns were published three times in the parish church of both parties.
Scotland alone among Reformed nations abolished not just saints' days, but also celebrations, including Christmas and Easter.	the Reformers banned the observance of Festivals and Saint Days. In this matter, however, the opinion of the people was not in step with that of the church.
Only in Scotland was punishment by humiliation – the public 'performing' of repentance – carried out with a special piece of furniture, known as the penitents' seat.	Scotland also introduced the sinners chair into church for the public humiliation of those parishioners who had offended the elders in some way.

Part C – The Treaty of Union, 1689–1740

7   How fully does Source A **explain the arguments for and against union with England? (9)**

Use the source and your own knowledge.

Candidates can be credited in a number of ways up to a maximum of 9 marks.

A maximum of 2 marks may be given for answers which refer only to the source.

Possible points which may be identified from the source include:

- The Kirk's alarm came from a real fear that by closer association with England, bishops would once again be imposed on the church.
- The treaty was also anathema to the Jacobites who rightly saw it as a major obstacle to their hope of one day restoring the Stuarts to the throne.
- Not all burghs and counties sent in petitions, but those that did were virtually all vehemently anti-union in content.
- Presbyterian ministers remained loud in their denunciations, vigorously condemning the proposed union as a profane threat to Scotland's historic reformed tradition.

Possible points of significant omission may include:

- There were fears from many burgh submissions that the Treaty would ruin manufacturing industries and erode laws and liberties.
- Burghs feared losing their rights and privileges such as their right to be represented in legislative power.
- There were fears that Scotland's history and pride would be lost and be taken over by a Greater England.
- There were understandable fears that the British parliament would favour English trade over Scottish.
- Presbyterian Protestants feared a British parliament dominated by the Anglican Episcopalian Church with bishops' seats in the House of Lords.
- English currency, weights and measures were to be introduced, which would be disadvantageous to Scotland.
- Public opinion was firmly against union with England.
- Scottish representation in a British parliament would be vastly reduced and the Scots would lose control of their affairs.
- Scots Episcopalians opposed union and Hanoverian succession – only the Stuart dynasty might restore episcopacy to the Scottish Church.
- It was hoped that there would be advantages in commerce and trade, particularly through access to English colonies in the Americas and India.
- Cross border trade would also hopefully improve with the loss of tariffs on the border.
- The protection of being in Great Britain meant that, for example, the Royal Navy would protect Scottish mercantile interests.
- There were common interests already with England in terms of religion and a common monarch.
- A Hanoverian succession offered security to Protestantism.

Any other valid points that meet the criteria described in the general marking instructions for this kind of question.

8   Evaluate the usefulness of Source B **as evidence of the passing of the Act of Union. (6)**

In making a judgement you should refer to:

- *the origin and possible purpose of the source*
- *the content of the source*
- *your own knowledge.*

Candidates can be credited in a number of ways up to a maximum of 6 marks.

Examples of aspects of the source and relevant comments:

Aspect of the source	Possible comment
Author: James Ogilvy, 1st Earl of Seafield	Useful as Ogilvy was a commissioner for the Union from 1702 and an active promoter of the Union from 1706, though his views did change.
Type of source: letter	Useful as a personal view of the progress of the Treaty though may be less useful owing to bias.
Purpose: to inform the English minister Godolphin of progress of the Act of Union	Useful as a record of events from the Scottish perspective, but also interesting as it is to Godolphin.
Timing: 7 November 1706	Useful as it dates from the time of the progress of the Act of Union when discussions of the detail of the Act were going on.

B

Content	Possible comment
My lord, since my last letter, we have carried by a majority of 32 votes the first article of the Union in the terms I formerly mentioned.	Useful as the first article of the treaty was the one that agreed the principle of the incorporating union, which the English commissioners were particularly keen to see.
we have had to make some alterations, which my Lord Commissioner … (has) found to be necessary so that the Union may be passed. I hope that we will be allowed to make these alterations.	Useful as a series of amendments or 'explanations' as they were added during the late autumn of 1706 to facilitate the progress of the Act.
The Kirk, which declares the Union inconsistent with their principles, it being contrary to the Covenant that the bishops sit in the Parliament.	Useful as the Kirk was one of the most important opposition groups to the Act of Union.

Points of significant omission may include:

- Scottish ministers/politicians were bribed through financial offers and positions in the House of Lords, for example.
- All the Articles were passed despite popular opposition outside the parliament.
- £20,000 was paid to various Scottish politicians as inducements.
- The Equivalent, a sum of £398,085.10s was granted to cover the taking on of English debt and to reimburse Scotland for losses suffered at Darien.
- Squadrone Volante's (or the New Party's) hold on the balance of power in the Scottish Parliament was key to Court Party's success.
- The leader of the opposition to Union, Hamilton, behaved most curiously and was not an effective leader. Some argue that he was in the pay of the pro-Union lobby.
- Opponents of Union disagreed with each other.
- The Court Party had a formidable party machine compared to the divided County Party.
- There were assurances that the British Parliament would support the Scottish economy over taxation.
- The Scottish Parliament was given the incentive of free trade with England and its colonies.
- There were last-minute concessions from the English on issues such as salt, wool and liquor.
- The Act of Security for the Kirk would allow the Church of Scotland to continue in its current form. This effectively ended the political role of one of the most effective anti-Union groups.
- Burghs and Royal Burghs were granted the right to remain, which was attractive to them.
- Scots laws and Scottish courts were to remain, which would keep a distinctive Scottish institution.
- English forces were moving north, creating fear of invasion if no treaty was agreed.

Any other valid points that meet the criteria described in the general marking instructions for this kind of question.

9   **Compare the views of** Sources C **and** D **about the effects of the Union, to 1740. (5)**

Compare the content overall and in detail.

Candidates can be credited in a number of ways up to a maximum of 5 marks.

Possible points of comparison may include:

Overall: Sources C and D agree about the initial impact of the Union on Scotland. There is agreement about the fact that optimistic forecasts were wrong and that the imposition of a malt tax, against the provisions of the Treaty, led to calls for repealing the Union and an eventual vote, which didn't succeed, but was close.

Source C	Source D
In spite of the optimistic forecasts of the unionist pamphleteers there was no sudden burst of prosperity after 1707.	Tax increases in Scotland were likely to bite deeply because the Scottish economy was still in the doldrums in the first decade after union, and those pamphleteers who had optimistically predicted an economic miracle were now proven wrong.
And in 1712 it was proposed, in defiance of the Treaty of Union, to apply the malt tax to Scotland.	
By the end of that year Scottish parliamentary representatives of all parties agreed that the only solution to these ills was the repeal of the Union.	In 1713 the House of Commons voted to apply the malt tax to Scotland in direct defiance of the provisions of the treaty itself.
The motion moving to dissolve the union was only narrowly defeated by four proxy votes;	Scottish peers and members of the Commons came together and agreed that the only solution was repeal of the treaty.
	The motion was put by the Earl of Findlater in the House of Lords in June 1713 and was only narrowly defeated by four proxy votes.

Answers B   119

Part D – Migration and Empire, 1830–1939

10 How fully does Source A **explain the experience of immigrants in Scotland? (9)**

Use the source and your own knowledge.

Candidates can be credited in a number of ways up to a maximum of 9 marks.

A maximum of 2 marks may be given for answers which refer only to the source.

Possible points which may be identified from the source include:

- Some of the local population looked upon the growth of ice-cream and Italian associations with considerable misgivings.
- The most vocal complaints came from the United Free Church who condemned the Italians for keeping their shops open on Sundays.
- It was alleged that moral as well as spiritual values were under threat.
- The police also added their weight to the opposition. Standards of behaviour, it was claimed, were low and were 'acceptable only to their alien owners and to people of loose moral habits'.

Possible points of significant omission may include:

- The integration of Italians was helped by the popularity of the businesses that they set up and owned, ice-cream and fish and chip shops.
- Italian immigrants also contributed to the growing leisure industry. Before the First World War, there were as many as 336 cafés in Glasgow.
- Many Italian families settled in many towns on the coast and in the main towns. The Nardini family developed what was to become the largest café in Britain in the town of Largs.
- The College of Italian Hairdressers was set up in Glasgow in the 1920s.
- Italian cafés got more approval from the temperance movement as the cafés generally did not sell alcohol.
- Immigrant Irish provided a workforce who often took the worst jobs.
- The Irish made a significant contribution to industrialisation in Scotland through their employment in the building of roads, canals and railways.
- The creation of separate Catholic schools in Scotland, mostly in the west of Scotland but also Edinburgh and Dundee, impacted on Scottish society.
- There was also an impact on Scottish sporting life. For example, Edinburgh Hibernian was founded in 1875 by Irishmen living in the Cowgate area of Edinburgh; Glasgow Celtic was set up in 1887 by Brother Walfrid, a Catholic priest. Dundee United was set up in 1909 with Irish Catholic support.
- Irish immigrants also brought the Protestant Orange Lodge Order to Scotland.
- Irish were important in the Scottish trades union movement, especially coalmining.
- Irish support helped develop the Labour Party in Scotland. Important political leaders like John Wheatley were responsible for the 1924 Housing Act which kick-started council-house building after the First World War.
- Jewish immigration: anti-Semitism was not a big problem, possibly because of the relatively low numbers of Jewish immigrants.
- Prejudice and discrimination affected the Jews in Scotland; like the Irish, Jewish immigrants were sometimes blamed for the spread of disease.
- Jewish immigrants living in poverty rarely got any help from local authorities; instead they relied on their own community, for example, the Glasgow Jewish Board of Guardians.
- The Jewish community was important to the development of the tailoring trade and tobacco industry, especially the production of cigarettes.
- Between 1860 and 1915, about 7,000 Lithuanians came to Scotland. Most were using Scotland as a stop-off point on their way to the USA or Canada.
- Scots complained about Lithuanians being dirty, immoral or strike breakers.
- Lithuanians were mainly employed in the coal and iron industries around Coatbridge.
- Lithuanians kept their own distinctive language and culture, setting up newspapers, social groups and shops that worked in the Lithuanian language.
- Many Lithuanians went to fight for Russia during the First World War; many never came back.
- After the First World War, the remaining Lithuanians were encouraged by the government to repatriate to Lithuania, especially those groups, for example women and children, who might be a burden on the state.
- Lithuanians gradually integrated into Scottish society, thus not leaving a lasting impact.

Any other valid points that meet the criteria described in the general marking instructions for this kind of question.

11 **Evaluate the usefulness of** Source B **as evidence of the impact of Scots on the Empire (6)**

In making a judgement you should refer to:

- *the origin and possible purpose of the source*
- *the content of the source*
- *your own knowledge.*

Candidates can be credited in a number of ways up to a maximum of 6 marks.

Examples of aspects of the source and relevant comments:

Aspect of the source	Possible comment
Author: James Mouat Garriock, a Scottish émigré from Lerwick	Useful as the author was typical of many Scottish emigrants; young single men in search of better lives abroad. Useful as it is a first-hand account of the experience of being a new émigré in Canada.
Type of source: letter from Garriock to his mother	Useful as it is a personal letter from someone with eyewitness experience of what life was like for emigrants like himself. Less useful as it may focus more on the negatives given the sympathetic nature of the audience; ordinary difficulties might be being exaggerated in search of assistance, either emotional or material.
Purpose: to give a personal experience of emigration in Canada	Useful as it shows success did not come quickly for many emigrants.
Timing: 1891	Useful as it is a contemporary document revealing the issues that new immigrants faced in getting themselves established in Canada.

Content	Possible comment
After my arrival I tried hard for work, but without success.	Useful as it shows that desirable work was not always easy to come by.
After about six weeks, I found a job for only two days surveying the harbour and bay but this job made me ill because of the sewage on the shore.	Useful as it shows that available jobs could be hazardous to health.
Many who have the means are leaving as fast as they can and going to the States.	Useful as it shows that many emigrants were unable to find success in Canada and so left for the United States.

Points of significant omission may include:

- Scots were important in the development of the fur trade, timber and agricultural industries.
- Farming was the most common career for the majority of emigrants up to the 1860s.
- Scots from Orkney and the Highlands dominated the fur trading companies of Canada through the Hudson's Bay Company and the North West Company.
- The Canadian government targeted Scots farmers to work on the vast lands of Canada's interior.
- Many Scottish immigrants found that while wages were higher, more work was expected for the money.
- Prominent Scots in Canadian finance included George Stephen who was President of the Bank of Montreal and helped raise $100 million to build the Canadian Pacific Railway, which unified the country.
- Scottish surveyors, like Sandford Fleming, helped map out the route for the railway.
- Scots also made significant contributions to railroad building across Canada.
- Scots made up the largest ethnic group in Nova Scotia.
- Scots had an impact on education; notable universities such as McGill and Queens, Kingston, Ontario were set up either with Scottish money or by Scottish scholars.
- Almost one-quarter of Canada's industrial leaders in the 1920s had been born in Scotland, and another quarter had Scottish-born fathers.
- Scots also dominated in politics; Sir John A. Macdonald was the first Canadian Prime Minister and Alexander Mackenzie was the first Liberal Prime Minster of Canada in the late nineteenth century.
- Other evidence of Scottish influence can be seen in the wide variety of place names, parks and other geographical features with Scottish connections.

Any other valid points that meet the criteria described in the general marking instructions for this kind of question.

12 **Compare the views of** Sources C **and** D **on the impact of empire on Scotland, up to 1939. (5)**

Compare the sources overall and in detail.

Candidates can be credited in a number of ways up to a maximum of 5 marks.

Possible points of comparison may include:

Overall: The sources agree that the Empire had a significant impact on Scotland, with Scots playing a full part in the running of the Empire. They also agree that the Empire had a significant impact on Scottish identity and employment opportunities.

Source C suggests that the Empire had a significant effect on Scots at home with active engagement with religion and the idea of Empire as a civilising influence. However, although Source D also highlights jobs and enthusiasm for the Empire, it stresses the link between Empire and national churches.

Source C	Source D
Personal connections, press coverage and the missionary movement in churches all combined to impress on Scots that they were part of an imperial enterprise. Empire had a significant impact on Scots at home.	So intense was the Scottish engagement with empire that it had an impact on almost every nook and cranny of Scottish life.
Among the many Scots for whom Empire provided jobs or professions, missionaries formed an important group.	Scottish professionals penetrated every corner of the Empire, so that in virtually every area of employment, Scots had a high profile.
perceptions of the Empire and of the colonial peoples, and of the role of Scots in the 'civilising mission'. Through the development of a Scottish missionary tradition and creation of national heroes amongst missionary figures.	The link between empire and the national churches also seemed strong. The cult of David Livingstone reached is height in the 1920s.
a claim of specific Scots contribution to Empire was generated and widely endorsed.	It was commonly asserted that imperial expansion only occurred after Union, hence it was a partnership with England in which the Scots had played their full part.

Part E – The Impact of the Great War, 1914–1928

13 How fully does Source A **explain the impact of the war on Scottish society? (9)**

Use the source and your own knowledge.

Candidates can be credited in a number of ways up to a maximum of 9 marks.

A maximum of 2 marks may be given for answers which refer only to the source.

Possible points which may be identified from the source include:

- By the summer of 1915, it was not uncommon to see women in highly visible roles at bank or post office counters, or working as ticket collectors.
- Edinburgh reported a sharp increase in women's employment in the capital.
- The process of putting women into jobs vacated by men was known as 'substitution' and by 1917 it was estimated that one in three women were substituting male workers' jobs.
- However, their efforts did not mean that they received equal pay: a male postman received 35 shillings a week while his female counterpart received 10 shillings less.

Possible points of significant omission may include:

- By 1916, 18,500 women were working in the heavy industries.
- Most jobs done by women were low or semi-skilled. Few women worked as engineers or directly in shipbuilding.
- The war helped women temporarily take on the jobs vacated by male workers who had gone to fight in the war.
- The late summer panic of 1914, over uncertainty in the economy, led to temporary unemployment for some 40 per cent of women workers in September 1914.
- By 1917, an estimated one in three women were substituting for male workers.
- Longer term, the changes in women's employment were temporary and by 1924, the Ministry of Labour was reporting a return to the pre-war status quo.
- The largest new employer of women in wartime was the munitions industry. The main munitions factories employing women were in Glasgow and Clydebank.

- The huge, purpose-built cordite factory at Gretna employed 9,000 women at its height.
- According to official guidelines, women were supposed to be paid a minimum of £1 a week with skilled women getting paid the same as men. However, this was not mandatory and employers often bypassed the regulation.
- A small engineering 'college for women' to produce aircraft engines was set up by Arrol-Johnston, Scotland's largest car manufacturer, at Tongland near Kirkcudbright, Ayrshire.
- Scottish Women's War Hospitals was set up by Elsie Inglis. A hospital was set up at Royaumont in France and started treating patients in January 1915.
- Helen Crawfurd, Agnes Dollan and Mary Barbour were leaders of the Glasgow Rent Strikes, 1915.
- Helen Crawfurd and Mary Barbour set up the Women's Peace Crusade in 1916 and, by summer 1917, a mass meeting attracted 14,000 protestors on Glasgow Green.
- The favourable performance of women in medicine during the war helped lead to doubling of the number of women studying medicine to 3,000 in 1919.
- Scottish universities continued to admit women medical students unlike in England where all but one university reverted to only accepting men.
- Women householders and wives of householders over the age of 30 were given the vote in 1918 partly as a result of changing attitudes during the First World War.

Any other valid points that meet the criteria described in the general marking instructions for this kind of question.

14 Evaluate the usefulness of Source B **as evidence of the impact of the war on food and rationing. (6)**

In making a judgement you should refer to:

- *the origin and possible purpose of the source*
- *the content of the source*
- *your own knowledge.*

Candidates can be credited in a number of ways up to a maximum of 6 marks.

Examples of aspects of the source and relevant comments:

Aspect of the source	Possible comment
Author: Dorothy Wiltshire, a young Scottish woman during the First World War	Useful as it is the first-hand experience of someone who, as a young woman, had to cope with the effects of food shortages and rationing.
Type of source: from an interview with Dorothy Wiltshire about her wartime experiences	Useful as it is an eyewitness account based on personal recollections of the problems of coping with food shortages and rationing. It may be more useful because it is intended to be an honest account of the most important things that happened to her. Less useful because over time her memory may have changed the emphasis of events, leading her to exaggerate the negatives.
Purpose: to record personal experiences of life in wartime Scotland	Useful as it is a personal account of the experiences of a key wartime impact on the lives of women.
Timing: 1970s	Useful as it is from the account of someone who experienced the First World War, reflecting on their experience with the benefit of hindsight — had time to think about their experience with better perspective. Less useful as hindsight may have changed the detail and emotions about the event.

Content	Possible comment
When you got to the top of the queue very often the door was shut and that was all for the day.	Useful as it shows how demand for food outstripped supply, leading to shops closing early.
She would get a sheep's head from the butcher, and make soup with the bone and a lovely pie with vegetables with the meat.	Useful as it shows women had to use parts of animals not normally used, making more use of vegetables.
During my lunch hour I used to go to try and get some shopping for mother but at that time nearly all the food was finished — even butter and marge.	Useful as it shows shortages of even basic foodstuffs such as butter and margarine.

Points of significant omission may include:

- Wartime restrictions on fishing reduced catches and pushed up prices so that, by 1918, white fish was rationed.
- The appointment of Scottish businessman, Sir Edward Geddes, as Controller of the navy in 1917 helped transform the dire state of merchant shipping and improve food supply from abroad.
- Many fishermen from the Western Isles joined the merchant navy, helping to keep the food supply going.
- Of 8,000 fishermen in the navy's trawler section, 2,000 came from the island of Lewis.
- By autumn 1916, food became more difficult to find and much more expensive.
- Government initiatives to increase the amount of land for growing food had limited effect in Scotland because a lot of land was given over to hill farming as it was only suitable for rough grazing.
- There were efforts to increase the numbers and size of allotments near cities, for example in Ballencrief.
- By the beginning of 1918, the Government introduced two 'meatless days' in Scotland, Wednesday and Friday; it was illegal for meat to be served in any public place on these days.
- By April 1918, rationing was in place in Scotland as across the rest of the country.
- Breaches of legislation could be punished by law under DORA (Defence of the Realm Act).
- The drinking of alcohol was limited during the war and this reduced the drinking of whisky and beer.
- DORA reduced the opening hours of pubs to only five and a half hours each day, with no opening on Sundays.
- Brewing and pubs were brought under government control in areas where munitions camps were being built. For example, in Scotland, in the areas around the naval base at Invergordon and Gretna, only 30 pubs and four off-licences were allowed.
- The pubs were deliberately very plain and not very comfortable. This had the effect of reducing convictions related to drunkenness by an average of 70 per cent.
- Some councils like Glasgow voted to stop serving alcohol at their functions and there was a ban on 'treating' – buying others rounds of drink. Pubs were not allowed to let their customers buy their drink on credit.
- Licensing laws after the war continued the wartime restriction with the 1921 Licensing Act.

Any other valid points that meet the criteria described in the general marking instructions for this kind of question.

15 Compare the views of Sources C **and** D **about the reasons for the rise of the Labour Party in Scotland after 1918. (5)**

Compare the sources overall and in detail.

Candidates can be credited in a number of ways up to a maximum of 5 marks.

Possible points of comparison may include:

Overall: Sources C and D agree.

Source C	Source D
'Red Clydeside' is at best only a partial explanation of the rise of Labour after 1918. It is uncertain how many of those involved were socialist revolutionaries.	The dominant image of Labour comes from the 'Red Clydesiders' elected in 1922. But even the 1922 election was not all it seemed: there was a strong strand of social conservatism in those elected.
The ILP lay behind the rents campaign, and the electoral breakthrough in Scotland can be related to the housing issue.	The politics of housing played a more important role in Labour's breakthrough: the wartime rent strikes raised the profile of Labour's distinctive message.
Influences other than war-time tensions on the Clyde helped Labour in the early 1920s.	By 1922, there was a resolution to the 'Irish question' and the ILP's support for state funded education for Catholics was important.
A major bonus for Labour was the support of the Irish Catholic community.	Irish support was also relevant to Labour's rise.

Section 2 – British – 20 marks

Part A – Church, State and Feudal Society, 1066–1406

16 To what extent was the most important role of the Church in medieval society political? (20)

Context: The Roman Catholic Church was the main stabilising force in Western Europe. The Church provided religious leadership as well as secular, or worldly, leadership.

Politics

- Throughout the period there was conflict between the Church and monarchs. The Church sought control over society and that included over secular rulers. This frequently led to conflict, such as the Investiture contest.
- Religious leaders as landholders had a role in maintaining and using troops for political reasons. For example, the role of Bishop Odo at the Battle of Hastings.
- Churchmen could rise to senior positions at the courts of monarchs due to their education.

Other factors

The importance of the Church in everyday life

- The local church was frequently the only stone building in villages illustrating its importance. Significant cathedrals, etc. were built in towns.
- The Church regulated everyday life through its acts of worship.
- The Church had a role as overlord for many peasants; they relied on it for work.

The importance of the Church within feudal society: saints, relics, crusades, salvation and pilgrimages

- The Church saw itself as a significant force for stability in medieval Europe.
- Through veneration of saints and the worshiping of relics, it provided visible symbols of religious power and examples of standards.
- Through Crusade and pilgrimages, it offered a path to salvation.

The differing roles of the secular and regular Church in:

Religion

- The primary role of the Church was the spiritual health of the population. As such it served the spiritual needs of medieval society.
- Regular clergy served the spiritual needs of society in monasteries, which were centres of learning as well as following different rules of life.
- Secular clergy were responsible for the day-to-day ministration of their flocks and their education in scripture, as well as performing important acts of worship.

Society and the economy

- The Church was a significant landholder and was exempt from many taxes.
- The Church had a role, therefore, as an employer and as a generator of economic wealth for the country, mostly though commercial activity.
- For example, Melrose Abbey had a sheep flock of at least 15,000 in the fourteenth century and exported wool to the Low Countries and Italy.

Any other relevant factors.

17 How important was the impact of the Civil War in the increase of central royal power in the reign of Henry II of England? (20)

Context: Henry II's reign was characterised by an increase in royal power, as he sought to control his patchwork inheritance using a variety of methods.

Impact of the Civil War

- Although Henry inherited a peaceful kingdom, it was a kingdom suffering the effects of the Civil War between Mathilda and Stephen.
- Henry's main concern was to recover his legitimate rights and destroy unlawful privileges as a first step to re-establishing orderly government after the Civil War.
- Henry inherited a country that had a lack of government due to the reign of Stephen.

Other factors

Growth of the nobility

- During the Civil War, the nobility had grown powerful, with some lords even controlling royal castles.
- Henry was remorseless in the destruction of adulterine castles and reclamation of royal strongholds that were now in baronial hands. For example, the campaign against Hugh Mortimer, the greatest of the Welsh Marcher lords, where Henry took his castles by force.

Cost of warfare

- Revenue was needed to fund the maintenance of royal castles as well as mercenary forces, when they were employed.
- Henry reviewed the role of sheriffs and bailiffs, removing those who were corrupt and replacing them with trusted men. The exchequer was restored and revenue collection made more efficient.

Need to develop the economy

Law and order

- Henry was committed to the restoration of law and order after Stephen's reign when disorder had increased.
- Henry believed that too few offenders were caught and too few of those put on trial were condemned.
- As a result he was a considerable legal reformer, making the law more efficient and regular through the use of assizes.

Effects of foreign influence

- Henry sought to recover his rights over foreign territory lost during his grandfather's time.
- The counties of Berry, Auvergne and Toulouse had fallen away from Aquitaine.
- The territory of Anjou was threatened by Blois. The Welsh princes and Scottish King were all threatening as well.

Any other relevant factors.

18 *Changing social attitudes were the most important reason for the decline of feudal society.*

How valid is this view? (20)

Context: Feudalism flourished between the eleventh and thirteenth centuries, but began to decline towards the close of the thirteenth century, ultimately disappearing by 1500AD.

Changing social attitudes

- Social mobility was increasing for several reasons, including the move to an economy based more on cash than service.
- In England the wars against France had brought riches to some, and enabled them to climb the social ladder.
- Expectations of social mobility increased throughout this period.

Other factors

The Black Death

- The Black Death reduced the population of England by roughly a third. Those peasants that survived saw their labour become a valuable commodity. Wage levels in England approximately doubled.
- Unable to find enough labour to work their demesne, lords found it more profitable to lease out the land. With smaller areas to farm, the lords had less need for the labour services provided by the serfs. Lords started to 'commute' these labour services. This meant that in return for a cash payment, peasants no longer had to work on the lord's demesne.

The Peasants' Revolt

- In England, the attempts of the Statute of the Labourers in 1351 to force peasants back into serfdom were widely and strongly resisted.
- Although the Revolt was defeated, its extent showed that the old feudal consensus had broken down.
- After the Peasants' Revolt the lords found it very difficult to retain the feudal system.

The growth of towns

- Towns offered greater opportunities for serfs in terms of jobs as freemen.
- The development of merchants and a middle class which paid tax reduced the King's reliance on feudal dues.

The growth of trade/mercantilism

- One effect of the Crusades was to encourage trade between the West and cities like Constantinople and Alexandria.
- Some lords realised that trade in wool was more profitable than relying on peasants. They diversified the use of their land as a result.

Any other relevant factors.

Part B – The Century of Revolutions, 1603–1702

19 To what extent were the policies of Charles I successful in Scotland? (20)

Context: Charles I was the second son of James I and VI of England and Scotland. His views on the divine right of kings soon put him at loggerheads with his Scottish subjects.

Political challenges

- Charles I caused political resentment because of his policies, which took power and land from Scottish nobles, as well as his decision not to visit Scotland until 1633, when he was crowned there.
- Charles I appointed bishops rather than nobles to the Scottish Privy Council.
- Charles I gave increasing power to bishops, which undermined the status of the Scottish nobility.
- The Stuart notion of the divine right of kings was chiefly ended by the Scots' opposition to Charles I's attempts to impose his will on the Scottish people.

Religious policies

- Charles I introduced William Laud, the Archbishop of Canterbury, to Scotland in 1633, and Laud proceeded to oversee Anglican practice in Scottish churches, which was resented by many.
- The King approved a unification of the Churches without consulting the Privy Council.
- The introduction of a new Service Book, a Scottish bishops' variation of the English Prayer Book, caused uproar when it was read at St Giles Cathedral in Edinburgh. There was widespread opposition across Scotland.

The Covenanters

- The Covenant demanded a Scottish Parliament and General Assembly free from the King's interference. It demanded the abolition of bishops, and called for a limit to the power of the King by increasing the role of Scotland's nobles and the Kirk, as well as the preservation of Presbyterianism in Scotland.
- Charles I did not deal with the Covenanters, helping cause the War of the Three Kingdoms.
- The English Parliament's treaty of alliance with the Scottish Covenanters, the Solemn League and Covenant of 1643, was a key feature of the change in fortunes of the King's enemies.

First Bishops' War

- The first Bishops' War took place in 1639. Charles I's failure to win led to a truce.
- The Pacification of Berwick appeared to give the Scots religious freedoms, but mutual suspicion continued between the Covenanters and Charles I.
- The King's desire for funds led to the recalling of the Short Parliament in England, which was quickly ended as it wished to discuss Charles' role in the eleven-year tyranny.

Second Bishops' War

- The second Bishops' War ended in humiliation as Charles I's forces were easily defeated by the Covenanters at the Battle of Newburn. The Treaty of Ripon of October 1640 ended hostilities.
- The resultant Treaty of London led to surprising concessions from Charles I to the Covenanters. He ratified the rejection of episcopacy, but his calling of the Long Parliament was to presage civil war.

Any other relevant factors.

20 How important was Cromwell's dominance as a reason for the failure to find an alternative form of government, 1649–1658? (20)

Context: Britain struggled to find a stable form of alternative government to monarchy in the years between 1649 and 1658 for a variety of reasons.

Cromwell's dominance

- Cromwell dominated politics throughout the period as he was one of the commanders of the New Model Army, signatory for the execution of King Charles I, member of the Rump Parliament and victor in Ireland.
- Cromwell raised taxation without consent and overrode a law he had helped to make, which protected Royalists from persecution.
- He passed progressive laws, but has been accused of being dictatorial and seeking to emulate monarchy, as seen by the nomination of his son Richard as his successor.

Other factors

The role of the army

- Army leaders were behind the creation of the Protectorate and the offer to Oliver Cromwell of the role of Lord Protector.
- Cromwell's power was based on his continuing popularity among the army.

- Creation of a military dictatorship from 1653 and the drawing up of military districts under the governance of major-generals during the second Protectorate from October 1656 illustrated the growing role of the army in governance.

Legacy of Civil War

- The Civil War led to lasting and bitter divisions in society.
- Supporters of the Protectorate were suspicious of Royalist plots as well as those from groups like the Fifth Monarchists and the Diggers.
- Despite Cromwell's desire for toleration of private worship, the culture of distrust probably helped lead to heavy handed army action against what was perceived to be opposition.

The effects of the execution of the King

- Cromwell was third signatory to the execution of the King. He was accused of regicide.
- With the death of the King came a lack of a check on the power of parliament. Without a king, Cromwell ruled on his own for two different periods during the Interregnum.

The role of parliament

- The Rump Parliament was more radical than Cromwell desired as well as its members arguing among themselves. This led to its removal.
- Quarrels between MPs and army officers were a feature of the Interregnum. Parliament stood in the way of toleration and thus prevented religious wounds healing.

Unpopular legislation

- Examples of unpopular legislation include: the Treason Law and Censorship Law introduced in 1649 and, in 1650, the Oath of Allegiance which was imposed for all men over 18.

Foreign policy

- A largely successful war was waged against both Holland and Spain, though it was costly and led to tax increases.
- The brutal legacy of dealing with rebellion in Ireland caused lasting resentment.

Any other relevant factors.

21 ***The Revolution Settlement of 1688–1702 successfully altered the balance of power between the monarchy and parliament.***
How valid is this view? (20)

Context: A series of agreements made between 1689 and 1701 legalised the division of power between parliament and the Crown and became known as the Revolution Settlement. This included the Bill of Rights, limiting the power of the monarch.

Religion

- The Toleration Act of 1689 provided for free public worship for all except Roman Catholics and Unitarians.
- Roman Catholics were still ineligible for elected posts in towns or parliament.
- Parliament now held more sway in religious matters, although the monarch still enjoyed the political advantages of being Head of the Church.

Finance

- Settlement made it impossible for the monarchy to exist financially independently of parliament.
- From 1689, parliament voted to give the Crown money as part of the Civil List system, which gave Parliament control over the distribution of money.
- The Settlement made it impossible for the Crown to raise money for any length of time without the approval of Parliament.

Legislation

- The legal settlement established parliamentary control over the legal system and courts.
- Judges could only be removed from their positions if parliament demanded this.
- Parliament now enforced its own control over judicial procedure. However, monarchs could still appoint judges who might be favourable to them.

Parliament

- The Triennial Act in 1694 was intended to keep MPs more closely in touch with public opinion.
- The Licensing Act was repealed in 1695, removing restrictions on the freedom of the press to report parliamentary criticism of the Crown.
- William and Mary had to agree to the Bill of Rights before they were given the throne, legalising the new relationship between Crown and parliament.

The succession

- The Bill of Rights declared that no Roman Catholic could become king or queen.
- Later, the Act of Settlement of 1701 stated that all future monarchs should be members of the Church of England.
- Parliament now governed the question of who ascended the throne.

Scotland

- The Claim of Right asserted that power flowed upwards from the people.
- The Settlement confirmed the position of the Kirk in Scotland as the Presbyterian Church.

The status of the army

- The Revolution Settlement meant that parliament gained partial control of the army. The monarch was not given enough money to maintain a standing army.
- Royal authority over military matters had now passed to the House of Commons.

Loopholes in the Settlement

- The monarch still held executive power and controlled foreign policy, declaring war and signing treaties. The monarch was still the source of patronage in the army and navy.
- The monarch still created peers, and could therefore control the House of Lords.

Any other relevant factors.

Part C – The Atlantic Slave Trade

22 How important was the slave trade to the British economy? (20)

Context: By the end of the eighteenth century, Britain was transforming from the leading trading nation to the first industrial power.

The importance of tropical crops and profits

- The climate of the West Indies was ideal for producing crops such as coffee, sugar and tobacco. The popularity of these products grew as Britain became addicted to the consumption of these status goods.
- The popularity of these products grew as Britain became addicted to the consumption of these high-status goods.
- Large profits were made and Britain's status in Europe and the rest of the world was enhanced.

The role of the trade in navigation

- The slave trade aided the growth of the both the Royal Navy and the United Kingdom's merchant navy.
- The Royal Navy grew out of the fight for control of the colonies and then protected British control and trading from these colonies.
- The Navigation Acts required that all overseas trade should take place in British ships, manned by British sailors when trading between British ports and the colonies.
- Additional laws limited the ability of other countries to compete with British traders; the 1733 Molasses Act, which banned foreign sugar being imported into North America and the 1739 Direct Export Act, which allowed plantation owners to ship goods directly to Europe.
- The development of the triangular trade.
- The slave trade trained experienced sailors, who could serve in the Royal Navy.
- There was a high casualty rate among sailors on slave trade ships.

The role of the trade in manufacturing

- The development of the cotton industry was integral to the development of the slave trade. Cities like Manchester exported cotton to Africa as part of the triangular trade. Cotton was the key industry that helped stimulate the industrial revolution.
- Manufactured goods made in Britain were traded for enslaved Africans. These included goods made in the new factories of the industrial revolution such as wool and metal goods, for example pots, pans and cutlery.
- Without the slave trade, planters would have struggled to meet the growing demands for the luxury tropical crops.

The role of the trade in the procurement of raw materials and trading patterns

- The slave trade provided the raw materials for industrial exports – and large profits – to Europe.
- Cities like Liverpool grew wealthy because its merchants could hold plantation cotton and other plantation goods like rum, then export directly to the rest of Britain and Europe. Bristol's wealth was based on plantation suga
- Other ports such as Glasgow prospered from selling goods and services to support slave traders.

Industrial development

- The slave trade was of importance to the development of the economy: financial, commercial, legal and insurance institutions emerged to support the activities of the slave traders; slave traders became bankers and many new businesses were financed by profits made from slave trading.

- The slave trade helped the development of Britain's transport infrastructure, canals and railways. Without transport, the industrial revolution would not have been possible.

- Wealth generated by the slave trade meant that domestic taxes could be kept low.

- The argument that the slave trade was the vital factor in Britain's industrialisation was put forward in Williams' 'Capitalism and Slavery' thesis.

- By the end of the eighteenth century, the industrial revolution had advanced and the slave trade's importance was in relative decline.

- Some historians have argued that only a small proportion of slave trade profits were directly invested in the industrial revolution, therefore its importance may have been overstated.

Wealth of ports and merchants

- Liverpool's wealth and power was based on its involvement in the slave trade. At the end of the eighteenth century, Liverpool controlled 60 per cent of the whole trade.

- Liverpool became a major shipbuilding centre as a result of the slave trade.

- Liverpool, London, Bristol and Glasgow all prospered from selling goods and services to support slave traders.

- Huge fortunes were made by merchants building country homes and endowing schools, universities and museums with the profits from the slave trade. Important merchant banks grew as a result of the slave trade.

Other factors

- Changes in agriculture were important in stimulating the industrial revolution. These created more food, which enabled the population to grow and to move away from the countryside to the towns.

- Profits from agriculture were used to invest in industry, canals and railways.

- Technological innovation was also stimulated, for example the development of water and steam power; new machinery; transport changes.

- Mineral and energy resources, particularly iron and coal. It was the technical innovations in overcoming the barriers to mass coal production that was one of the biggest stimulants of industrial growth.

- The economy was doing well which prevented dissent and helped create political stability.

- Much of the profits of slavery were spent in maintaining ostentatious living, for example landed estates.

Any other relevant factors.

23 *The slave trade had a negative impact on African societies.*

How valid is this view? (20)

Context: The slave trade had been carried out in Africa for centuries; however, the arrival of the Europeans completely transformed the nature and scale of the trade.

The slave sellers and the European 'factories' on the West African coast

- Europeans mostly stayed in the coastal areas, leaving the capture of slaves to Africans. In the areas where slavery was not practised, for example among the Xhosa people of southern Africa, European slave-ship captains were unable to buy African captives.

- European 'factories' were developed on the coast to control the slave trade.

- The development of slave factories enabled the scale and frequency of the trade to increase.

The development of slave-based states and economies

- Enslavement by Africans could be used as a punishment for a crime or as payment for a family debt, or most commonly of all, it was the result of being captured as a prisoner of war.

- The arrival of European and American ships offering trading goods in exchange for captives gave an added incentive to the existing slave trade, often leading to abductions in order to make more money.

- Some societies preyed on others to obtain captives in exchange for European firearms, in the belief that this was the only way to protect themselves from attack by rivals and enemies who already had such weapons. As a result, states such as Dahomey, which was organised around the slave trade, became more powerful.

The destruction of societies

- Initially there was not massive disruption to African societies with rich and powerful individuals benefiting from receiving consumer goods and gold in return for captives.

- By the end of seventeenth century European demand for African captives became so great that they could only be acquired through raiding and warfare. Large areas of Africa were devastated and societies disintegrated.
- An estimated 10 million people were transported from Africa over the course of the eighteenth century. Many of those enslaved were the most productive and economically active sections of the population and this had a negative economic impact, leading to falls in production of food and other goods.

The development of foreign colonies

- West Africa grew poorer by its relationship with Europe as the enslaved Africans and other resources that were taken from Africa helped create the economic development and wealth of Europe and their colonies. The transatlantic trade also contributed to the impoverishment of Africa, which aided the subsequent colonial conquest of Africa by the European powers.

Roles played by leaders of African societies in continuing the trade

- African slave sellers grew wealthy by selling African captives to European traders on the coast. They were able to deal on equal terms with European traders who built 'factories' on the West African coast to house captives before selling them on to the slave-ship captains, who in turn transported the captives to the colonies of the New World.
- On the African side, the slave trade was generally the business of rulers or wealthy and powerful merchants, concerned with their own selfish or narrow interests, rather than those of the continent. At that time, there was no concept of being African – identity and loyalty were based on kinship or membership of a specific kingdom or society, rather than to the African continent.
- States actively engaged in slavery, particularly Dahomey, grew in power and influence.

Any other relevant factors.

24 To what extent was the decline in the economic importance of slavery the main reason for the success of the abolitionist campaign in 1807? (20)

Context: At the end of the eighteenth century, even as slave owning remained profitable, there were growing demands for the abolition of the trade and slavery itself.

Decline in economic importance of slavery

- As a result of the war with France, the slave trade declined by two-thirds.
- The industrial revolution had increased the importance of manufactured British goods and agriculture; Britain became less dependent on trading foreign goods.
- The slave trade became less important in economic terms – there was less demand for large numbers of slaves to be imported to the British colonies.
- There was a worldwide over-supply of sugar and British merchants had difficulties re-exporting it.
- There was growing competition from parts of the Empire like India, where crops like sugar were being produced on a bigger scale and more cheaply.

Other factors

Effects of slave resistance

- Successful slave rebellions like in Saint-Domingue (Haiti) increased the general fear of slave revolts.
- Abolition of the slave trade would mean slave conditions would have to improve because slaves would become more valuable. There were concerns that unless conditions improved, more slave revolts would follow.
- In Jamaica a substantial number of runaways lived in the mountains, outside the control of the authorities. Successive attempts to bring them under control had failed, which made it harder to maintain slavery without changes.

Military factors

- The abolition of the slave trade would undermine Napoleon's effort to restore French control in the Caribbean; the abolition campaign helped British interests.
- The 1805 Act banning any slave trade between British merchants and foreign colonies was aimed at attacking French interests by limiting their ability to engage in a lucrative trade.

Religious revival

- The religious revival of the late eighteenth century was at the heart of the anti-slavery movement. Many of the early leaders came from non-Conformist Churches such as Quakers and Methodists or Presbyterians and Baptists.
- Methodist leaders like John Wesley had criticised slavery, influencing abolitionists like John Newton.
- Early Quaker leaders translated their religious belief in the equality of all men before God into general humanitarian concerns. The Quakers were hugely important to the Society for the Abolition of the Slave Trade; nine of its original members were Quakers.

- In the eighteenth century, there was a religious revival that led to a rise in a fervent kind of Christianity: Evangelical Christianity. Evangelicals were concerned with morality and the impact of sin in causing mankind to fall out of God's favour. Evangelical Christians were especially important in the abolition movement, for example, William Wilberforce, Thomas Clarkson and Granville Sharp.

- Some Quakers had close links with the slave trade through banking and finance, for example Barclays Bank and Barings Bank.

- The Church of England had links to the slave trade through missionary organisations like the United Society for the Propagation of the Gospel (USPG), which owned slave plantations in Barbados.

Campaign of the Anti-Slavery Society

- Thomas Clarkson toured ports and cities connected with the slave trade to obtain witnesses for the parliamentary investigations of the slave trade which provided Wilberforce with convincing evidence for his speeches.

- The society published books and pamphlets, for example eyewitness accounts from former slaves such as Olaudah Equiano.

- The Anti-Slavery Society ran campaigns to boycott goods produced by slaves in the West Indies, such as sugar and rum, and supported the selling of products like sugar which had not been produced by slave labour.

- Public meetings and lecture tours involving those with experience of the slave trade, for example John Newton, were held and churches and theatres were used for abolitionist propaganda.

- The Anti-Slavery Society organised petitions and subscription lists supporting the abolition of slavery. Also artefacts and illustrations with anti-slavery messages were produced, for example Wedgwood pottery.

- Members lobbied MPs to get promises that they would oppose the slave trade in parliamentary debates.

- Effective moderate political and religious leadership among the abolitionists influenced major figures such as Pitt and Fox to support their cause; abolitionists gave evidence to parliamentary commissions.

Role of Wilberforce

- Wilberforce spent eighteen years putting forward the arguments of the Society for the Abolition of the Slave Trade in parliament.

- Wilberforce's speeches in parliament were effective in drawing attention to the cause.

- Wilberforce's Christian faith had led him to become interested in social reform. He linked the need to reform factory conditions in Britain with the need to abolish slavery and the slave trade within the British Empire.

- Wilberforce collaborated with other abolitionists to achieve his aims, including the Quakers, Thomas Clarkson and Olaudah Equiano.

Any other reasonable factors.

Part D – Britain, 1851–1951

25 *By 1928, Britain had successfully become a democratic country.*

How valid is this view? (20)

Context: The growth of democracy in Britain was a gradual process and marked by a switch in emphasis from the rights of stakeholders or property owners to equality and fairness for all citizens.

The widening of the franchise, 1867–1928

- 1867 Reform Act: Increased the number of men with the vote to 1.5–2.5 million (one in three). There were new voters from burghs, but the right to vote was still based on property value and MPs were still unevenly distributed; there were too many counties and small burghs at the expense of industrial areas. Thus political power still remained with the landowners, tenant farmers and middle classes.

- 1884 Representation of the People Act: Made the franchise in the counties the same as that in the burghs. The electorate doubled to 5 million (two in three) men could vote. This Act gave the vote to the skilled working class, but the vote was still linked to a complex set of property qualifications, excluded several groups such as women.

- 1918 Representation of the People Act: Now most men over the age of 21 and women over the age of 30 could vote, but voting registration issues had not been resolved by the time of the 1918 election and plural voting, for example at universities, still existed.

- 1928: All men and women over the age of 21 were now allowed to vote, but undemocratic anomalies existed – plural votes and the university constituencies were not abolished until 1948 and the voting system was still 'first past the post' in the UK.

Other measures relating to the distribution of seats

- 1867 Reform Act: Minor redistribution of seats, which was the redistribution of just 52 MPs.

- 1885 Redistribution of Seats Act: The vast majority of constituencies now had only one MP. Boundaries were redrawn to approximately equal constituencies, which largely solved the north/south imbalance. This created a recognisably modern electoral system.

Corruption and intimidation

- The voting system had been 'open'. Voting was also marked by drinking, mob action and the 'influence' of wealthy landowners. The South of England was over represented.
- 1872 Ballot Act: Intimidation declined but corruption was not wiped out because voting could take place over several days and there were still too few voters; election agents were able to work out who had voted for which candidates and act accordingly.
- In rural areas, landowners could still assert influence – ballot boxes for different villages were counted separately so election agents could observe how many votes were cast for the other side.
- 1883 Corrupt and Illegal Practices Act: This set a maximum expenditure according to the size of the electorate, and returns of election expenditure were required. This was very effective.
- 1884 Representation of the People Act: This extended the size of the electorate in most constituencies to a size where bribery was not feasible.

Widening membership of the House of Commons

- The property qualification to be an MP was abolished in 1858.
- Payment for MPs began in 1911, enabling working-class men to sit.

The Role of the House of Lords

- 1911 Parliament Act: Lords could only delay bills from the House of Commons for two years rather than veto them completely. They had no control over money bills.

Choice and participation in democracy

- The spread of socialist ideas and trades unionism led to the creation of the Labour Representation Committee in 1900 and the parliamentary Labour Party by 1906. This party included more working-class MPs and represented the interests of the working class, thereby offering a wider choice to the electorate.
- Individual political parties developed national political organisations to make sure their 'message' got across to the electorate, for example the development of the National Liberal Federation, Conservative Central Office, Primrose League. This led to the participation of more ordinary people in politics.
- Thanks to the 1870 (1872) Education Acts, there was a great increase in literacy. There was also a great increase in the range and variety of daily newspapers. Railways spread information nationally and were important to the growth of democracy.

Any other relevant factors.

26 How important were the social surveys of Booth and Rowntree as a reason why the Liberals introduced social welfare reforms, 1906–1914? (20)

Context: By the early twentieth century, urbanisation and population growth had created social problems too big for local solutions. In addition, the old system of poor relief proved unable to cope with the numbers of people seeking help.

Concerns over poverty – the social surveys of Booth and Rowntree

- The reports of Charles Booth and Seebohm Rowntree showed that the main causes of poverty were irregular employment, low pay, unemployment, sickness and old age. These were factors that were mostly out of an individual's control.
- Booth's seventeen-volume survey of London revealed that almost one-third of the capital's population lived in poverty.
- The extent of poverty was confirmed in Rowntree's survey of York, which although relatively prosperous, revealed similar levels of poverty in a main regional town.

Municipal socialism

- Local council-led action on social reforms seemed to show what could be done if solutions were centrally planned and funded. The example of Birmingham was highlighted; Joseph Chamberlain implemented a series of reforms improving public services between 1873 and 1875. His reforms inspired Beatrice Webb, one of the leaders of the Fabian movement, who wanted more government actions to solve social problems.

Foreign examples

- Bismarck, Germany's Prime Minster, had introduced a very successful system of social security. Liberal politicians such as Lloyd George wanted to introduce similar reforms in Britain, partly to show that Britain was 'keeping up' with Germany.

National efficiency

- By the end of the nineteenth century, Britain's share of world trade was in relative decline because other countries like the USA and Germany had industrialised. The government was worried because Britain's wealth depended on an export-led economy.
- The government believed that unless the health and educational standards of Britain's workers improved, Britain's position as a strong industrial power would be threatened.

Fears over national security

- The government was worried when almost 25 per cent of the volunteers to fight in the Boer War were rejected because they were physically unfit to serve in the armed forces. In Manchester, two out of every three volunteers were medically unfit to fight. There was concern that the nation's 'fighting stock' of young men was so unhealthy.

- The Boer War broke out in 1899 in South Africa. It took the British Army nearly three years to defeat an irregular army of Boer farmers. There was concern as to whether Britain could survive a war or protect its empire against a far stronger enemy in the future.

- Concerns about national security and national efficiency coalesced into worries about Britain's future financial and economic security.

The rise of New Liberalism

- New Liberal ideas were not important issues in the general election of 1905. When Prime Minister Campbell Bannerman died in 1908, the door was opened for new 'interventionist' ideas.

- Leading New Liberals were Winston Churchill and David Lloyd George. Both were interested in social reform and were young, ambitious and keen to make their mark on politics. The New Liberals argued that state intervention was necessary to liberate people from social problems over which they had no control.

Party advantage

- Since 1884, many more working-class men had had the vote and the Liberals had tended to attract many of those votes. Social reform was a means of continuing to appeal to these voters.

The rise of Labour

- By 1906, the newly formed Labour Party was directly representing the interests of the working class, the largest social group in Britain. Thanks to democratic reform more members of the working class had the vote. Liberals would have to devise polices which would keep the support of the working class if they were to retain their vote.

Any other relevant factors.

27 To what extent were the Labour social welfare reforms, 1945–1951, effective in meeting the needs of the British people? (20)

Context: The 1942 Beveridge Report was instantly popular on its publication. It identified key social problems and proposed solutions which seemed to offer meaning and hope in the fight against the Nazis during the Second World War.

The aims of the Welfare State

- The 1942 Beveridge Report identified the five 'Giants' of poverty: Ignorance, Idleness, Squalor, Disease and Want.

- Beveridge offered a vision of Britain's future offering help to all, 'from the cradle to the grave'.

- The Labour government also nationalised 20 per cent of industry – the railways, mines, gas and electricity. The government directly employed people in growth industries where success was measured by the amount of work done and people employed, not productivity.

Ignorance

- Reform was started by the wartime coalition government led by Churchill. The 1944 Education Act raised the school-leaving age to fifteen. Wider measures to improve learning were implemented, with public health measures such as the introduction of school milk, etc.

- Labour introduced a two-tier secondary schooling whereby pupils were split at the age of eleven (twelve in Scotland) depending on their ability. The more academic pupils who passed the eleven-plus exam went to grammar schools (senior secondaries in Scotland) and the rest to secondary moderns.

- Those who went to grammar schools were expected to stay on past the age of fifteen and this created a group of people who would take senior jobs in industry, while those in the secondary moderns would leave, taking practical jobs, thus solving the skills shortages in the country.

- In theory, children of all backgrounds could get equal opportunities in life. In practice, the system created a bigger division between the poor and the rich because children from better off backgrounds got more help and support in passing the exam to get to grammar schools. In many cases, the existing inequalities between the classes were increased rather than reduced.

- Labour kept to their promise of extending the school-leaving age, despite severe economic problems and pressure to postpone the measure.

- Labour expanded university education through the introduction of grants so all could attend in theory.

Idleness

- The need to rebuild Britain after the war meant unemployment was basically non-existent, so the government had little to do to tackle idleness.

- Expansion of university education after the war led to a 60 per cent increase in student numbers between 1945 and 1951. This provided more skilled workers and allowed people from less advantaged backgrounds to pursue a higher education, helping to keep unemployment down.

- The Labour government also nationalised 20 per cent of industry – the railways, mines, gas and electricity. The government directly employed people in growth industries where success was measured by the amount of work done and people employed, not by productivity.

Squalor

- There was a great shortage of housing as the war had destroyed and damaged thousands of homes. The housing shortage was compounded by limited attempts to improve housing in the inter-war period; most house building had been for private owners and little had been done about slum housing.

- The job of tackling the housing shortage was given to Bevan's Ministry of Health, which was already overstretched setting up the new Health Service.

- Labour's target for housing was to build 200,000 new homes a year. 157,000 pre-fabricated homes were built to a good standard, but the full target was never met.

- Bevan encouraged the building of council houses rather than privately funded construction.

- The New Towns Act of 1946 aimed to target overcrowding in the increasingly built-up older cities. By 1950, the government had designed twelve new communities.

- The Town and Country Planning Act attempted to get rid of slums by providing local communities with more power for building developments and new housing.

- However, by 1951 there was still a huge shortfall in British housing.

Disease

- The National Health Service (NHS) was set up in 1948 and was the first comprehensive universal system of health care in Britain.

- The NHS dealt effectively with the spread of disease. Some of Britain's most harmful diseases were almost wiped out by the NHS's programme of vaccinations.

- The NHS also offered childcare, the introduction of prescriptions, health visiting and provision for the elderly. Treatment was free at the point of need, which meant people did not have to pay to get medical help.

- The NHS was almost too successful. The demand from the public was overwhelming; the estimated member of patients treated by the NHS almost doubled. Costs could no longer be funded out of general taxations, so prescription charges were introduced by 1951.

Want

- The 1946 National Insurance Act provided comprehensive insurance to give sickness and unemployment benefits and covered for most eventualities. It was said to support people from the 'cradle to the grave' which meant people had protection against falling into poverty throughout their lives. This was very effective as it meant that if the breadwinner of the family was injured, their family was less likely to fall into poverty. However, a criticism of the Act was that the benefits were only granted to those who made 156 weekly contributions.

- The 1948 National Assistance Board was set up to provide help for those not covered by the National Insurance Act. This acted as a safety net to protect these people. However, many people still lived on incomes below subsistence level, showing the problem of want had not completely been resolved.

Any other relevant factors.

Part E – Britain and Ireland, 1900–1985

28 To what extent did the First World War have an impact on Ireland? (20)

Context: The First World War brought economic demand to Ireland. The islands' positive engagement in the war was changed by events in 1916.

Irish attitudes to the First World War

- Irish support for the war was strong in 1914. The image of Germany invading Catholic Belgium elicited much sympathy in Ireland.

- Ulster gave strong support for the war, partly to demonstrate loyalty to the Empire.

- In the south of Ireland, almost 200,000 volunteered, showing support for the war.

The Nationalist movement 1914–1916

- The Nationalist movement split over its policy at the beginning of the First World War.

- Most Nationalists, including John Redmond, supported the war effort.

- A minority of Irish Volunteers as well as the Irish Republican Brotherhood opposed the war.

- The Catholic Church opposed the war from 1915 and called on Redmond to drop his support for the war.

The Easter Rising

- April 1916 saw an armed rising by around 1,200 Irish Republicans aiming to end British rule in Ireland.
- British troops were more heavily armed and put down the insurrection.
- The rebels surrendered unconditionally.

Changing attitudes towards British rule after 1916

- British actions after the Rising encouraged the growth of Sinn Féin and saw the eclipse of constitutional Irish Nationalists.
- There were mass arrests of Sinn Féin members and the leaders of the Rising were executed after court martials.
- The Irish public grew increasingly hostile to the British and sympathetic to the rebels. This was further encouraged by stories of British atrocities that grew after the Rising.
- Sinn Féin's support grew and it won 73 seats in the 1918 general election.

Anti-conscription campaign

- The British government attempted to impose conscription in Ireland in April 1918.
- There was widespread opposition in Ireland from the Church, trades unions and Nationalists.
- Sinn Féin in particular gained much sympathy and support for their role in the campaign.

Decline of the Nationalist Party

- John Redmond's enthusiastic support for war alienated some supporters. His death in 1918 led to a loss of leadership.
- The Nationalists were poorly organised by 1918 and local party branches had declined, in contrast to the young and vibrant Sinn Féin organisation.

Rise of Sinn Féin

- The actions of Sinn Féin and its association with the anti-conscription campaign and Easter Rising led to an upsurge of support for the party as evidenced by its success in the 1918 general election and subsequent formation of the Dáil.

Any other relevant factors.

29 How important were divisions in the Republican movement as a reason for the outbreak of the Irish Civil War? (20)

Context: When the British commander admitted that the British could only control all of Ireland by imposing martial law, the British negotiated an end to the War of Independence, but disagreements about the future relationship between Britain and Ireland spilled over into conflict.

Divisions in the Republican movement

- The Anglo-Irish Treaty caused divisions.
- Pro and anti-Treaty factions emerged around Michael Collins and Eamon de Valera.
- The split was very personal as both sides had fought together during the War of Independence.

Other factors

The Anglo-Irish Treaty

- The Treaty provided for a self-governing Irish state that would have its own army and police force.
- However, the Treaty also meant that the Irish were to remain in the Empire as a dominion. This was too much for Republican Irish nationalists.

Partition

- The Treaty also allowed Northern Ireland to opt out of the new state and remain with the rest of the United Kingdom, which it did.
- In 1920, this split was recognised in the Government of Ireland Act, which was intended to create two self-governing territories in Ireland, with six counties in the north and 26 in the south.

Dominion status

- The Anglo-Irish Treaty meant that Ireland became a dominion of the British Empire, rather than being independent of Britain.
- This was not popular with many Irish people who wanted full independence from the United Kingdom.

The role of Collins

- Michael Collins was part of the negotiation team that agreed the Anglo-Irish Treaty with the British.
- Collins was frustrated at a lack of instruction from the Irish government over whether to accept the Treaty or not.
- Collins recognised that the Treaty was a half-way house, but argued that it gave Ireland, 'the freedom to achieve freedom'.

The role of de Valera

- Eamon de Valera was the first President of Dáil Éireann.
- He gave the Irish negotiators the power to make agreements without reference to the Cabinet back in Ireland.
- He opposed the Treaty, claiming he had not been consulted on its provisions.
- When the treaty was ratified by a narrow majority, he resigned as President.

Any other relevant factors.

30 *The role of the British Army was the most important obstacle to peace between 1968 and 1985.*

How valid is this view? (20)

Context: Northern Irish politics became increasingly sectarian during this period. Developing trouble led to the deployment of British troops.

The role of the British Army

- The British Army was initially deployed to improve security in Northern Ireland against a background of increasing communal violence.
- Aggressive tactics by the army led to disillusionment with them in the Catholic community.
- Examples of aggressive actions such as Bloody Sunday and the Fall Curfew encouraged support for the paramilitaries.

Other factors

Economic differences

- Economic discrimination against the Catholic population existed for much of this period in terms of jobs, although this began to break down as the period went on, especially in the 1970s and beyond.
- Certain sectors favoured Protestants, such as engineering and shipbuilding.

Religious and communal differences

- Religious differences were significant as Northern Ireland was dominated by the Protestant majority, over its Catholic minority.
- Religious differences were enhanced by differing communal traditions as well as language and sporting differences.
- These differences were further compounded by political polarisation, frequently along religious lines: Catholic Sinn Féin and Protestant Ulster Unionist Party, for example.

Hardening attitudes

- Attitudes hardened from the late 1960s as intercommunal violence grew.
- Paramilitary groups formed to protect their own communities and attack their opponents.
- Paramilitary groups become more extreme with the emergence of the Provisional IRA, for example.
- There was loss of sympathy among some groups owing to the indiscriminate nature of the violence.

British government policies

- Government policy alienated many in Northern Ireland, especially in the Catholic community.
- Internment or detention without trial started in 1971 with little success.
- The number of violent deaths grew.

Direct rule

- Direct rule of Northern Ireland was imposed in 1972 after the British government decided to remove control of security from the Northern Irish government, which promptly resigned.

The role of the Irish government

- The Anglo-Irish Agreement of 1985 gave the Irish government a role in the governance of Northern Ireland for the first time. This led to improved co-operation between the British and Irish governments and paved the way for the Good Friday Agreement thirteen years later.

Any other relevant factors.

Section 3 – European and World – 20 marks

Part A – The Crusades, 1071–1204

31 How important were overpopulation and famine as motives for Christians from different classes to take the cross? (20)

Context: The religious wars we call the Crusades were successful in motivating Christians from all walks of life to travel to and attempt to control the Holy Land. That so many went was down to a variety of factors.

Overpopulation and famine

- Demographics influenced the Crusades; as the population grew so did the need for resources to support them.
- Several famines in Europe have also been suggested as a possible motive.
- The Holy Lands were commonly seen as being lands of plenty, therefore attracting crusaders.

Other factors

Religious motives

- Urban II wished to reunite the two branches of Christianity and the Crusades offered him the chance to do this.
- Outrage at Muslim actions and 'atrocities' in their expansion west, particularly the taking of Jerusalem, galvanised Christians into action.
- Urban II offered remission of sins for those going on Crusade, which was attractive to knights who were trained in the art of killing.

The desire to acquire territory in the Holy Land

- The desire for land was undoubtedly a motivation for some, especially younger sons who did not stand to inherit their father's land. During the First Crusade this motive was clearly behind the actions of Bohemund and Baldwin, who struck off on their own and seized land at Antioch and Edessa.

Peer pressure

- Some knights were undoubtedly motivated by expectation put on them to do the right thing by going on Crusade; this conferred status on the family of the Crusader.
- Stephen of Blois who was married to the daughter of William I of England is a good example. He returned home in 1098 without having fulfilled his crusading vow to forge a way to Jerusalem. He was pressured by his wife Adela into making a second pilgrimage, and joined the minor crusade of 1101.

Seeking fame and riches

- The knightly class produced men who were good at killing. The desire to make a name for oneself was undoubtedly a motivation to go on Crusade. Crusades provided an opportunity to kill for God and seek fame.
- The East was seen as being wealthy so the desire for riches would have motivated some.

The sense of adventure

- The Crusades offered a chance of adventure to peasants who would otherwise have had a life of toil on the land for a lord. It offered excitement and opportunity.

Any other relevant factors.

32 *The Christian defeat at Hattin was the main reason for the fall of Jerusalem in 1187.*

How valid is this view? (20)

Context: The success of the First Crusade led to Christian control of Jerusalem, and the creation of a number of Crusader States. These states were always threatened by their more numerous Muslim neighbours.

The Christian defeat at Hattin

- The military defeat of the armies of Jerusalem by Saladin's forces at the Battle of Hattin destroyed the main Christian army in the Holy Land. This left Jerusalem unprotected.
- Saladin was ruthless in the aftermath of victory, slaughtering all members of the militant orders and personally killing Reynald of Chatillon, though Guy was allowed to surrender and enter captivity.

Other factors

The death of Baldwin IV

- Baldwin IV died in March 1185. He had skilfully used a mixture of military and diplomatic means to keep Saladin at bay.
- A short power struggle after the death of his chosen successor, his nephew, in August let Guy de Lusignan assume the throne, abetted by Sibylla. Guy would pursue a much more aggressive policy towards Saladin.

Divisions among the Crusaders

- There were divisions between the faction around Guy de Lusignan and his wife, and the faction around Raymond III of Tripoli.
- Some Crusaders actively sought to open hostilities with their Muslim neighbours; examples include Reynald of Chatillon with his attacks on Muslim pilgrims and the Knights Templar with their uncompromising attitude.

The lack of resources of the Christian States

- The Christian Crusader States of the Middle East always suffered from their relative isolation from their support areas in the west. Except for the First Crusade, they also lacked support from the Byzantine Empire.
- There was a constant need for men, which was never really dealt with.
- Massive fortifications were used to redress the military imbalance which existed between the Crusaders and Muslims, for example Crac de Chevaliers.

Unification of Islamic states under Saladin

- One of the main reasons that the Crusader States survived for as long as they did was divisions in the Muslim world.
- Saladin militarily managed to unite the Muslims of Syria and Egypt, and effectively surrounded the Kingdom of Jerusalem, putting it in a very weak military position.
- Saladin kept his disparate forces united with the common enemy of the Christian kingdom.

Any other relevant factors.

33 The crusading ideal declined in the years up to the Fourth Crusade in 1204.

How valid is this view? (20)

Context: The Crusading movement was remarkably long lived historically. However, the movement had long been suspect in terms of the motives of some Crusaders. As time went on, the Crusades became less successful.

The Fourth Crusade

- Instead of heading for the Holy Land as was originally intended, the Fourth Crusade ended up attacking Constantinople, the capital of the Byzantine Empire.
- Crusader leaders had been persuaded to help Alexios Angelos by diverting to Constantinople and placing his deposed father on the throne of Byzantium. The Crusaders would then continue to the Holy Land after picking up rewards.
- However, when payment was not made, the Crusaders and their Venetian allies attacked and plundered Constantinople. They set up a series of weak Latin kingdoms in parts of Byzantium in the aftermath of their successful attack.

Role of Venice

- Venice effectively managed to get the Fourth Crusade into debt by selling them huge amounts of equipment that they could not afford to pay for.
- The Doge of Venice proposed that the debt be paid off by the Crusaders attacking the city of Zara, a Christian city that had been Venice's, but was now controlled by the King of Hungary.
- The Venetians supplied the ships for the Fourth Crusade, but hoped to divert it to a more suitable target for their ambitions.
- Byzantium was a competitor for maritime trade in the Middle East.

Co-existence of Muslim and Crusading States

- The survival of the Crusader States, for up to 200 years in the case of the Kingdom of Jerusalem, shows that there must have been times of peace and co-existence between Muslims and Crusaders.
- Examples include the Treaty of Mutual Protection signed between King Alric of Jerusalem and the Emir of Damascus, prior to the Second Crusade.

The corruption of the crusading movement by the Church and nobles

- Popes were willing to use crusades against Christians, such as the Albegensian Crusade against the Cathar heretics of Languedoc (Toulouse and southern France) in 1209–1229.
- There are many examples of nobles using the Crusades for their own ends; for example, Bohemond and Baldwin in the First Crusade, and the hijacking of the Fourth Crusade.

Effects of trade

- Trade links directly into the Fourth Crusade and the influence of Venice in persuading the Crusaders to change their plans.
- Pisa and Genoa both had a lot of influence in events during the Third Crusade; they both used trade rights as a bargaining chip to get what they wanted.

Any other relevant factors.

Part B – The American Revolution, 1763–1787

34 How important was the Boston Massacre as a reason for the colonists' moves towards independence? (20)

Context: In the aftermath of the Seven Years' War, relations between the colonists of the Thirteen American Colonies and the mother country, Britain, began to decline.

Boston Massacre

- The Boston Massacre occurred in 1770 when British soldiers reacted to attacks by an American mob by shooting into the crowd, leading to the deaths of five colonists.
- The subsequent inquiry and trial led to the acquittal of six of the soldiers and the conviction for manslaughter of two others.
- The term 'massacre' was used by the likes of Paul Revere to fuel opposition to the British in the Thirteen Colonies.

Other factors

Disputes over taxation

- The British attempted to impose taxation on the colonies in the aftermath of the Seven Years' War. They argued that taxation was needed to pay for the British Army's role in the war and subsequent stationing in America to defend the colonies.
- Colonists argued that they had already paid tax through the Navigation Acts and that it was simply unfair to pay taxes imposed on them by the British Parliament. 'No taxation without representation' became a familiar protest during this time.
- The Stamp Act stated that an official stamp had to be bought to go on any printed matter. Colonists subsequently refused to pay for this and the Act was repealed.
- Townshend Duties were placed on glass, tea, paper and lead, in 1767.

Punishment of Massachusetts

- The Boston Tea Party was a political protest by the Sons of Liberty in Boston, on 16 December 1773. The demonstrators, some disguised as Native Americans, in defiance of the Tea Act of 10 May 1773, destroyed an entire shipment of tea sent by the East India Company.
- This led to the imposition of laws by the British that were meant to punish Massachusetts.
- The acts took away Massachusetts' self-government rights, which led to growing resistance in the Thirteen Colonies.

British intransigence

- The British were unwilling to compromise with the colonists, for example the re-imposition of the Navigation Acts and Declaratory Act, which maintained that Britain had the right to tax colonists.

Rejection of Olive Branch Petition

- The Olive Branch Petition was a plea to George III to prevent further conflict as well as pledging loyalty. George III rejected the colonists' last attempt at compromise, declaring them to be traitors.

Influence of Thomas Paine

- Thomas Paine was the author of the influential pamphlet 'Common Sense', which argued in favour of independence.
- His views were radical for the time as he was a republican, but his views were extremely important in the eventual setting up of the American constitution.

Any other relevant factors.

35 To what extent did the League of Armed Neutrality change the global nature of the war? (20)

Context: The American War of Independence quickly developed a global significance as various European powers reacted to the pressures that it put on commercial activity and used it as an opportunity to gain revenge on the dominant British.

League of Armed Neutrality

- The nations of Russia, Sweden and Denmark agreed to the First League of Armed Neutrality, which declared that they could trade with belligerent nations at a state of war.
- They were willing to use force to protect their shipping from stops and seizures that the Royal Navy made.
- The League stayed out of the war, and was a purely defensive measure.

French intervention

- Smarting from their defeat in the Seven Years' War, the French entered the war on the side of the American colonists.
- The French contribution to the American war effort was significant in terms of training, loans and weapons, as well as direct participation by army and naval forces. Their contribution was central to the colonist's success at Yorktown.
- Britain found itself effectively taking part in a world war.
- The entry of the Dutch and Spanish into the war stretched Britain's naval resources around the world once again.
- However, the bulk of the war between Britain and the colonists took place on land.

Control of the sea

- Although the war was largely on land, control of the sea mattered, especially for Britain, which needed to get supplies and troops to America from the British Isles.
- The development of the naval conflict led to a drain on the resources of Britain as its naval forces dwarfed those of the other powers, but when the forces of the other powers combined, they were a threat.

Worldwide nature of war

- Britain used over 7,000 German mercenaries – Hessian soldiers – in the war.
- Views in Britain changed as the war progressed as, with increasing European involvement, some Parliamentarians questioned Britain's ability to win a prolonged war.
- Canadians also played a role in the conflict. Canada was invaded by colonist forces on two occasions, but both failed and cost the Americans the support of many of those who had sympathised with them in Britain.

Any other relevant factors.

36 *The political impact of the American Revolution was significant.*

How valid is this view? (20)

Context: The American Constitution was supposed to be the antidote to the tyranny that had passed for British rule of the Colonies. Its system of checks and balances was designed to ensure that no one part could dominate.

The experience of rule by Britain

- British rule seemed unfair to colonists as they were ruled by the King and parliament with no representation of their own and no way to influence decision making.
- There was a real fear of tyranny by monarchy, so the American system was designed to prevent this.

Significance of the Constitution

- The deliberate separation of Legislature, Executive and Judiciary was designed to create the checks and balances the system needed.
- The Bill of Rights established the rights for individuals in states within a federal union of all states. It set out clear lines of authority between federal government and individual states. This would avoid central government exerting a controlling power over people's lives.
- The Constitution was aimed at men and excluded women and slaves from notions of equality.

Executive: the role of President

- Executive power was vested in the elected President, and his Vice-President and Cabinet.
- The President acted as Head of State and Commander-in-Chief, but would have no vote in the law-making process, although he could suggest and veto legislation.
- Members of the Executive could be removed from office by the electorate or the other branches of government (impeachment) if it was felt they were not doing their job properly.

Legislature: Congress

- Legislative power lay in the hands of an elected Congress which was divided into two Houses, the Senate and the House of Representatives.
- Congress passed laws and raised taxes, as well as having responsibility for international trade, war and foreign relations.
- Congressional elections were held regularly to ensure that congressmen remained in touch with the people they served.

Judiciary: Supreme Court

- Judicial power was granted to the Supreme Court of the USA.
- The Supreme Court acted as the highest court of appeal in the country. It also debated the legality of new laws passed by Congress.

- Supreme Court judges were nominated by the President and their appointment was ratified by Congress after a rigorous checking process. Appointees to the Supreme Court could be removed from their position if they acted improperly.

Any other relevant factors.

Part C – The French Revolution, to 1799

37 *The effects of the American Revolution were the main reason for French Revolution in 1789.*
How valid is this view? (20)

Context: By 1789, there were many different sources of discontent against the French monarchy.

The American Revolution

- French financial and military support for the American colonists had a direct impact on the financial crisis that enveloped the French monarchy in 1789, as it increased the already huge debt.
- The American Revolution was fought to free the country from tyranny and sought to protect individual rights. The irony was not lost on many of the French soldiers who came home.
- The French Declaration of the Rights of Citizens was modelled, in part, on the American Declaration of Independence.

Other factors

Role of the bourgeoisie

- The bourgeoisie were a politically frustrated group as they could not access political power unless they bought a noble title.
- They resented paying the taxes demanded of the Third Estate.
- They were the group who engaged with the Enlightenment and provided the main leadership for the Revolution when it happened.

The economic crisis of 1788–1789

- There was unrest among both the peasantry and urban workers in Paris because of grain shortages and rising inflation.
- Economic problems led to growing unemployment.
- Restless peasantry and urban workers provided the mass support for change as they blamed the nobles and monarchy for their problems.

Financial problems of the Ancien Regime

- The monarchy suffered from crippling debt owing to several factors, which led it to call the Estates-General, which increased the simmering resentment of many groups in France.
- Tax collection was inefficient and corrupt. Attempts at reform met resistance from entrenched groups and led to the dismissal of reformist ministers like Calonne.
- The tax burden fell on the Third Estate, who resented the exemptions of the First and Second Estates.
- The lavish lifestyle of the Royal Court did not encourage loyalty to the Crown.

Influence of the Enlightenment

- The ideas of the Enlightenment had an impact on the bourgeoisie who liked the ideas developed by Montesquieu and others.
- The philosophes encouraged political debate among the bourgeoisie and sympathetic members of the nobility.

The political crisis of 1788–1789

- The calling of the Estates-General in August 1788 was an attempt to raise finance by the King, but it unleashed political forces which would lead to the monarchy's destruction.
- The Cahiers de doléances revealed the depth of dissatisfaction with the existing order, especially among the bourgeoisie and the peasantry.

Actions of Louis XVI

- Louis was out of his depth in the ensuing political crisis and contributed to his own fall through several actions.
- He called the Estates-General, which led to the widespread criticism of the monarchy.
- Rumours of his closing the meeting halls that the Estates met in led to the Tennis Court Oath.
- The creation of the National Assembly by the Third Estate showed political power had shifted.

Any other relevant factors.

38 How important was the role of Robespierre as a reason for the Terror, 1792–1795? (20)

Context: Threats from abroad to protect the monarchy and the possibility of foreign invasion radicalised the revolution.

The role of Robespierre

- Robespierre came to control the important Committee of Public Safety in 1793.
- He believed that the 'general will' of the people sanctioned the use of terror against the Revolution's enemies.
- He purged various groups including monarchists, Hebertists and Dantonists.
- Robespierre assumed increasing powers to deal with opponents, such as the Law of 22nd Prairial (June 1794).

The threat of counter-revolution

- Robespierre could swiftly take control because of the creation of the organs of terror by the Convention, owing to their fear of counter-revolution.
- The Girondins were concerned by a restless population in areas like the Vendée as well as the émigrés. They created the Committee of Public Safety and Revolutionary Councils, for example.
- These would become the mechanisms of terror once the Jacobins were in power.

The outbreak of war

- Other European powers looked on at events in France with growing concern. The Austrian Emperor saw his sister beheaded and other monarchs saw the Revolution as a threat; war ensued.
- War put pressure on the Convention to mobilise the nation against its enemies, using the Levée en masse, for example.

The threat of invasion

- Early military reverses, and the loss of their commander Doumirez, led to concerns about loyalty at home.
- The external dangers France faced radicalised the Revolution. Victories emboldened the Convention to end monarchy, but it also encouraged their monarchical enemies.
- It was pressure from mass demonstrations in Paris which intimidated the Convention into adopting terror as 'the order of the day'.

Political rivalries

- France saw its revolution become progressively more radical in the context of war and the rivalries of the various political groups was important in this radicalisation.
- The contest between the Girondins and Jacobins is of particular importance.

Religious and regional differences

- Parts of France were conservative and did not approve of the Revolution. Civil war broke out in the Vendée. The rising was brutally suppressed. Many women and children were drowned in the Loire at Nantes.
- Under the Civil Constitution of the Clergy, priests had to swear an oath of loyalty to the state. Many refused and became leaders of resistance.

Any other relevant factors.

39 To what extent did the urban workers gain most from the French Revolution? (20)

Context: The French Revolution made a huge impact on French society. It made profound changes to the way society was organised and had varying impacts on the various groups that made up society.

The urban workers

- The urban workers made up the feared Parisian mob, which roused itself at various times during the French Revolution. Examples include the storming of the Bastille and the march on Versailles, which had a huge symbolic and actual impact on the power of the monarchy.
- Longer term, although the Revolution enshrined certain rights, the urban workers were affected by military service, inflation and food shortages.
- Economically they gained little as trades unions were banned after the passing of the Chapelier Law in May 1791.

Impact on other groups in French society

The peasantry

- The peasantry did make some gains due to the French Revolution.
- The ending of feudalism in August 1789 freed the peasants from the legal and financial burdens placed on it.
- The nationalisation of Church land as well as the transfer of land from the nobility and clergy to the peasantry was an advantage to peasants who could afford to buy the land.

The bourgeoisie

- The bourgeoisie probably benefited the most from the French Revolution.
- Most of the political forms of the Revolution, starting with the Declaration of the Rights of Man, saw political power put into the hands of the bourgeoisie through this period. Most voting qualifications were based on property ownership, for example.

- Economically, they benefited from the ending of feudal practices as they could afford to exploit the new commercial opportunities that arose.
- Promotion based on ability benefited the educated middle classes.

The First Estate

- The Revolution had a huge negative impact on the better-off clergy as their economic rights and political status were lost.
- The Civil Constitution of the Clergy passed in July 1790 meant that the Church was now subordinate to the French Government.
- Earlier the Church had been stripped of its land holding and the tithe had been abolished.
- The monastic orders were devastated and the clergy became state employees.

The Second Estate

- Aristocratic tax and status privileges were removed by the Revolution.
- The ending of feudalism in August 1789 saw the status of the nobility in France collapse.
- In 1790, outward displays of 'nobility' such as titles and coats of arms were forbidden by law.
- In 1797, after election results suggested a pro-royalist re-emergence, the Convention imposed alien status on nobles and stripped them of their French citizenship.

Any other relevant factors.

Part D – Germany, 1815–1939

40 *By 1850 supporters of nationalism had made significant progress in their aims.*

How valid is this view? (20)

Context: By 1850 the forces that were favourable to the idea of German unification had grown, but opposition was still very strong, especially from Austria.

Supporters of nationalism

- Liberal nationalists believed a united Germany should have a Liberal constitution that would guarantee the rights of citizens. Such ideas were popular during the nationalist risings of 1848.
- Economic nationalists thought unity would remove the trade barriers between states and this would allow economic growth and prosperity.
- Prussia formed a customs union in 1818 that, by the 1830s, was called the Zollverein; the Zollverein helped nationalist ideas to spread as people saw the practical benefits of co-operation.
- Nationalist ideas were spread by philosophers, historians, poets and dramatists who influenced the literate middle classes, especially students: Jahn and the Burschenschaten movement; Wartburg in 1817; Hamburg in 1832; Young Germany in 1833; the Rhine Movement in 1840.
- Fichte described Germany as the Fatherland where all people spoke the same language and sang the same songs.
- German poets and authors, such as the Grimm brothers, and composers such as Beethoven, encouraged feelings of national pride in the German states.
- In 1830, anti-French feelings promoted 'the watch on the Rhine' and nationalist festivals such as Hambach (1832) also encouraged nationalist feelings.

Opponents of nationalism

- One-fifth of the population of the Austrian Empire were German; the Austrian Emperor feared nationalism would encourage them to break away and join Germany. There was Austrian supremacy over Prussian proposals as seen in the Treaty of Olmütz.
- In 1815, Metternich became worried about the growth of liberal and nationalist student societies and cracked down on them, using acts like the Carlsbad Decrees, which banned student societies and censored newspapers.
- The particularism of the various German states had a strong tradition of independence. Bavaria, for example, had a proud independent history.
- Popular apathy to unification was strong as most Germans were peasants.
- France and Russia feared that a strong, united Germany would be a political, economic and military rival to them.
- There were divisions among the nationalist movement as seen in the Frankfurt Parliament and arguments over Gross or Kleine Deutschland.
- The nationalists collapsed in 1848–1849, as traditional rulers reasserted control.

Any other relevant factors.

41 How important were the actions of Napoleon III in the unification of Germany, by 1871? (20)

Context: After the failure of Liberal nationalism, Germany unified under the leadership of the powerful Prussian state, led by Bismarck.

The actions of Napoleon III

- France was considered to be the pre-eminent European military power and under the leadership of Napoleon had intervened decisively in the Italian peninsular.
- Napoleon over-reacted to the Hohenzollern candidature, which allowed Bismarck to provoke the French into declaring war on Prussia.
- Napoleon's leadership of the French army was poor as it was decisively defeated at Sedan.

Other factors

Prussian military strength

- The Prussian army was well armed, efficient and well led by von Roon and von Moltke.
- The Prussian army was to be the architect of unification with its victory in wars against Denmark, Austria and France.

Prussia's economic strength

- Prussia benefited from the Congress of Vienna with the acquisition of the industrial Rhineland.
- The Prussian customs union and Zollverein had transformed the once agricultural country into an economic powerhouse with efficient railways, and an industrial economy.
- A thriving economy gave Prussia the financial muscle to fund her army and dominate the smaller German states.

The decline of Austria

- Austrian attempts to rival Prussia economically did not work.
- Austria stagnated economically and her army also declined in its effectiveness in the 1840s.
- Defeats by France in Italy and in the Seven Weeks' War saw Austria's influence decline.

Role of Bismarck

- Bismarck was the chief minister of Prussia over this period and manipulated events skilfully.
- He oversaw military reforms and ignored the liberal Prussian Parliament.
- He engineered the war with Denmark over the disputed territory of Schleswig-Holstein.
- After the war with Austria, he offered a generous peace which kept Austrian friendship.
- Bismarck manipulated events over the Hohenzollern candidature and the Ems telegram.

The attitude of other states

- Most states in Europe were happy to see a divided Germany.
- Britain was preoccupied with her Empire and not unsympathetic to the forces of nationalism.
- Austria and France misjudged Prussia and Bismarck, to their cost.

Any other relevant factors.

42 To what extent was the crushing of opposition the main reason why the Nazis were able to stay in power, 1933–1939? (20)

Context: The Nazis ruled Germany with a mixture of oppression and popular policies.

Crushing of opposition

- Once elected to power, the Nazis moved swiftly against their political opponents.
- The Communist Party was crushed.
- The SPD (Social Democratic Party) and other political parties were banned.
- State governments were brought into line.
- The Nazis used the SA and concentration camps against opponents.

Other factors

Success of economic policies

- The Nazis claimed economic success with a massive reduction in unemployment.
- Huge public works were undertaken, such as the autobahns.
- Re-armament stimulated the economy.
- Long term, the artificial stimulus of the economy was probably unsustainable.

Success of social policies

- The Nazis implemented a range of social policies to control all sections of society.
- Trades unions were banned and the German Labour Front, under Robert Ley, was created.
- Huge investments in youth organisations, such as the Hitler Youth, were made.
- Education was controlled.
- The Strength through Joy movement was created.
- A concordat with the Catholic Church was reached; a reichsbishop was appointed as Head of the Protestant Churches.

Success of foreign policy

- Military re-armament took place.
- Re-occupation of the Rhineland occurred.
- Anschluss, the annexation of Austria into Nazi Germany in March 1938, took place.
- The Nazis occupied the Sudetenland.
- Breaking the terms of the Versailles Treaty was popular.

Establishment of a totalitarian state

- Between 1933 and 1934, the Nazis converted a democracy into a totalitarian state; only the Nazi Party was allowed.
- The Gestapo, SS (an elite force of troops) and SA were used to police Germany and remove opponents to the regime.
- Anti-Nazi judges were dismissed and replaced with those favourable to the Nazis.
- An all-embracing law which allowed the Nazis to persecute opponents in a 'legal' way was enacted: Acts Hostile to the National Community (1935).

Fear and state terrorism

- Fear/terror, through the Nazi police state and the Gestapo, was widespread.
- Concentration camps were set up to detain opponents.
- The SS was used to control the German public.

Propaganda

- Joseph Goebbels co-ordinated the manipulation of the media to sell the Nazi story.
- Radio, cinema and rallies disseminated Nazi propaganda to every community.

Any other relevant factors.

Part E – Italy, 1815–1939

43 *Nationalism in Italy had significantly grown by 1850.*

How valid is this view? (20)

Context: Support for Italian nationalism grew in the years before 1850. There were groups that supported greater integration of the Italian states, but significant opposition as well, particularly from Austria.

Supporters of nationalism

Educated middle class

- The Risorgimento saw 'patriotic literature' produced by novelists and poets including Pellico and Leopardi. These inspired the educated middle class.
- Thinkers such as Gioberti, Balbo and Mazzini promoted ideas for an Italian national state, which also inspired nationalism among the middle classes.

Liberals

- Some liberals believed that unification was a way to a fairer Italy.
- Some businessmen were keen to build a unified state to develop a more efficient economy.
- The creation of one system of weights, measures and currency across Italy appealed.

Popular sentiment

- The invasions of Italy by Napoleon and the spreading of the ideas of the French Revolution, such as liberty, led to popular demands for freedom. These demands also came from those who wanted to see a state that could not be so easily dominated by foreigners, especially the Austrians.
- Nationalist groups were created: Mazzini's Young Italy, and secret societies, for example the Carbonari.
- A unifying culture was encouraged through the idea of a unified language as well as the operas of Verdi and Rossini.

Opponents of nationalism

Austria

- The Austrian army was used to crush any attempts to remove Austrians from Italian soil.
- Austria maintained a powerful military presence in Italy through the Quadrilateral fortifications.
- Lots of examples of the Austrian army in action including the crushing of Carbonari revolts in the Kingdom of Naples, 1820–1821 and in Piedmont in 1821. During the 1848–1849 revolutions, the Austrian army defeated Charles Albert twice, retook Lombardy and destroyed the Republic of St Mark.

Italian princes and rulers

- Individual rulers were understandably opposed to nationalism as they would lose power.
- They used censorship, police and spies, as well as the Austrian army, to crush revolts in 1820–1821, 1830 and 1848–1849.

Attitude of the peasants

- Most of the population was illiterate and indifferent to politics and nationalist ideas. They did revolt during bad times, such as 1848, but this was caused by bad harvests and poor economic times, and not nationalistic views.

Position of the Papacy

- The Nationalist movement was optimistic about the new Pope, Pius IX, who they hoped would be sympathetic to nationalism, but these hopes were dashed when Pius IX denounced the Nationalist movement during the 1848–1849 revolutions.

Failures of the 1848–1849 revolutions

- The 1848–1849 revolutions failed for numerous reasons, such as the power of the Austrians, but more importantly the lack of co-ordination by and co-operation between the Nationalist leaders who did not agree completely; for example, Charles Alberts disliked Mazzini.
- There was a reluctance to ask for international help, indeed the French crushed the Roman Republic.

Any other relevant factors.

44 To what extent was the unification of Italy achieved by 1870 due to the role of Cavour? (20)

Context: Italy was unified due to a variety of factors, such as the spread of new ideas following the French Revolution, the development of effective leadership and foreign intervention.

Role of Cavour

- As Prime Minister of Piedmont-Sardinia, Cavour played a deft hand diplomatically, coming to agreements with Prussia and developing the alliance with France.
- He took Piedmont into the Crimean War on the side of France and Britain.
- The eventual unification was a Piedmontese creation.

Other factors

Rise of Piedmont

- Piedmont developed economically under Cavour's leadership, for example making free trade treaties with Britain and France.
- Cavour managed to increase Piedmont's trade by 300 per cent.
- The development of railways and canals facilitated economic expansion.
- Piedmont was the natural political leader of the Unification movement.

Role of Garibaldi

- Garibaldi was a committed Nationalist and fought in the War of Liberation for Victor Emmanuel.
- His role was crucial in north–south unification with his military successes in Sicily and Naples.
- Garibaldi handed over his 'conquests' to Victor Emmanuel at Teano.

Role of Victor Emmanuel II

- The King was supportive of Cavour. Victor Emmanuel of Piedmont and Cavour realised foreign help was needed to drive the Austrians from Italy.
- The King 'managed' Garibaldi very well in 1866, preventing a diplomatic crisis.

Decline of Austria

- Austria's position was in decline in economic and military terms, especially when compared to their rival in Germany: Prussia.
- Austria was isolated diplomatically. Russia had been an ally until the Crimean War and Austria's neutrality in it.

Attitudes and actions of Napoleon III

- Napoleon III had a secret meeting with Cavour at Plombières in July 1858. In the formal treaty of January 1859, Napoleon III promised 200,000 men to fight for Piedmont if Austria attacked.
- The defeat of the Austrians at Magenta and Solferino were French victories. Austria handed Lombardy to France, who gave it to Piedmont.
- Napoleon did not intervene over Garibaldi's expedition. He accepted Cavour's invasion of the Papal States to stop Garibaldi reaching Rome, which also allowed the Piedmontese to defeat the Papal army, taking The Marches and Umbria.
- The Italians took Rome after the defeat of Napoleon by Prussia in 1870.

Importance of foreign intervention

- French intervention in the War of Liberation of 1859 was crucial as it facilitated the two main victories.
- Britain refused a joint naval blockade with France to stop Garibaldi crossing the Strait of Messina which was crucial for Garibaldi's success.

Any other relevant factors.

45 How important were social controls as a reason why the Fascists were able to stay in power, 1922–1939? (20)

Context: Mussolini was the Fascist leader of Italy between 1922 and 1939. His control of Italy was a mixture of repression and acceptance.

Social controls

- Control of the workers and the economy was achieved through the 22 corporations that were set up in 1934.
- Workers were provided with a wide range of benefits, such as insurance, but strike action was banned.
- For most people the regime offered stability and, for the middle classes, protection from communism.
- The young were encouraged to join youth movements, such as the Avanguardista, which aimed to create energetic soldiers and willing mothers.

Other factors

Fear and intimidation

- The secret police, the OVRA, was established in 1927 and the death penalty was reintroduced. Brutal tactics were used, but relatively few people were imprisoned and killed.
- Local blackshirt militias terrorised those inclined to oppose the Fascists. Made up of ex-soldiers, their tactics involved forcing people to drink castor oil and making them eat live toads.
- Creation of a special tribunal of army and militia officers to try even minor offences, which controlled the population.

Establishment of the Fascist State

- Emergency powers were given to Mussolini in 1922. He set up alternative power structures that opposed the parliament, such as the Fascist Grand Council.
- Acerbo law transformed Italy into a single constituency that Mussolini could manipulate in the 1926 general election.
- Democracy was ended in 1926 when all opposition parties were banned. By 1929, all the trappings of a Fascist dictatorship existed.

Crushing of the opposition

- The opposition was weak and divided. The Liberals divided into four factions and the Left into three.
- Groups were unlikely to work together against the Fascists.

- Opportunities to move against the Fascists were lost, such as after the murder of Matteotti.
- The King backed Mussolini at key moments.

Propaganda

- Fascist control of the media meant the populace heard a pro-Fascist message.
- Mussolini developed a cult of personality as the great leader.
- Slogans such as: 'War is to a man, what childbearing is to a woman' transmitted Fascist ideas, reinforcing the macho stereotype.

Foreign policy

- Mussolini was initially extremely popular with a successful foreign policy, up until 1938.
- Foreign policy successes in 1923, such as the Corfu Incident, which led to the Italian occupation of the island with little fighting.
- Mussolini's prestige was boosted by the invasion of Abyssinia in 1935, giving the appearance of his developing an Italian empire.
- Participation in the Spanish Civil War enabled Mussolini to boost Italy's pretensions as a military power.
- Mussolini's foreign prestige was boosted by his role as key negotiator in the Munich Agreement of 1938 between Germany and the Western Allies.

Relations with the Papacy

- Lateran treaties/concordats with the Papacy enabled acceptance of the Fascist regime by the Catholic majority. Many Catholics supported Mussolini's promotion of 'family values'.
- Priest salaries were paid for by the government.
- Religious education in schools could be given only by Church-approved teachers.
- The appointment of bishops had to have government approval.

Economic and social policies

- Fascists developed the Italian economy in a series of public works and initiatives, for example the 'Battle for Grain' and the 'Battle for Land'.
- Fascism crushed organised crime, with most Mafia leaders in prison by 1939.
- Wars in Ethiopia and Spain cost huge amounts of money for a poor country like Italy.

Any other relevant factors.

Part F – Russia, 1881–1921

46 How important was discontent with repressive government and its policies as a cause of the 1905 revolution? (20)

Context: When he ascended to the throne in 1894, Tsar Nicholas II was determined to maintain the power of the Romanov dynasty. He dismissed growing demands for more popular participation in government as 'senseless dreams'.

Discontent with repressive government and its policies

- Although reluctant to rule when he came to the throne in 1894, Nicholas II was determined to maintain autocratic rule.
- Nicholas was out of touch with the people he ruled, never visiting the poor rural villages or the factories in the cities.
- Nicholas was a family-orientated man, dominated by his wife and preoccupied with his son's haemophilia. He appointed all his ministers and based his decisions upon the censored reports they sent to him.
- There was discontent among almost all sections of Russian society.
- The middle class were aggrieved at having no participation in government, and angry at the incompetence of the government during the war with Japan.
- There was propaganda from middle-class groups. Zemstvas (local councils) called for change and the Radical Union of Unions was formed to combine professional groups.
- University disturbances occurred in 1899. The government was unwilling to accept that the protests were a genuine desire for reform and treated them as an attack on the Tsar's authority.
- The gentry tried to convince the Tsar to make minor concessions.
- Political groups did not really play a role, although they encouraged peasant unrest, and strikes in the urban areas.
- Russification: The national minorities were aggrieved at the lack of respect for their cultures, languages and religions, and the imposition of the Russian language.
- The national minorities harboured a great desire for independence or at least greater autonomy and began to assert themselves. Georgia, for example, declared its independence.
- The Minister of the Interior (in charge of police and internal security), Vyacheslav von Plehve, was assassinated in 1904.

Working class discontent

- Russia was undergoing massive economic expansion; there was an average of 8 per cent growth per annum thanks to the economic policies of Sergei Witte. The rate of expansion put more strain on the living and working conditions of the factory workers.

- There were periodic downturns in which workers were made unemployed. At the start of the 1900s there was industrial recession which caused a lot of hardship for the working class.

- The working class's complaints were long hours, low pay, poor conditions, the desire for a constitutional government and an end to the war with Japan.

- There was a wave of strikes in January 1905 with nearly half a million people on strike – ten times the number who had participated in the previous decade.

Discontent among the peasantry

- The massive economic growth had been paid for largely by grain exports, which often led to starvation in the countryside. Worsening economic conditions had caused famines in 1897, 1898 and 1901.

- The peasants had several grievances, such as high redemption payments, high taxes, Land Hunger and poverty.

- There was a wave of unrest in 1902 and 1903, which had gradually increased by 1905. There were various protests such as timber cutting, seizure of lords' land –sometimes whole estates were seized and divided up, labour and rent strikes, attacks on landlords' grain stocks.

- Political opposition groups encouraged peasants to boycott paying taxes and redemption payments, and refuse to be conscripted to the army.

Economic problems

- Economic recession between 1899 and 1903 led to growing unemployment throughout the Empire.

- Russia remained mainly a backwards country. By 1900, fewer than a quarter of the population could read.

Military defeat in the war against Japan

- Russia had initially launched the war in 1905 against Japan to distract the public from domestic troubles by rallying patriotism.

- The war with Japan was a failure and humiliation for the country, which was made worse by the heavy losses suffered by the Russian army.

- The incompetence of the government during the war made social unrest worse.

- Troops suffered from low morale after the defeat and complained about poor pay and conditions. There were some sporadic but unco-ordinated revolts.

- There were mutinies by troops waiting to return from the war and on the Trans-Siberian Railway.

- In June 1905, the battleship *Potemkin* mutiny in Odessa took place, although the planned general mutiny did not follow. The mutiny itself was prompted as much by poor conditions for the sailors on board as political discontent.

- Most of the troops remained loyal (unlike in 1917).

Bloody Sunday

- On 22 January 1905, Father Gapon, an Orthodox priest, attempted to lead a peaceful march of workers and their families to the Winter Palace to deliver a petition asking the Tsar to improve the conditions of the workers. Marchers were fired on and killed by troops.

- Many people saw this as a brutal massacre by the Tsar and his troops. Bloody Sunday greatly damaged the traditional image of the Tsar as the 'Little Father', the Guardian of the Russian people.

- Reaction to Bloody Sunday was strong. There was nationwide disorder: strikes in urban areas and terrorism against government officials and landlords, much of which was organised by the Social Revolutionaries.

Any other relevant factors.

47 To what extent was the February Revolution in 1917 caused by the role of Tsar Nicholas II? (20)

Context: By February 1917, discontent and opposition to the Tsar had reached almost all sections of Russian society.

Role of Tsar Nicholas II

- The Tsar was seen as a weak ruler as he was too easily influenced by the Tsarina, Rasputin and his ministers. The Tsar appeared to be more interested in his family than in the issues facing Russia.

- Once the crisis of 1905 had passed, the Tsar 'rolled back' most of the concessions made, making them reforms in name only, for example the Duma. Political repression drove opposition underground and bred resentment for the future.

- The Tsar had stubbornly tried to maintain autocracy at all costs and had resented the work of loyal minsters like Witte and Stolypin because, in modernising Russia, they impacted on his absolute power. The Tsar preferred the advice of ministers who flattered his status.

- In September 1915, the Tsar took personal control of the armed forces, which left him personally responsible for any defeats.
- During 1916 and 1917, Nicholas II ignored advice and warnings from Rodzyanko, Chair of the Duma, and he failed to understand the severity of events in February 1917.
- By February 1917, the Tsar had lost control of the armed forces as well as the support and loyalty of the Russian people, which contributed to the February 1917 Revolution.

Inherent weaknesses of autocracy

- Government by a single authority figure was unsuitable for coping with the demands of running a modern, industrial war; there are too many responsibilities.
- Key appointments to the military and the government were based on the personal favour of the Tsar and, as a consequence, inept government ministers severely hampered the war effort and thus reduced support for the Tsar.
- The Tsar's taking of personal control of the armed forces in 1915 exposed the frailty of the autocracy and its dependence on the personality and ability of the ruler.
- The Tsar alienated many of his natural supporters among the aristocracy with his tolerance of his wife's association with Rasputin, as well as his poor management of the war effort. Without their support, including those in High Command, the frailty of the autocracy became apparent.

Role of Tsarina Alexandra

- In September 1915, the Tsar left the Tsarina in charge, which was not welcomed in Russia, as she was German.
- Her relationship with Rasputin was viewed with suspicion; his disreputable behaviour tainted the royal family.
- The Tsarina allowed Rasputin to act as her personal advisor and influence the appointment and dismissal of government ministers. This alienated many of the nobility and led to the assassination of Rasputin in December 1916.

Discontent among the bourgeoisie

- There had been long-term discontent as Nicholas II seemed unwilling to share his power despite promises (October Manifesto and Fundamental Laws). The Duma had limited powers and the Tsar dissolved them and changed the franchise.
- The middle classes despaired at the inept running of the war. Many were mobilised by military defeats caused by the shortages of weapons and munitions in 1915 and by the high casualties caused by the lack of medical facilities, even at home.
- Despite opposition from the government, industrialists in the Association of Industry and Trade co-ordinated the setting up of a network of War Industry Committees in 1915. The committees co-ordinated war production and had some success, even collaborating with worker representatives. However, when the military situation improved in 1916, the government harassed the committees, leading to growing opposition to the regime among industrialists.
- Key members of the War Industry Committee were often members of moderate political parties such as the Octobrists.

Discontent among the working class

- The war exacerbated long-term discontent among industrial workers.
- The inadequate transport system was unable to cope with the supply demands of the military as well as the needs of the Russian economy and society.
- There was a lack of food, made worse by the transport problems and the loss of agricultural land to the Germans. As a result, in the cities there were long queues and bread riots, culminating in the International Women's Day protest in Petrograd.
- The military situation led to a decrease in the effectiveness of censorship; more information and opposition views could be read openly.

Peasant discontent

- The war put extra demands on the peasantry with the requisitioning of horses and the conscription of men. Agricultural output decreased. Russia's huge casualties impacted most on the peasants.
- As the war went on, land seizures by peasants became more common.

Impact of the First World War – military defeat and economic problems

- After initial victories against the Austro-Hungarians in 1914, Germany reinforced the Eastern Front. The war did not go well for Russia and they suffered many defeats. Russia also lost control of Poland in 1915, which was a severe blow to Russian pride.
- The Russian army lacked vital resources, including adequate medical care, and this led to high fatalities and casualty rates.
- Defeats were caused by incompetent officers, some of whom failed to use basic codes when communicating and who even refused to co-operate with each other.
- The decision by the Tsar to take personal control of the war in 1915 was promted by the need to take back control of the war from his own generals, who had been increasingly following their own judgements.

- The Tsar's personal command of the army did not alter the pattern of military defeats, and he began to lose control of and support from the armed forces. The generals forced his abdication at Pskov.
- The war was costing 17 million roubles a day and Russia had to get loans from Britain and France. Economic problems such as heavy taxes, high inflation and price rises meant that many Russians were living in poverty.

Any other relevant factors.

48 *The role of Trotsky was the main reason for the victory of the Reds in the Civil War.*

How valid is this view? (20)

Context: The Bolsheviks managed to cling on to power after the October Revolution. However, after the signing of the peace treaty with the Germans at Brest-Litovsk in April 1918, growing opposition led to civil war.

Role of Trotsky – organisation of the Red Army

- Trotsky supervised the formation of the Red Army, which became a formidable fighting force of 3 million men.
- He recruited ex-Tsarist army officers for their military expertise, but had them and their families monitored by political commissars to ensure their loyalty.
- Trotsky's headquarters was a heavily armed train, which he used to ceaselessly travel around the country.
- He used conscription to gain troops and would shoot any deserters.
- Trotsky helped provide an army with great belief in what it was fighting for, which the Whites did not have.

Use of terror

- The Cheka was set up to prevent opposition to the Reds and fight counter-revolution after 1918.
- Chekist agents could act as they pleased; there was no need for proof of guilt for punishment to be exacted.
- There was persecution of individual people who opposed the Reds as well as whole groups of people, which helped to reduce opposition due to fear.
- The Cheka often brutally murdered their victims, for example packing the lungs and mouths of victims with mud.
- Some of the first victims of the Cheka were leaders of other political parties.
- In 1921, Lenin gave the Cheka more latitude in how they operated. Estimates vary as to the number of victims during the Civil War, up to 250,000.

Propaganda

- The revolutionary slogans of the Reds were more persuasive than those of the Whites, who offered a return to the old Tsarist regime. Many ordinary Russians preferred to support the Reds as they offered at least the possibility of improvement. Peasants were especially fearful of the loss of their land.
- The Whites were unable to take advantage of the brutality of the Reds to win support as they often carried out similar atrocities.

Superior Red resources

- The Reds were in control of a concentrated area of western Russia, which they could successfully defend due to the maintenance of their communication and supply lines.
- Once the Reds had established defence of their lines, they could repel and exhaust the attacks by the Whites until they scattered or surrendered.
- The Reds controlled the major industrial centres in their land (Moscow and Petrograd), so had access to factories to make weapons. Control of the railways meant they could transport troop supplies quickly and efficiently and in large numbers to the critical areas of defence or attack.
- The decisive battles between the Reds and Whites were near railheads.
- Having the two major cities of Moscow and Petrograd in their possession meant that the Reds controlled the administrative centres of government.

Unity of the Reds

- The Reds were under the leadership of Lenin, who was responsible for the introduction of War Communism. He was a skilled delegator and ruthless political operator. The cult of Lenin as an infallible leader grew at this time.
- Lenin imposed War Communism; this was the relaxation of strict communist economic policies to improve industrial and agricultural production. Peasants were forced to sell their grain to the Reds, so the communists were able to ensure that their troops were well supplied.

Disunity among the Whites

- The Whites were an unco-ordinated series of groups whose morale was low. In the Ukraine, there was a separatist nationalist opposition nicknamed the 'Greens' and in Siberia, there was a Social Revolutionary controlled government that opposed both the Whites and the Reds.

- The Whites were a collection of socialists, liberals, moderates, etc. who all wanted different things and often fought among themselves due to their political differences. All of the Whites shared a hatred of communism but other than this they lacked a common purpose.

- There were at least three important White generals, Kolchak, Yudenich and Denikin, but no overall Commander-in-Chief or clear chain of command.

- No White leader of any measure emerged to unite and lead the White forces, whereas the Reds had Trotsky and Lenin.

- The Whites were too spread out geographically to co-ordinate attacks and put consistent pressure on the Reds. As a result, the Reds were able to fight one attacking force at a time.

- The Whites were not as well supplied and fed as the Reds because they did not have easy access to supplies or credit.

Effects of foreign intervention

- The British, French and Japanese all sent forces in 1920, supposedly to help the Whites fight against the Reds. However, the calibre of the soldiers was not high. The Japanese never left Siberia and the British and French headed for areas which contained industrial assets lost in the October Revolution, for example the British headed for Baku, centre of the Russian oil industry. Few foreign troops directly engaged with the Reds.

- The supplies and number of soldiers given by the allies was not enough to make a significant difference to the outcome of the war.

- Foreign intervention was a propaganda coup for the Bolsheviks, who were able to claim that the foreign 'invaders' were imperialists trying to overthrow the revolution and invade Russia.

Any other relevant factors.

Part G – USA, 1918–1968

49 How important were the activities of the Ku Klux Klan as an obstacle to the achievement of civil rights for black people up to 1941? (20)

Context: In the century after emancipation in 1863, black Americans struggled to translate their freedom into equal rights and opportunities.

Activities of the Ku Klux Klan

- The Ku Klux Klan was a racist organisation formed after the American Civil War to prevent former slaves achieving equal rights in the southern states. The Klan was suppressed by 1872, but there was a resurgence after the First World War.

- Their methods including beatings, torture and lynching, were designed to spread fear and intimidation among mainly blacks, but also any other group demonstrating behaviour or attitudes of which the Klan disapproved.

- Roosevelt refused to support a federal bill to outlaw lynching in his New Deal in the 1930s because he was concerned such a measure would undermine support for the New Deal in the South.

- Activities took place at night – men in white robes, with guns, torches and burning crosses caused maximum fear in victims.

- The 'second' Klan grew most rapidly between 1910 and 1930 in cities such as Detroit, Memphis, Dayton, Atlanta, Dallas and Houston; white Southerners did not like that urbanisation was forcing them to live in closer proximity to black people.

- Klan membership in Alabama dropped to less than 6,000 by 1930.

- In the late 1940s, small independent units continued to be active in places like Birmingham, where members launched a reign of terror by bombing the homes of upwardly mobile African Americans.

- Klan activities in the 1940s led to continued migration of black Americans from the South to the North.

Other factors

Legal impediments

- Jim Crow Laws were laws passed in the Southern states to negate the constitutional amendments guaranteeing equal rights to black people after the Civil War. These laws segregated black people from white people in everything from restaurants to transport. The most serious restriction was in education where separate schools ensured most black Americans did not have access to the education needed to get good jobs.

- The Plessey v. Ferguson Supreme Court decision of 1896 upheld state racial segregation laws for public facilities as long as they were 'separate but equal'.

- Successive attitudes of presidents to segregation and black rights reinforced the status quo. For example, President Wilson openly approved the 1915 film *Birth of a Nation*, directed by D.W. Griffiths, which celebrated the founding of the Ku Klux Klan.

Lack of political influence

- In the 1890s, loopholes in the interpretation of the 15th Amendment were exploited to allow states to impose voting qualifications. For example, in the 1898 case of Mississippi v. Williams, voters were required to understand the American Constitution; however, the Grandfather Clause was applied, so a literacy test for voting was applied to black people, but not poor whites, because their 'grandfathers' had had the right to vote.

- Most black people in the South were sharecroppers, which meant they did not own land; some states identified ownership of property as a voting qualification.

- Black people were essentially disenfranchised, particularly in the South, and could not elect anyone who would oppose the Jim Crow Laws.

Divisions in the black community

- Some leading black thinkers, like Booker T. Washington, promoted accommodationist ideas – black people should be prepared to 'prove their worth' before getting equal treatment – and were regarded as 'Uncle Toms' by many.

- W.E.B. DuBois, a leading black academic, believed in full civil rights and political representation and helped found the NAACP (National Association for the Advancement of Colored People) – a national organisation whose main aim was to oppose discrimination through legal action. In 1919, he launched a campaign against lynching, but it failed to attract most black people and was dominated by white people and well-off black people.

- Marcus Garvey promoted Black Pride – he founded the UNIA (Universal Negro Improvement Association) which aimed to get black people to 'take Africa, organise it, develop it, arm it, and make it the defender of Negroes the world over'.

Popular prejudice

- Slavery created the stereotype of black Americans as poor, ill-educated and/or ignorant. The status of black Americans was stigmatised, and this was the basis for the racism that persisted.

- Many white Americans reacted badly to population change that led to closer daily proximity to black people. After the First World War, millions of African Americans relocated from the South to the industrial centres of the North in search of jobs and better opportunities, particularly in cities such as Boston, Chicago and New York (Harlem). Racial tensions exploded, most violently in Chicago, and lynchings – mob-directed hangings, usually racially motivated – increased dramatically in the 1920s.

Any other relevant factors.

50 *The New Deal was a success for America in the 1930s.*

How valid is this view? (20)

Context: By the time President Roosevelt took office in 1933, one-quarter of all Americans were unemployed because of the Great Depression. He acted swiftly to try to boost the economy, boost jobs and give help to the poor.

The First New Deal 1933–1934

- The response of Republican President Hoover to the Great Depression following the Wall Street Crash had been ineffective. Roosevelt and the Democrats aimed to show the benefits of a more interventionist government approach.

- 'Alphabet Agencies' were launched, giving relief and recovery in the first 100 days of the Roosevelt presidency; for example, the Federal Emergency Relief Administration (FERA), Tennessee Valley Authority (TVA) and Public Works Administration (PWA) provided relief and work.

- The Economy Act, 1933, sought to balance the budget. Wages of state employees were cut by 15 per cent and the savings were spent on relief programmes.

- The unpopular Prohibition laws were lifted to raise revenue.

The Second New Deal 1935–1937

- Various measures were put in place to improve living and working conditions.

- The National Labour Relations Act ('Wagner Act'), 1935, protected the rights of workers to collectively bargain with employers.

- The Banking Act, 1935, established the Federal Bank Deposit Insurance Corporation, which insured deposits up to $5,000, and later, $10,000.

- The WPA (Works Progress Administration), 1935, launched a programme of public works across America. By 1938 it provided employment for 3 million men (and some women).

- Rural electrification in 1936 provided loans to electrify rural areas of America.

- The Social Security Act, 1935, provided a state pension scheme for the old and widows, as well as help for the disabled and poor children.

The role of Roosevelt and 'confidence building'

- Roosevelt used the mass media to increase direct communication with the American people; over 30 'fire-side chats' were broadcast from March 1933 to restore the nation's confidence.

- Roosevelt declared that 'the only thing we have to fear is fear itself'.
- The Emergency Banking Act, 1933, allowed the Federal Government to check banks were well run and credit worthy, only allowing 'sound' banks to reopen.
- By the end of 1933, many small banks had closed or were merged.
- Most depositors got much of their money back.

The role of the Federal Government

- The New Deal increased the role of the Federal Government in directing the economy and in the daily lives of the American people.
- The Federal Government strengthened the power of organised labour.
- The Federal Government took on the role of regulator between business, labour and agriculture.
- There was dissatisfaction at the increase of federal power; legal challenges in the Supreme Court; opposition from state governments, especially in the South; and employers' groups formed the Liberty League opposed to the New Deal.

The economic effects of the New Deal

- New Deal measures provided help for those most in need, however debate continues about its impact on economic recovery.
- One of the fastest periods of GDP (gross domestic product) growth in US history was during Roosevelt's first term as President. However, a downturn in 1937–1938 raised questions about how sustainable the policies were.
- The New Deal did help stimulate the economy in some ways. Between 1933 and 1939, GDP increased by 60 per cent from $55 billion to $85 billion; the number of consumer products bought increased by 40 per cent while private investment in industry increased by five times in just six years.
- However, unemployment remained at 14 per cent or above of the working population.
- In the later 1930s, re-armament was important in reducing unemployment and revitalising the American economy, particularly after the mini-slump of 1937.

Any other relevant factors.

51 To what extent was the Civil Rights movement effective in meeting the needs of black Americans, up to 1968? (20)

Context: The Second World War had stimulated renewed demand for black civil rights. By the 1960s, these demands were becoming more vocal.

Aims of the Civil Rights movement

- The Civil Rights movement was mainly peaceful and intended to bring civil rights and equality in practice, not just in the Constitution, to all non-while Americans.
- Some Black Radical movements had more separatist aims.
- The disparate objectives within the movement sometimes diffused its clarity and purpose.

Role of the NAACP in desegregation – methods and tactics

- National Association for the Advancement of Colored People (NAACP) lawyers fought the Brown v. Topeka Board of Education, 1954.
- The NAACP helped organise the Montgomery Bus Boycott, 1955.
- The NAACP was important in mobilising student demonstrations.
- The implementation of key legal decisions was, in some places, delayed for many years owing to political opposition and entrenched attitudes.

Role of CORE in desegregation – methods and tactics

- The Congress of Racial Equality (CORE) organised sit-ins and Freedom Rides during 1961.
- CORE helped organise the March on Washington.
- CORE was instrumental in setting up Freedom Schools in Mississippi.
- CORE faced increasing criticism in the later 1960s as campaigning failed to secure civil rights and equal opportunities in black peoples' everyday lives.

Roles of the SCLC and Martin Luther King in desegregation – methods and tactics

- Martin Luther King was leader of the Southern Christian Leadership Conference (SCLC), set up in 1957 after the success of the Montgomery Bus Boycott (1956) to co-ordinate the actions of local protest groups.
- Little Rock, Arkansas, saw desegregation in 1957 following national publicity.
- Birmingham, Alabama 1963: use of water cannon: Reaction of Kennedy, role of Martin Luther King in pressuring the administration.
- In August 1963, a March on Washington took place. Martin Luther King made his famous 'I Have a Dream' speech amid massive publicity.

- Martin Luther King encouraged non-violent protest, as exemplified by sit-ins and Freedom Rides.
- Martin Luther King believed that the Civil Rights Act of 1964 'gave Negroes some part of their rightful dignity, but without the vote it was dignity without strength'.
- In March 1965, King led a march from Selma to Birmingham, Alabama, to publicise the way in which the authorities made it difficult for black Americans to vote easily.
- King came under increasing criticism in the late 1960s for failing to secure meaningful civil rights and equal opportunities in the lives of everyday black people.

Changes in federal policy

- Truman used presidential executive orders to appoint black candidates and order to equality of treatment in the armed services. Kennedy signed an executive order in 1962 outlawing racial discrimination in public housing.
- The president ordered the use of the army/National Guard to uphold the law: examples include, Eisenhower at Little Rock to protect nine African-American students enrolled in a Central High School; Kennedy at Oxford, Mississippi to protect black student, James Meredith.
- Landmark legislation was passed: Johnson and the 1964 Civil Rights Act banning racial discrimination in any public place; the Voting Rights Act of 1965: by the end of 1965 over 250,000 black people were newly registered to vote, there was also government support for Affirmative Action.

Social, economic and political changes

- The Civil Rights Acts of 1964 and 1965 improved political rights but were irrelevant to black people in the cities of the North who already had these freedoms.
- There was little improvement in the economic rights for black Americans in the North, for example in equal pay.
- The Watts riots, Los Angeles, were shocking because rioters burnt the homes in their own neighbourhood.
- There were splits in the Civil Rights movement and increasing criticism of Martin Luther King by Black Radical movements.
- The SCLC non-violent campaign was met by race riots. The promised housing initiative by the Mayor of Chicago (1966) to ease tension never started.
- Urban poverty and de facto segregation was still common in cities. Martin Luther King's campaign to attack poverty largely failed.

Rise of Black Radical movements

- After 1966, there was a divergence in the Civil Rights movement between non-violent and more radical action.
- Stokely Carmichael and Black Power.
- Malcolm X publicised the increasing urban problems within the ghettos of America. He became famous for the slogan: 'By any means necessary.'
- The Black Panthers were involved in self-help schemes providing food, clothing and other services in poor black neighbourhoods.
- The Kerner Commission of 1968 recognised that US society was still divided.
- The most prominent activists within the Black Panthers were arrested, impacting on the effectiveness of the movement.

Any other relevant factors.

Part H – Appeasement and the Road to War, to 1939

52 How important were pacts and alliances in the methods used by Germany and Italy to pursue their foreign policies from 1933? (20)

Context: From 1933 onwards, both Germany and Italy became more assertive in the pursuit of their expansionist foreign policies.

Pacts and alliances

- The German–Polish Non-Aggression Pact between Nazi Germany and Poland, signed on 26 January 1934, normalised diplomatic relations between Poland and Germany, and promised peace for ten years. Germany gained respectability and calmed international fears.
- The Rome–Berlin Axis was a treaty of friendship signed between Italy and Germany in October 1936.
- The 'Pact of Steel' was an agreement between Italy and Germany, made in May 1939, guaranteeing immediate aid and military support in the event of war.
- The Anti-Comintern Pact was signed between Nazi-Germany and Japan in November 1936. The pact was notionally directed against the Communist International (Comintern) but was clearly aimed at the Soviet Union. In 1937, Italy joined the Pact.
- In the Munich Agreement, September 1938, Italy collaborated with Germany in the negotiations, leading to Hitler gaining the Sudetenland and weakening Czechoslovakia.

- In the Nazi–Soviet Non-Aggression Pact of August 1939 both Hitler and Stalin bought time for themselves. Hitler secured his eastern border in the event of a war in Western Europe. It seemed war in Europe over Poland was unlikely. Poland was to be divided up among Germany and Russia. Britain had lost the possibility of alliance with Russia.

Economic and military diplomacy

- Italy and Germany used economic influence and pressure, for example on south-Eastern European states.
- In the Anglo-German Naval Treaty of 1935, Germany was allowed to expand its navy. The Versailles Treaty was ignored in favour of bi-lateral agreements. This was a gain for Germany.
- German re-armament took place openly from 1935. This was done with speed and on a large scale, and included conscription.
- The emphasis was on air power and the growing threat from the air.
- By 1939, Hitler had an army of nearly 1 million men, over 8,000 aircraft and 95 warships.
- Aid supplied to Franco (Spain) was tactically important to Hitler, not only for testing weapons but also because it gave access to Spanish minerals.
- Italy had naval ambitions in the Mediterranean – 'Mare Nostrum' – that challenged British naval supremacy.
- Hitler's gamble and timing paid off when German remilitarisation of the Rhineland took place with a lack of Allied resistance despite his generals' opposition.
- In the Spanish Civil War, aid was given to the Nationalists, allowing the testing of weapons and tactics, for example with the aerial bombing of Guernica.

Fascist strategies employed in the crises between 1933 and 1939

Disarmament Conference

- Hitler withdrew from the League of Nations and Disarmament Conference, 1934, effectively preventing any agreement on the issue. This reduced the League of Nations to a 'talking shop'.

Rhineland

- Prior to remilitarisation of the Rhineland, Hitler made an offer of a 25-year peace promise. In this way, diplomacy was used to distract and delay reaction to Nazi action.
- The invasion took place over the weekend to ensure a 'fait accompli' when foreign governments returned to work on Monday morning.
- Hitler acknowledged that use of military force had been a bluff.

Abyssinia

- Italian invasion of Abyssinia, 1935. Example of clear provocation by Italy. Military performance was relatively poor against very poorly equipped enemy.
- The failure of the League of Nation to apply meaningful economic sanctions due to the desire of the British to maintain a good relationship with Italy.
- The abortive Hoare–Laval Pact discredited French and British diplomacy.

Austria

- There was an attempted coup in 1934 to try and achieve Anschluss.
- Hitler's blustering and bullying of Schuschnigg, the Austrian leader prior to 1938.
- When the Anschluss did happen, it appeared to be genuinely popular in Austria.

Fascist strategies – Sudetenland and Munich

- Hitler used the discontent of ethnic Germans in the Sudetenland to incite a crisis.
- Hitler's attempts to bully Czech leaders was not successful.
- Chamberlain met Hitler three times in desperate diplomatic attempts to avoid war.
- The Munich Agreement satisfied German demands for the Sudetenland, but did not consult the Czech government about this decision. Hitler was unhappy that this agreement did not let him invade a country.
- The German army occupied the Czech areas of Bohemia and Moravia in March 1939.

Poland

- In Poland in 1939 Hitler used the same tactics of escalating demands and provocation.
- A faked border attack by Poland on Germany was used as the excuse for invasion in September.

Any other relevant factors.

53 To what extent was British foreign policy successful in containing Fascist aggression, 1935 to March 1938? (20)

Context: In the 1930s, British foreign policy was constrained by economic and political factors. Appeasement aimed to resolve disputes by the reasonable settling of grievances.

Aims of British foreign policy

- The main aim of British foreign policy, Appeasement, was the preservation of peace. Up until March 1938 (and later), this was achieved.
- Conflicts that did occur (Abyssinia, Spain) were on the periphery of Europe/the Mediterranean.

Abyssinia

- Mussolini's plans for a new Roman Empire in the Adriatic, the Mediterranean and North Africa were a blow to British foreign policy, which aimed to keep Mussolini as an ally.
- The Stresa Front (1935) was initially successful.
- The Hoare–Laval Pact, 1935, brought public outcry at Franco-British attempts to facilitate Italian aggression; this led to Hoare's resignation.
- The imposition of limited sanctions on Italy did not appease Mussolini, and drove him closer to Hitler. The policy failed to aid Abyssinia. Britain ignored a direct appeal for help to the League of Nations from Haile Selassie.

Rhineland

- Hitler was successful in reintroducing conscription and re-arming from 1933 but, by the late 1930s, Germany's potential enemies were re-arming at a faster rate. The growth of the Luftwaffe was a serious challenge to Britain's security.
- Hitler was successful in remilitarising the Rhineland – more as a result of bluff, clever timing and French/British weakness than German military strength.

Naval Agreement

- The Anglo-German Naval Agreement (1935) successfully limited German naval strength to 35 per cent of British. However, Hitler was more focused on building up army and air force strength. Britain actively undermined the Treaty of Versailles and the League of Nations.

Non-intervention

- Britain's main aim was to prevent this war spreading to the rest of Europe and the world, and in this it was successful.
- The policy of non-intervention was sponsored by Britain; it also guaranteed that Britain would be on good terms with the victors.
- The policy was openly breached by Germany and Italy, and to a lesser extent the Soviet Union.
- British intelligence passed on details on Republican shipping to the Nationalists.
- Resolute action did end attacks on British merchant shipping.

Anschluss, 1938

- The attempted Nazi coup in 1934 which aimed to achieve Anschluss failed due to Italian opposition.
- The annexation of Austria was successful in 1938, although the invasion itself was chaotic and inefficient.
- Geography would have prevented serious opposition to the invasion, even had Britain wanted to act, which it did not.

Any other relevant factors.

54 *Changing attitudes to Appeasement were the main reason for the outbreak of war in 1939.*

   How valid is this view? (20)

Context: By 1939, Appeasement had failed to settle German grievances and Hitler showed no sign of letting up in his demands for more territory.

Changing British attitudes to Appeasement

- Czechoslovakia did not concern most people in Britain until the middle of September 1938, when some began to object to a small democratic state being bullied. Most of the press and the population went along with the Munich Agreement out of relief at the avoidance of war; however, levels of popular opposition are often underestimated.
- German invasion of the remainder of Czechoslovakia in spring 1939 consolidated growing concerns in Britain.
- The German annexation of Memel (largely German, but in Lithuania) further showed Hitler's bad faith.
- Actions convinced the British government of the growing German threat in south-Eastern Europe.
- Along with France, Britain gave guarantees to Poland and promised action in the event of threats to Polish independence. However, the British government was well aware that it was unlikely to be able to honour promises made to the Poles.

Other factors

Occupation of Bohemia and the collapse of Czechoslovakia

- After the German invasion of Czechoslovakia in March 1939, the British and French governments could no longer fool themselves and had to admit that Hitler's word was worthless and his aims went beyond the incorporation of ex-German territories and ethnic Germans into the Reich.
- Support was promised to Poland and Rumania.
- The British public accepted that all attempts to maintain peace had been exhausted.
- Chamberlain felt betrayed by the Nazi seizure of Czechoslovakia, realised his policy of Appeasement towards Hitler had failed, and began to take a much harder line against the Nazis.

Developing crisis over Poland

- Hitler's aims for the destruction of Versailles included regaining Danzig and the Polish Corridor.
- The British and French made a decision to stick to their guarantees to Poland.

British diplomacy and relations with the Soviet Union

- Stalin knew that ideology and geography would inevitably lead to Hitler's attack on Russia.
- Stalin invited Lord Halifax, the British Foreign Secretary, to go to Russia to discuss an alliance against Germany.
- Britain refused as they feared Russian communism, and they believed that the Russian army was too weak to be of any use against Hitler.
- In August 1939, the British and French eventually sent a low-level military mission to discuss an alliance with Russia. Owing to travel difficulties it took five days to reach Leningrad. The talks broke down over the issue of Russian troops in Poland.
- Stalin was unimpressed with the lack of status of the mission; this confirmed Stalin's suspicions regarding the British, that they were willing to try any tactic to ensure the Germans attacked eastwards instead of west. He felt they could not be trusted, especially after the Munich Agreement, and that they would leave Russia to fight Germany alone.
- The failure of the Franco-British mission to Russia led directly to Stalin opening talks with the Nazis who seemed to be taking the Russians seriously, sending Foreign Minister von Ribbentrop and offering substantive concessions.

Position of France

- France had signed an agreement with Czechoslovakia offering support if the country was attacked. However, Hitler knew that the French would do nothing without British support.
- The French military, and particularly their air force, had been allowed to decline in the years after 1919.
- After Munich, the French were more aggressive towards dictators. In 1939, they were keen to reprise their military alliance with Russia; however, French foreign policy was tied to the British and their actions.

Nazi–Soviet Pact

- The Nazi–Soviet Pact was unexpected – it was the result of Hitler and Stalin's self-interested motives.
- The Pact established diplomatic, economic and military co-operation, and the division of Poland.
- Hitler was freed from the threat of Soviet intervention and war on two fronts.
- Hitler now felt able to attack Poland because he rightly assumed that Britain and France would not go to war over Poland without Russian assistance.
- Hitler's foreign policy aims, the destruction of the Versailles settlement and *lebensraum* in the East probably mean the Nazi–Soviet Pact should be seen more as a factor influencing the timing of the outbreak of war rather than one of its underlying causes.
- In the longer term, Hitler would probably still need to expand eastwards to sustain Germany's militarised economy.
- Hitler believed that the British and French were 'worms', whose promises over Poland would turn out to be empty because of their previous policy of Appeasement and avoidance of war at all costs.
- Hitler believed that delaying war would mean the balance of military and economic advantage would shift against Germany.

Invasion of Poland

- On 1 September 1939, Hitler and the Nazis faked a Polish attack on a minor German radio station in order to justify a German invasion of Poland. An hour later, Hitler declared war on Poland, blaming the 'attack'.
- France and Britain had a defensive pact with Poland. This forced France and Britain to declare war on Germany, which they did on 3 September.

Any other relevant factors.

B

Part I – The Cold War, 1945–1989

55 *Soviet policy that was used to control Eastern Europe was successful.*

How valid is this view? (20)

Context: In the aftermath of the Second World War, the Red Army effectively occupied large parts of Eastern Europe. It created a series of sympathetic states that helped it maintain a buffer zone, and theoretically, showed the success of communism. The Soviet Union used a variety of methods to control the satellite states.

Desire for reform in Eastern Europe

- By the 1950s and 1960s, the satellite states were performing poorly economically, when compared to their western counterparts.
- Repressive policies followed by Stalinist leaders of the satellites led to a desire for reform.
- Nikita Khrushchev seemed to offer hope of reform with his policy of 'many roads to socialism' and attacks on the policies of Stalin.

Policy towards Poland (1956)

- Polish workers went on strike over wage reductions and poor housing conditions.
- Gomulka eventually emerged as leader; he supported limited reform.
- Soviet policy was initially to threaten, but then to negotiate with the new Polish leadership.
- This led to no direct Soviet intervention as Polish reforms were limited and Poland remained communist and part of the Warsaw Pact.

Policy towards Hungary (1956)

- Encouraged by the Poles, Hungarians demanded change, which increasingly got out of hand.
- Initial Soviet military intervention led to their withdrawal, due to opposition.
- Soviet policy was to support the new leader, Nagy, to begin with; however, Nagy announced Hungary was to withdraw from the Warsaw Pact and hold free elections.
- A massive Soviet military intervention crushed the rising.

Policy towards Berlin (1961)

- Berlin was occupied by the four allied victors at the end of the war. It had an open border between East and West Berlin.
- Poor economic conditions and repression encouraged many Berliners and others from the East to walk over the border to the West.
- The Soviets agreed to the East German plan to build a wall around West Berlin.
- The wall dealt with the issue of population movement: communism was maintained.

Domestic pressures

- Khrushchev had encouraged reform within limits. He struck hard against opponents who questioned the orthodoxy of communism.

International context

- Criticism of Soviet actions spurred the Soviets to show strength against what was seen frequently as foreign-encouraged plots.

Military and ideological factors

- The Soviet Union could not afford to see their buffer zone breached or have communism be seen to fail, hence their intervention.

Any other relevant factors.

56 **To what extent did the USA lose the war in Vietnam due to the strengths of North Vietnam? (20)**

Context: The policy of containing the spread of communism led to American intervention in many parts of the world. Intervention in Vietnam grew massively under the presidency of Lyndon B. Johnson.

Strengths of North Vietnam

- North Vietnam had good leadership in the form of Ho Chi Minh, as well as effective military leadership and goals defined by General Giap.
- The North was a communist dictatorship, with a strong nationalistic tone, and was effective in mobilising its people.
- North Vietnam could rely on the help of the Soviet Union and China, for example an effective air-defence system was developed.

- The Viet Cong were motivated with a strong ethical code of behaviour towards the peasants when they operated in the South. In areas they controlled, peasants were given land.

Other factors

Weaknesses of South Vietnam

- The South Vietnamese government leadership was corrupt.
- The dominance of the Catholic elite was strong in the government and in military leadership.
- The South Vietnamese military was strong on paper, but suffered from poor morale and motivation.
- It was difficult for Americans to justify upholding a clearly flawed and unpopular regime.

Difficulties faced by the US military

- The US army was designed to fight a conventional war and had to change rapidly to deal with jungle warfare against a guerrilla army.
- The US army encountered difficulty in dealing with the Viet Cong as they merged into the local population and utilised a range of booby traps that lowered the morale of US troops.
- Military methods used by the USA were blunt and did not capture the hearts and minds of the local population. For example, the use of napalm and Agent Orange was indiscriminate and caused long-term problems for the local population.

Changing public opinion in the USA

- War was initially popular in the USA, but changing public opinion led to a political reaction as the USA was a democracy.
- Rising numbers of body bags, the increasing length and cost of war, plus its brutality were there to see on the television. The impact of the Tet Offensive was also significant in changing views in the USA.
- Protests took place across America, particularly in the universities, but were also headed-up by prominent figures like Muhammad Ali.
- Johnson did not stand for re-election and Nixon was elected on a ticket of Vietnamisation of the conflict.
- There was still significant support among sections of the population, but there was a loss of political will to increase American involvement.

International isolation of the USA

- No significant NATO ally supported US action in Vietnam, despite US pressure.
- Those countries that did, such as Australia, came under pressure to withdraw their own troops as the war went on.

Any other relevant factors.

57 How important was Western economic strength as a reason for the end of the Cold War? (20)

Context: As the 1970s and 1980s progressed, it looked as if the Cold War may reform with the new leadership of Gorbachev, but no one foresaw the collapse of communism in the late 1980s.

Western economic strength

- The economic strength of the West allowed it to sustain large military spending as well as show the East a better quality of life.
- An example of Western economic strength is the threat of the Strategic Defence Initiative. While militarily a little implausible, it was backed by formidable finance and technology.
- The Marshall Plan was important in the immediate post-war period in ensuring economic stability and growth in the West.

Other factors

Soviet economic weakness

- The Soviet economy was geared to heavy industrial production and servicing its large military.
- The lack of quality consumer goods did not demonstrate a superior economic model.
- Some East European states looked to the West to modernise their economies and even borrowed large sums of money during détente, which was not encouraging economically.
- When another arms race beckoned, Gorbachev recognised that the Soviet Union could not compete.

Defeat of the Soviet Union in Afghanistan

- The Soviet Union intervened in Afghanistan to rescue a sympathetic Marxist government.
- They got bogged down in a war with the Western funded and armed Mujahideen.

- The war was expensive and used up valuable resources.
- Eventual Soviet withdrawal showed the limits of Soviet military power.

Role of Mikhail Gorbachev

- Gorbachev became leader of the Soviet Union in 1985.
- He wished to reform the communist system to better the lives of the people.
- His policies of Perestroika and Glasnost encouraged people to criticise the political system.
- He engaged with the USA in a desire to reduce the risk of conflict, so he could readjust the Soviet economy.
- He was behind the decision to withdraw the Soviet military from Afghanistan in 1988.
- His decision to withdraw Soviet military support for the satellite state regimes was very important.

Role of Ronald Reagan

- Reagan rejected détente and brought a combative approach to the Cold War.
- Openly critical of the 'evil empire', his presidency saw growth in military expenditure as well as the proposed 'Star Wars' programme, which threatened a new arms race.
- Reagan could be personally charming and changed tack after meeting Gorbachev and receiving intelligence that the Soviets genuinely believed they were going to be attacked.

Collapse of communism in Eastern Europe

- With the loss of Soviet military support, the Eastern European states rejected communism.
- Poland elected Solidarity into government in 1989. Other states soon followed.

Any other relevant factors.

[End of marking instructions for Practice Paper B]

Practice Paper C

Section 1 – Scottish – 20 marks

Part A – The Wars of Independence, 1249–1328

1 Compare Sources A **and** B **about the succession problem in Scotland. (5)**

Compare the content overall and in detail.

Candidates can be credited in a number of ways up to a maximum of 5 marks.

Possible points of comparison may include:

Overall: The sources agree on the death of the maid of Norway and its implications for Scotland. There is also agreement on the actions of Robert the Bruce and his followers in raising their military forces. Agreement also exists about the implications of this with an outbreak of open warfare, though Source B also adds an appeal to Edward to come and sort out the problem.

Source A	Source B
The bad news from the north reached the Scottish government early in October. Queen Margaret had died in Orkney on her way to Scotland.	But a sad rumour spread among the people that our lady was dead and because of this the kingdom of Scotland is troubled and the community perplexed.
Robert Bruce, in his seventieth year or thereabouts, had arrived unexpectedly with a strong body of armed men. It was rumoured that his friends the earls of Mar and Atholl were raising their forces.	When the rumour was heard Sir Robert Bruce came to the meeting with a large number of followers to confer with some who were there.
It looked as though the guardianship would collapse and the question of succession be settled by open war between the claimants.	But the earls of Mar and Atholl are collecting their army and some other nobles of the land have been persuaded to join their party.
	Because of that there is a fear of a general war and a large-scale slaughter unless the Most High, through your active involvement and good offices, administer a quick cure.

2 How fully does Source C **explain the role of William Wallace and Scottish resistance? (9)**

Use the source and your own knowledge.

Candidates can be credited in a number of ways up to a maximum of 9 marks.

A maximum of 2 marks may be given for answers which refer only to the source.

Possible points which may be identified in the source include:

- The decisive move was the linking up of the opposition in Moray with a rising in the shires to the east of the Spey and in the important burgh of Aberdeen.
- It was the first and last pitched battle which William Wallace won.
- That was why the community entrusted him with sole guardianship of the realm in the spring of 1298.
- Wallace deserves to be remembered as a patriot and a charismatic warlord.

Possible points of significant omission may include:

- Resistance to the English grew in the south-west, and in the north-east of Scotland.
- William Wallace and Andrew Murray brought leadership to the Scottish resistance.
- Scottish guerrilla tactics in their early resistance had moved towards a pitched battle at Stirling, under the combined leadership.
- The nobles Bruce and Steward started an armed revolt against Edward at Irvine.
- Andrew Murray took castles at Inverness, Elgin and Aberdeen.
- Murray eventually removed all English garrisons north of Dundee.

- William Wallace was present at the killing of Sir William Heselrig, the English Sheriff of Lanark.
- The Scottish were victorious at the Battle of Stirling Bridge, 11 September 1297.
- Wallace and Murray were appointed Guardians.
- Wallace invaded the north of England, around Carlisle and Newcastle.
- The English were increasingly unable to administer Scotland as the resistance developed.
- The English could not replace their officers in Scotland and found it difficult to collect taxation.
- The Scots set up their own administration systems showing their success in pushing the English out.

Any other valid points that meet the criteria described in the general marking instructions for this kind of question.

3   **Evaluate the usefulness of** Source D **as evidence of the reasons for the rise and triumph of Robert the Bruce. (6)**

In making a judgement you should refer to:

- *the origin and possible purpose of the source*
- *the content of the source*
- *your own knowledge.*

Candidates can be credited in a number of ways up to a maximum of 6 marks.

Examples of aspects of the source and relevant comments:

Aspect of the source	Possible comment
Author: John of Fordun	Useful as he was a secular priest who was well informed about events during the Scottish Wars of Independence. Less useful as he was a Scottish nationalist so some of his writing may be biased. In general he is considered to be fairly reliable.
Type of source: Chronicle	Useful as one of the first attempts to write a continuous history of Scotland.
Purpose: to record events in the history of Scotland	Useful as the Chronicle was created to inform people of the history of Scotland.
Timing: c.1350	Useful as although John was not present during the Wars of Independence his work was within living memory of the events. It is likely that he was well informed about events.

Content	Possible comment
He advanced with his army against the enemy to the battle ground. When the opposing party saw him they were all afraid and fled.	Useful as the source shows the decisive defeat of Bruce's internal enemies, the Comyns, at the Battle of Inverurie.
King Robert ravaged the earldom of Buchan with fire; and of the people, he killed whom he would, and to those whom he would have live, he granted life and peace.	Useful as the source illustrates the ruthless methods employed by Bruce when dealing with his enemies. Also useful as it illustrates that he could be magnanimous.
And from that day the king gained ground and became ever more strong himself; while the opposition was daily losing confidence.	Useful as it indicates these events were a turning point for Bruce in his struggles to be undisputed King of Scotland and to defeat his enemies.

Possible points of significant omission may include:

- Details of raids into the north of England by Bruce or his lieutenants in 1315, 1316, 1318, 1322, 1323 and 1328.
- Raids may have brought wealth and exercised Bruce's soldiers, but they were less successful in bringing Edward II to the negotiating table. The south of England was where the main English magnates and wealth lay, and the north of England was a long way away for many of them.
- The death of Edward I in 1307 meant he was succeeded by Edward II who was less interested in Scotland and was not the military leader that his father had been.
- Bruce was supported by key groups in Scotland such as the Church.

- Military success of the Scots over the English at Bannockburn and the Battle of Old Byland where the English King was almost captured.
- The Scots' campaign in Ireland under Edward Bruce and Thomas Randolph.
- Diplomatic recognition of Bruce's kinship from France in 1310.
- The weakness of the English government of Isabella and Mortimer after the removal of Edward II.
- The Treaty of Edinburgh recognised Robert the Bruce as King of Scotland in his own right.

Any other valid points that meet the criteria described in the general marking instructions for this kind of question.

Part B – The Age of the Reformation, 1542–1603

4 Compare the views of Sources A **and** B **about the Reformation of 1560. (5)**

Compare the sources overall and in detail.

Candidates can be credited in a number of ways up to a maximum of 5 marks.

Possible points of comparison may include:

Overall: Sources A and B agree that the Reformation's immediate cause was a riot in Perth which led to the sacking of Catholic religious houses. They also agree that Knox was made a protestant minister in Edinburgh and that the deployment of English military forces was important in the success of the Reformation.

Source A	Source B
In St John's Church at Perth, on Thursday 11 May, Knox preached a sermon which led to a riot in which church ornaments and furnishings were destroyed.	The Reformation crisis of 1559 was sparked off by a riot in Perth.
The houses of the Black and Grey Friars and the Carthusian monks were also destroyed.	The town's religious houses were sacked within nine days of Knox's return to Scotland from France and Geneva on 2 May.
John Knox was appointed minister of the capital on 7 July.	entered the capital, where Knox was installed as its first Protestant minister on the seventh of the month.
English troops under Lord Grey entered Scotland in support of the Congregation, at the end of March.	The arrival of an English fleet in January 1560 and an army two months later proved to be the decisive factor.

5 How fully does Source C **explain the relationship between the monarch and Kirk in the reign of James VI? (9)**

Use the source and your own knowledge.

Candidates can be credited in a number of ways up to a maximum of 9 marks.

A maximum of 2 marks may be given for answers which refer only to the source.

Possible points which may be identified in the source include:

- By the middle of 1592, the fragile relationship between the Crown and the Kirk was once again clear.
- The king did not see the religious and ecclesiastical world in the terms in which most of the Kirk saw it.
- James did not share the fervour which most of the Kirk appears to have borne against Catholicism.
- This factor unified the Kirk, and their belief that it was the ministers' job to ensure the godly conduct of government, created an atmosphere of conflict with the Crown rooted in the king's disinclination, as far as the Kirk saw it, to purify the nation.

Possible points of significant omission may include:

- James believed in his divine right to rule, which put him at odds with the Kirk; views of Andrew Melville that the King should be accountable to the authority of the Kirk.
- In Trew Law, James appears frustrated by the lack of respect he receives from his subjects; while in Basilikon Doron, James is determined to bring Scotland's remote localities under more direct royal control.
- Relations with the Kirk deteriorated after 1592, leading to conflict in 1596.
- The Second Book of Discipline (1578) established a vision of a Presbyterian Kirk but the Black Acts (1584) subsequently stated the supremacy of the monarch in all matters.
- The Golden Act (1592) recognised the recovery of Presbyterian influence within the Kirk but it did not reduce the power of the monarch.
- The establishment of Presbyteries in 1581 meant there was a possible challenge to royal authority.

- James sought to extend the power of the monarch and bishops over the Kirk by: having bishops recognised as moderators of Presbyteries; allowing bishops to hear cases of excommunication/deposition of ministers, visit parishes, appoint schoolmasters; giving the monarch the power to determine the time and place of the General Assembly (which James used as a means of maintaining support with the Assembly meeting in the North East where there was less resistance to his ideas).
- James also faced challenges to his authority from Catholics. In 1594, James ordered the suppression of a rebellion by the Catholic earls of Huntly and Errol.
- Rebellion in December 1596; James fled from Edinburgh, but this made him more determined to control the Kirk.
- In 1597, Andrew Melville was deposed as Rector of St Andrews.

Any other valid points that meet the criteria described in the general marking instructions for this kind of question.

6 **Evaluate the usefulness of** Source D **as evidence of the impact of the Reformation on Scotland, to 1603. (6)**

In making a judgement you should refer to:

- *the origin and possible purpose of the source*
- *the content of the source*
- *your own knowledge.*

Candidates can be credited in a number of ways up to a maximum of 6 marks.

Examples of aspects of the source and relevant comments:

Aspect of the source	Possible comment
Author: committee including John Knox	Useful as written by leading reformers of the Scottish Reformation.
Type of source: work of ecclesiastical order	Useful as an official document defining the new Church organisation.
Purpose: to define the organisation and workings of the Protestant Church	Useful as it shows the attempt to set up a Presbyterian Church.
Timing: 1560	Useful as a contemporary document from the time of the Protestant Reformation in Scotland.

Content	Possible comment
We ought to be careful that they have knowledge to profit from that which ought to be most dear to us, to wit, the kirk and our Lord Jesus.	Useful as it shows the intention that the new Church should educate the young in the teachings of the Bible.
Of necessity therefore we judge it, that in the towns every kirk have one Schoolmaster appointed, such a one at least as is able to teach Grammar, and the Latin tongue.	Useful as shows the desire to introduce an educational structure focused on literacy.
In the countryside, either the reader or the minister there appointed, must take care over the children and youth of the parish, to instruct them.	Useful as another point showing the intention of the new Church to ensure education for all in Scotland.

Possible points of significant omission may include:

- The aim of a school in every parish in Scotland was not achieved owing to lack of funds, but literacy of the population did improve.
- Clergy or readers were encouraged to educate the young in the word of God.
- The treatment of the Catholic clergy was relatively lenient. They were allowed to keep two-thirds of their revenues for life.
- The Kirk Session sought to police the morals of their congregations, through the introduction of the sinning stool, for example. It was also concerned with control of events such as weddings.
- The observation of Catholic festivals was actively discouraged; for example, Easter and Christmas were abolished as festivals.
- There were changes to the act of worship as Protestant practices were introduced.
- English rather than Latin was used for services. The Bible was translated and was available in English, which made it accessible to those who spoke English.
- Changes to church buildings, such as the removal of statues, etc. were made. They were replaced with plain parish kirks.

- Scotland changed from being a Catholic country to being a Protestant one, albeit with a small Catholic minority.
- Trade with Europe continued throughout this period, for example with the Dutch.

Any other valid points that meet the criteria described in the general marking instructions for this kind of question.

Part C – The Treaty of Union, 1689–1740

7 **Compare the views of** Sources **A and** B **about worsening relations between Scotland and England. (5)**

Use the sources and your own knowledge.

Candidates can be credited in a number of ways up to a maximum of 5 marks.

Possible points of comparison may include:

Overall: Sources A and B agree about the purpose and range of acts brought in by the Scottish Parliament that had an impact on relations with England. The Act of Security was designed to allow for Scottish independence in choosing a monarch on the death of Anne. The Act anent reserved powers to declare war and peace with the Scottish Parliament. Economic measures, such as the Wine Act and Wool Act, impacted on important trades that were designed to further Scottish independence of action.

Source A	Source B
the parliament of 1703 was considerably less compliant than its predecessor and against the wishes of the pro-Hanoverian Court, passed an Act of Security, which meant that Scotland would not be bound to support England's nomination for a successor to Queen Anne.	An Act of Security, passed in open defiance of the Court party, stated that the Scots Parliament had the right to decide on Queen Anne's successor and that England and Scotland could not have the same sovereign in the future.
The Act anent (concerning) Peace and War, which reserved to the Scottish parliament the right after Anne's demise to declare war and conclude peace.	The Act anent (concerning) Peace and War, which gave the Scots Parliament the right to declare war and make peace if the two nations continued to share a sovereign after Anne's death.
Economic warfare was opened with the Wine act.	A third measure, the Wine Act, formally permitted trade with France during the war.
This was followed in 1704 with the passage of an act which forbade the import but allowed the export of wool, steps which were judged by English woollen merchants to be hostile.	The Wool Act passed during the session the following year, was regarded as openly hostile by England in allowing the export and prohibiting the import of wool.

8 **How fully does** Source C **explain the passing of the Act of Union? (9)**

Compare the content overall and in detail.

Candidates can be credited in a number of ways up to a maximum of 9 marks.

A maximum of 2 marks may be given for answers which refer only to the source.

Possible points which may be identified in the source include:

- The opposition, which embarked on delaying tactics from the outset, succeeded in postponing serious consideration of the first of the Articles for a month.
- Article 1 (on the principle of incorporating union) was passed on 4 November by 116 votes to 83.
- The ministry on the same day brought before the House a bill guaranteeing the Presbyterian settlement of the Church.
- On 16 January 1707, the Treaty was ratified with a majority of 43.

Possible points of significant omission may include:

- Scottish ministers/politicians were bribed through financial offers and positions in the House of Lords, for example.
- All the Articles were passed despite popular opposition outside the parliament.
- £20,000 was paid to various Scottish politicians as inducements.
- The Equivalent, a sum of £398,085.10s was granted to cover the taking on of English debt and to reimburse Scotland for losses suffered at Darien.
- Squadrone Volante's (or the New Party's) hold on the balance of power in the Scottish Parliament was key to the Court Party's success.
- The leader of the opposition to Union, Hamilton, behaved most curiously and was not an effective leader. Some argue that he was in the pay of the pro-Union lobby.
- Opponents of the Union disagreed with each other.
- The Court Party had a formidable party machine compared to the divided County Party.

- There were assurances that the British Parliament would support the Scottish economy over taxation.
- The Scottish Parliament was given the incentive of free trade with England and its colonies.
- There were last-minute concessions from the English on issues such as salt, wool and liquor.
- The Act of Security for the Kirk would allow the Church of Scotland to continue in its current form. This effectively ended the political role of one of the most effective anti-Union groups.
- Burghs and Royal Burghs were granted the right to remain, which was attractive to them.
- Scots laws and Scottish courts were to remain, which would keep a distinctive Scottish institution.
- On key issues for the Scots, the English commissioners were willing to make concessions. They were more concerned with Article 1 and having an incorporating union. They were flexible on the economic articles.
- English forces were moving north, creating fear of invasion if no treaty was agreed.

Any other valid points that meet the criteria described in the general marking instructions for this kind of question.

9   **Evaluate the usefulness of** Source D **as evidence of the effects of the Union, to 1740. (5)**

In making a judgement you should refer to:

- *the origin and possible purpose of the source*
- *the content of the source*
- *your own knowledge.*

Candidates can be credited in a number of ways up to a maximum of 6 marks.

Examples of aspects of the source and relevant comments:

Aspect of the source	Possible comment
Author: George Lockhart of Carnwarth	Useful as he was the pro-Jacobite MP for Edinburgh and had been deeply involved in the 1715 rising.
	Less useful as he could be biased in his reporting of the condition of Scotland in 1725.
Type of source: letter	Useful as a personal view of the situation in Scotland.
Purpose: to inform the Old Pretender of conditions in Scotland likely to help in a successful Jacobite rising	Useful as it provides advice as to what might have been needed to incite a Jacobite rising.
Timing: 18 December 1725	Useful as the source was written eighteen years after the Act of Union when its effects, both positive and negative, were being felt across Scotland.
	Also useful as it was written after the failed Jacobite rebellion of 1715, but deals with the likelihood of Jacobite rebellion.

Content	Possible comment
I have mentioned this because your friends are not so numerous as they were in 1715.	Useful as recognition that outright support for Jacobitism had declined since the abortive, and badly led, attempt to secure the Crown for the Stuarts in 1715.
However, the opposition to the Union daily increases and that is the way in which Scotsmen will be roused to help your cause.	Useful as it seeks to exploit the opposition to Union as a method of raising support for the Jacobite cause.
as soon as your army lands, a manifesto should be published with respect to religion and containing an assurance of your design to maintain the two kingdoms in their ancient independent state by dissolving the union.	Useful as it recognises some of the contentious issues since Union, such as religion, and seeks to exploit the desire to decouple England and Scotland.

Possible points of significant omission may include:

- Numerous Scottish weights and measures were replaced with new imperial or 'Union' ones.
- There was an overall increase in taxation. Duties rose five-fold, for example.
- More efficient tax collection systems were introduced which led to resentment.
- There was a loss of toll revenue from old cross-border trade.
- Darien investors were fairly quickly reimbursed with money from the Equivalent.

- The introduction of the new Malt tax was fiercely opposed and there were even riots.
- Smuggling increased massively as a result of the increases in taxation.
- Higher taxes had a huge impact on some Scottish industries, such as paper production, shoe-making, candle-making and the important linen and wool industries.
- There was a significant rise in Scottish merchant trade; huge expansion in mercantile trade in coal, salt and grain and an increase in vessels needed to facilitate this trade.
- There was an increase in land improvement, such as enclosures.
- There was an increase in transatlantic trade as previous restrictions were removed.
- Fast growing west-coast ports, such as Port Glasgow and Greenock, were testament to improved access to the plantations in the Caribbean.
- Scottish tobacco merchants increased their trade, though real growth happened after 1740.
- There were fewer Scottish mercantile losses as they benefited from the protection of the Royal Navy.
- Many ex-Jacobites become bond servants in the colonies.
- There was an expansion of jobs for Scots in the 1720s, especially as a result of Walpole's policies, which reflected a more conciliatory approach to Scotland from British politicians; for example, in the British armed forces and as doctors.
- The reintroduction of patronage in 1712 led to resentment among the Presbyterian community who had assumed that Union would entrench their view of religion. They welcomed George I, however, when he succeeded Anne as a protector of Protestantism.
- There was immediate widespread opposition to Union across Scotland, not just in the Highlands.
- Initially there was much political opposition and there was a motion to repeal union in 1713, though it did, just, fail.
- The Whig party were dominant in Scotland.
- The office of Secretary of State was abolished from 1725.
- The Scots Privy Council was abolished in 1708.
- There was a desire for restoration of the Stuart dynasty.
- There were invasion scares in 1708 and 1719 in support of the Jacobites.
- There was resentment towards George I after 1714.
- The Jacobites rose in strength in 1715, but were poorly led and ultimately failed.

Any other valid points that meet the criteria described in the general marking instructions for this kind of question.

Part D – Migration and Empire, 1830–1939

10 Compare Sources A **and** B **about the reasons for emigration of Scots. (5)**

Compare the sources overall and in detail.

Candidates can be credited in a number of ways up to a maximum of 5 marks.

Possible points of comparison may include:

Overall: The sources agree that the Scots emigrated for a variety of social, economic and cultural reasons, mostly means and opportunity.

Source A suggests that the most effective encouragement for emigration came from emigrants happy with their move. However, Source B highlights the incentive of owning land and the promotion of emigration through the popular press.

Source A	Source B
Scots were lured overseas by a variety of economic, social and cultural incentives.	Emigration was not caused so much by poverty – as by the lure of opportunity.
The recurring promise of independence through landownership was a powerful attraction, particularly to those whose security and prospects and been eroded by the commercialisation of farming in Scotland.	A primary incentive was the possibility of owning land that was cheap to acquire and plentiful whereas in Scotland even wealthy farmers were dependent on their landlords.
The skilled working class sought higher wages and better working conditions overseas, especially in the United States.	Canada and Australasia were magnets for those who wished to work the land, but rural tradesmen and industrial workers tended to opt more for the USA.
Throughout the nineteenth century guidebooks and newspapers poured forth a torrent of advice and encouragement, generally trying to steer emigrants in the direction of Canada.	The weekly People's Journal … was specially designed to promote the interests of the working classes and virtually every issue had articles on emigration worldwide, providing advice on changing employment conditions and opportunities available overseas.

C

11 How fully does Source C **explain the impact of Scots emigrants on the Empire? (9)**

Use the source and your own knowledge.

Candidates can be credited in a number of ways up to a maximum of 9 marks.

A maximum of 2 marks may be given for answers which refer only to the source.

Possible points which may be identified in the source include:

- Many Scots emigrants like those from England had a decided advantage over the peasant masses that flocked across the Atlantic in their millions from Ireland, Central and Eastern Europe and the Mediterranean.

- The economic, social and religious development of Scotland ensured that its emigrants spoke mainly Scots-English, were usually Protestant, literate and often highly or semi-skilled in the practices of an advanced industrial and agrarian economy.

- They were also drawn abroad for the most part, not by crisis or disaster, but by a desire to exploit opportunities and achieve aspirations not easily satisfied at home.

- Unlike many other nationalities, Scots rarely experienced systematic prejudice or discrimination in the new lands and offered them skills which were much in demand there.

Possible points of significant omission may include:

- The consistently high level of Scottish emigration over the time period helped create a sustained pattern of impact across many countries of the Empire.

- The Empire created jobs for the growing Scottish population.

- Administering the Empire created opportunities for younger sons of well-off families who otherwise might have struggled to maintain their social and economic status.

- The Empire helped stimulate the growth of Scottish education; it helped create jobs for young men from the professions like medicine and the law, for example the Atlantic slave trade.

- Scotland made a great contribution to church missionaries in the Empire and, as a result, Scots from poor backgrounds had the chance to get the education and jobs which lifted them from poverty.

- Some Scots went on to have a remarkable impact on the countries they went to and become internationally renowned figures, for example David Livingstone.

- There was an impact on Scottish identity: Scottish engagement in the Empire's trade and missionary work helped create a sense of united identity with England.

- Many Scots made huge fortunes abroad, for example Andrew Carnegie.

- The reputation of the Scottish military and the Scottish martial traditions rested on the role the Scots played in the conquest of Empire. For example, the role of the Scots in supressing the Indian Rising of 1857.

- Scots helped develop the overseas investment boom through joint stock companies and investment trusts. One of the first set up was the Scottish American Investment Trust in 1873. By 1914, there were 853 registered trusts in Edinburgh.

- Scots had a big impact in countries like England; the first Labour Prime Minister was James Ramsay Macdonald, from Lossiemouth in Moray. Others were successful inventors like John Logie Baird (television) and David Napier (engineering).

- Successful businessmen were benevolent; for example, Andrew Carnegie sold his business in 1801 and went on to donate most of his wealth to charity, funding education and libraries around the world including back in Scotland.

- John Muir from Dunbar helped found the national park system in the USA and influenced many in the conservation movement with his writings.

- Scots were prominent in the USA in skilled jobs such as shipbuilding, construction, granite-working, engineering and mining.

- Scots were important in the development of the fur trade, timber and agricultural industries in Canada.

- Farming was the most common career for the majority of emigrants up to the 1860s.

- Scots from Orkney and the Highlands dominated the fur trading companies of Canada through the Hudson's Bay Company and the North West Company.

- There were also prominent Scots in Canadian finance; George Stephen was President of the Bank of Montreal and helped raise $100 million to build the Canadian Pacific Railway, which unified the country.

- Scots made significant contributions to railroad building across Canada.

- Scots had an impact on education; notable universities such as McGill in Montreal and Queen's in Kingston, Ontario were set up either with Scottish money or by Scottish scholars.

- Almost one-quarter of Canada's industrial leaders in the 1920s had been born in Scotland, and another quarter had Scottish-born fathers.

- Scots also dominated in politics; Sir John A. Macdonald was the first Canadian Prime Minister and Alexander Mackenzie was the first Liberal Prime Minster of Canada in the late nineteenth century.

- In Australia and New Zealand, Scots were successful at introducing new farming methods for sheep.

- Scots in Australia and New Zealand were important in whaling, mining and engineering. Examples are James and Alexander Brown who produced most of the coal in New South Wales, Australia.
- Andrew Fisher, from Ayrshire, emigrated to Australia to work in the coal mines and trades unions. He went on to become Prime Minister of Australia three times between 1908 and 1915.
- Scots were deeply implicated in the harsh treatment of Aboriginals in Australia, stealing their lands for the development of farming, and murdering natives.
- Nearly all the money to finance India's jute factories came from Scotland. The first jute mill was opened by Scots at Serampore, India in 1855.
- One-third of Scottish emigrants returned to Scotland, indicating that, for whatever reason, emigration was not successful for all.

Any other valid points that meet the criteria described in the general marking instructions for this kind of question.

12 Evaluate the usefulness of Source D **as evidence of the contribution of Jewish immigrants to Scotland, to 1939. (6)**

In making a judgement you should refer to:

- *the origin and possible purpose of the source*
- *the content of the source*
- *your own knowledge.*

Candidates can be credited in a number of ways up to a maximum of 6 marks.

Examples of aspects of the source and relevant comments:

Aspect of the source	Possible comment
Author: J. Tobias, son of Jewish family from the Gorbals, Glasgow	Useful as it is based on the first-hand experience of someone who grew up in the Jewish community in Glasgow.
Type of source: interview with J. Tobias	Useful as oral history from someone who knew the situation of the Jewish community in Glasgow.
Purpose: to record the poverty and employment of his family	Useful as it shows how his family's economic situation was hard despite his father setting up his own business.
Timing: 1976	Useful as it is from someone who is reflecting on the contribution his family made to Scotland. Less useful as feelings and emotions about the hardships experienced may have become exaggerated over time.

Content	Possible comment
The poverty was absolutely diabolical.	Useful as it shows the hardships the Jewish community experienced in Glasgow.
He went to a Jewish company of merchants and they supplied him with an anvil, bellows and equipment to start up on his own.	Useful as it shows the support and help given by the Jewish community to support their own.
He started his own business in 1900 in MacFarlane Street in the Gallowgate and many a week he'd come home with hardly a penny in his pocket after he'd paid one or two bills. It wasn't easy going.	Useful as it shows the continuing hardship experienced by Jewish immigrants despite their doing better for themselves.

Possible points of significant omission may include:

- Early Jewish immigrants tended to be well educated and settled in the West End of Glasgow.
- Large numbers of Jewish immigrants arrived in Scotland between 1880 and 1914. Most of these were poor, fleeing religious and economic persecution in the Russian Empire.
- Jewish immigrants tended to work in jobs such as door-to-door selling or ran their own businesses.
- Common Jewish businesses included tailoring and tobacco, especially the making of cigarettes.
- A feature of the Jewish communities was to have their own synagogues, reading rooms and societies for helping the poor.
- Nearly all the shops and businesses in the Gorbals were Jewish.
- Scottish trades unions complained about Jewish immigrants undercutting wages.

trades unions also complained about Jewish involvements in the sweated trades: industries that paid very low wages and forced their workers to work long hours.

- Resentment against Jewish immigration gradually grew; in 1905 the *Daily Record* and *Mail* complained about the Alien danger represented by poor Jewish immigration.
- The large number of poorer Jewish immigrants did create some racial tension in places like Glasgow.
- However, numbers of Jews in Glasgow was not more than 15,000 in the inter-war period; although anti-Semitism existed, it was never widespread.
- Many Jews used Scotland as a stopping off point on their way to the USA because Scotland was relatively cheap and easy to reach from the continent. As a result, the Jewish population in Scotland was never large.
- By the 1930s, a distinct Jewish identity was disappearing as Jews integrated more with the local population. The Yiddish language began to die out as did Yiddish newspapers.

Any other valid points that meet the criteria described in the general marking instructions for this kind of question.

Part E – The Impact of the Great War, 1914–1928

13 Compare the views of Sources A **and** B **about voluntary recruitment in Scotland at the beginning of the war. (5)**

Compare the sources overall and in detail.

Candidates can be credited in a number of ways up to a maximum of 5 marks.

Possible points of comparison may include:

Overall: The sources agree that there was an initial enthusiasm for volunteering in Scotland at the start of the First World War.

Source A suggests that there was a variety of reasons why men volunteered, including the appeal by Lord Kitchener. However, although Source B also suggests that Kitchener's appeal was important, it highlights that the surge of recruits was promoted by concerns about unemployment.

Source A	Source B
As war was declared, men rushed to enlist. Their reasons were as complex and varied as their backgrounds.	Recruitment was a mixture of individual decisions, information and opportunity.
Others saw it as relief from unemployment or the chance of escape, however temporary, from a life of drudgery.	There was a pool of recruits from these industries because of the threat or reality of unemployment.
The demand for manpower was immediate, with Lord Kitchener making a direct appeal to the patriotism of the people of Scotland.	An appeal was made by Lord Kitchener, for new recruits to be organised into new battalions of existing regiments.
This call for manpower was responded to enthusiastically, with crowds of volunteers filling the recruiting offices.	54% of all the Scottish volunteers of 1914–1915 had enlisted by the end of 1914. This was the period in which influential institutions and social groups were most enthusiastic about the war.

14 How fully does Source C **explain the wartime effects of the First World War on Scottish industry and the economy? (9)**

Use the source and your own knowledge.

Candidates can be credited in a number of ways up to a maximum of 9 marks.

A maximum of 2 marks may be given for answers which refer only to the source.

Possible points which may be identified in the source include:

- The West of Scotland played an important part in military production. The Clyde contained 90% of Scottish shipbuilding and marine engineering in 1914.
- The Great War created considerable activity in Scotland's heavy industries, especially in the Glasgow and Lanarkshire areas.
- There were technological gains ... in shipbuilding where production processes were simplified by the Ministry of Shipping.
- Wartime pressure to increase the speed of production led to the introduction of pneumatic and electrical tools. There were similar advances in the munitions industry.

Possible points of significant omission may include:

- The 1915 Munitions Act created a state industry for armaments production. It had oversight of all industries connected to the making of weapons, even controlling the movement of skilled workers.

- Glasgow had a skilled engineering workforce which meant that such workers were very valuable in wartime.
- Clyde shipyard experienced a boom with the three leading yards winning orders worth over £16 million.
- Inefficient working practices meant that the shipyards did not always make huge profits.
- Shortages of skilled workers prevented ships being built faster.
- Shipyards faced competition for workers from the munitions factories.
- The Glasgow shipyards had to extend their policy of providing flats near their yards for key workers; foremen could rent flats with two or three rooms and an indoor toilet.
- The influx of workers and the use of women put a strain on industrial relations with several strikes in 1915.
- The steel, jute and coal industries also experienced a boom during the war years.
- Edinburgh's rubber industry thrived during the war; it was brought under the control of the Ministry of Munitions.
- All rail companies came under the control of the government and a non-strike agreement was negotiated for the duration.
- East-coast ports were closed to trade and kept open only for limited fishing; only the catching of herring remained constant throughout the war.
- In September 1914, the Admiralty took control of all shipping, including the fishing fleet.
- After an initial slump at the start of the war, agriculture thrived, with industries such as sheep farming doing especially well.
- Wages for farm workers and skilled shepherds boomed, owing to the shortage of supply.
- The amount of food and crops being grown dropped dramatically, leading to a sharp increase in the prices of basic foods. For example, the prices of fish and eggs had risen by 100 per cent by 1916.
- The wartime boom masked the long-term decline of the heavy industries before 1914.
- The post-war economic slump led to the collapse of Dundee's jute industry and to high unemployment in other sectors.

Any other valid points that meet the criteria described in the general marking instructions for this kind of question.

15 Evaluate the usefulness of Source D **as evidence of the impact of the war on Scottish politics. (6)**

In making a judgement you should refer to:

- *the origin and possible purpose of the source*
- *the content of the source*
- *your own knowledge.*

Candidates can be credited in a number of ways up to a maximum of 6 marks.

Examples of aspects of the source and relevant comments:

Aspect of the source	Possible comment
Author: Robert Irvine, a Scottish soldier during the First Word War	Useful as from someone well-informed about the problems in Glasgow through news from home. Less useful as his knowledge is based on second-hand information from other sources.
Type of source: an interview with Robert Irvine	Useful as oral history from someone who was personally involved in politics, so would be well-informed about what trades union activists were doing as a result of the war. It is a personal recollection so the source may be more useful because it is intended to be an honest account of what happened.
Purpose: to record the personal experiences of the impact of the war on politics	Useful as it is a record of how events at home had an impact on the politics of those at home and away fighting.
Timing: 1963	Useful as it is from the account of someone who had direct experience of radical politics in Glasgow, reflecting on their experience with the benefit of hindsight — had time to think about their experience with better perspective. Less useful as hindsight may have changed the detail and importance of the events.

Content	Possible comment
The married men … were … resentful, because they were getting letters from their womenfolk that the landlords were putting up rents and so forth.	Useful as it shows the importance of the rent disputes to the war effort; impact on men fighting.
Gradually this resentment spread … General Haig had written to Lloyd George: 'For heaven's sake, resolve your war there in Glasgow and Scotland or you'll lose the battle here.'	Useful as it shows the seriousness of the situation and how seriously the government took the events on 'Red Clydeside'.
Clyde Worker's Committee and shop stewards did have some impact on the troops fighting because the more we experienced the folly of war, the more we appreciated the work that our comrades at home were doing at home.	Useful as it shows how the events on 'Red Clydeside' and the attitudes to the war were linked.

Possible points of significant omission may include:

- Industrial tensions rose as a result of the rising costs of living and wages which did not keep pace.
- The 1915 Rent Strike disputes fed into disgruntlement with employers over pay and working conditions, especially the introduction of women workers.
- There was a series of disputes and strikes in 1915: 'Tuppence an Hour' strike, February 1915; Fairfield's dispute 1915; dilution of labour – Clyde Workers' Committee.
- After the 1915 Munitions Act, most strikes were supressed and the government tried to keep workers happy enough so they didn't interrupt war production.
- The 1915 Rent Restriction Act was passed as a result of social and industrial unrest.
- The Clyde Workers' Committees tried to give union representation for workers' grievances throughout the war. This was important in the demands for a '40 hour' week in 1919.
- Police charged demonstrators, leading to rioting and made attacks and arrests of the demonstration's leaders at the Battle for George Square, January 1919.
- John Maclean was an influential and respected communist who called for a workers' revolution during the First World War. He was well-known as a public speaker but lacked a political party with which to put across his views outside of Glasgow.
- Some activists, like Helen Crawfurd, set up the Women's Peace Crusade in 1916.
- Helen Crawfurd later helped set up the Communist Party in Britain in 1920.
- Most Labour MPs elected after the First World War were moderate and had been supporters of the war.
- The First World War settled many key political issues like Irish nationalism; most workers switched their support to the Labour Party which favoured a gradual approach to change.

Any other valid points that meet the criteria described in the general marking instructions for this kind of question.

Section 2 – British – 20 marks

Part A – Church, State and Feudal Society, 1066–1406

16 *David I was successful in his attempts to increase royal power in Scotland.*

How valid is this view? (20)

Context: David I succeeded to the throne of Scotland in 1124. He brought feudal ideas with him from his time in England and Normandy. These were introduced with a variety of success in parts of Scotland.

Introduction of feudal landholding

- Military feudalism was introduced in the south-west, Lothians and across North-East Scotland.
- David brought allies with him in the form of French and English knights who were used to the idea of feudalism. They were often given difficult areas to police for David.
- There were some clashes with traditional the Celtic system of mormaers of Scotland. They were used to their own power and operated in an independent way, for example the earls of Moray.
- It was more difficult to penetrate the west and north of Scotland in terms of introducing feudalism, though David did have positive relations with many of the traditional earls in places like Fife.

Development of independent military forces

- The introduction of feudal landholding allowed David to develop an effective military force. For example, it helped him subdue Moray and dominate the north of England, though it performed poorly at the Battle of the Standard and did not merge well with the more unruly Celtic elements of his army.

Developing the economy

- Burghs with preferential trading rights were introduced, in order to generate income. Burghs produced important revenue from their system of taxes, rents and fines. Examples include Stirling and Perth.
- Silver coinage and moneyers (people who mint corns) were introduced.

Law and order

- Royal power was practically expanded or reinforced with the development of existing royal castles such as Roxburgh, particularly around the burghs, as well as grants of lands to allies, for example, in Moray, to a Flemish knight.
- David also extended his power through intermediaries such as alliances with the powerful earls of Orkney.
- Royal justice expanded as King David granted Scottish magnates the right to hold their own court in his name.
- Judicial officers such as the Justiciar (supreme judges) were appointed.

Development of government

- The rudimentary development of government, such as sheriffs, as well as offices like Chamberlain and Chancellor, aimed to secure revenues and expand royal justice. However, there is also evidence of retention of the old systems with Gaelic terms and officials.

Church development

- David is associated with Church developments, especially the introduction of the Roman form of religion as compared to the existing Celtic one.
- Lands were granted to several monastic orders, such as the Cistercians.
- There was sensitivity to local needs as well. Local saints, such as St Mungo were praised.

Any other relevant factors.

17 To what extent were King John's attempts to increase royal authority successful in England? (20)

Context: John succeeded to the English throne on the death of his brother Richard. In a controversial reign, he struggled to hold the Angevin Empire together as well as face the challenges of his own magnates.

Loss of Normandy

- The loss of Normandy to Philip II of France by 1204 led to the collapse of much of the Angevin Empire. Much of John's foreign policy was geared to the recovery of the lands north of the Loire.
- The only sizeable land mass controlled by John in France was the Duchy of Aquitaine.
- John found it difficult to secure the assistance of English barons in his attempts to regain his French lands.

Military power

- John was a reasonable military commander; an example of this is the victory at the Battle of Mirabeau.
- John made use of mercenaries in his armies.
- The Royal Navy was established during John's reign.
- John built up alliances with other groups who were suspicious of the growth of Capetian power, such as the counts of Boulogne and Flanders.
- However, John's allies were eventually defeated at the Battle of Bouvines in 1214.

Royal administration

- Record keeping and tax gathering improved during John's reign.
- John was very active in the administration of England and was involved in every aspect of government.
- Many roles in government were filled by new men, which did cause resentment among English barons.

The economy and taxation

- Relentless conflict led to a demand for revenue and John was active in raising taxation.
- 'Scutage' was implemented eleven times in seventeen years, far more frequently than under Richard or Henry.
- John created a new tax on income and movable goods in 1207, which produced £60,000.
- He also created a new set of import and export duties, payable directly to the Crown.
- John implemented the confiscation of the lands of barons who could not pay or refused to pay.
- There were improvements in the quality of silver coinage.

Relationship with the barons

- There was much resentment at the increases in taxation.
- There was also resentment at the expectation of service in France, especially from northern barons.
- The failure of military campaigns led to open revolt in 1215.
- Magna Carta was negotiated to end the revolt. This attempted to define rights, etc. but was never actually implemented by either side.

Relationship with the Church

- John fell out with Pope Innocent III on the appointment of a new archbishop of Canterbury.
- This led to John's excommunication, which actually helped him seize Church revenue.
- Reconciliation occurred when John made England a fief of the Papacy, which led to ecclesiastical support for John.

John's personality

- John could be petty and vindictive; there are many examples of his poor treatment of allies and enemies.
- John's harsh treatment of prisoners after the Battle of Mirabeau offended the sensibilities of many of his allies, particularly William de Roches of Anjou, who eventually sided with Philip of France.
- There is debate over what John did with his nephew Arthur, though most think John murdered him.

Any other relevant factors.

18 How important was the growth of towns as a reason for the decline of feudal society? (20)

Context: Feudalism flourished between the eleventh and thirteenth centuries, but began to decline towards the close of the thirteenth century, ultimately disappearing by 1500AD.

The growth of towns

- Towns offered greater opportunities for serfs in terms of jobs as freemen.
- The development of merchants and a middle class which paid tax reduced the King's reliance on feudal dues.
- The growth of towns led to the development of a market economy and the transition from a barter- to a money-based economy.

Other factors

Changing social attitudes

- Social mobility was increasing for several reasons, including the move to an economy based more on cash than service.
- In England, the wars against France brought riches to some, and enabled them to climb the social ladder.

The Black Death

- The Black Death reduced the population of England by roughly a third. Those peasants that survived saw their labour become a valuable commodity. Wage levels in England approximately doubled.
- Unable to find enough labour to work their demesne, lords found it more profitable to lease out the land. With smaller areas to farm, the lords had less need for the labour services provided by the serfs. Lords started to 'commute' these labour services. This meant that in return for a cash payment, peasants no longer had to work on the lord's demesne.

The Peasants' Revolt

- In England, the attempts of the Statute of the Labourers in 1351 to force peasants back into serfdom were widely and strongly resisted.
- Although the Revolt was defeated, its extent showed that the old feudal consensus had broken down.
- After the Peasants' Revolt, the lords found it very difficult to retain the feudal system.

The growth of trade/mercantilism

- One effect of the Crusades was to encourage trade between the West and cities like Constantinople and Alexandria.
- Some lords realised that trade in wool was more profitable than relying on peasants. They diversified the use of their land as a result.

Any other relevant factors.

Part B – The Century of Revolutions, 1603–1702

19 *Religious issues were the main reason for the outbreak of civil war in England.*

How valid is this view? (20)

Context: Charles I was the son of James I. He believed in the divine right of kings and this led to confrontation over matters such as his perceived lack of support for Reformed Protestantism and his power over parliament. However, other issues also contributed to the outbreak of civil war.

Religious matters

- England was a predominantly Protestant country with a significant number of Puritans. Puritans were well represented in parliament.
- It was felt that Charles favoured Catholicism, as his marriage to the French Catholic Henrietta Maria and her observance of mass seemed to confirm.
- Charles' Bishop of Canterbury, Archbishop William Laud, was widely considered to be a crypto-Catholic.
- Charles' support for high church bishops and Anglican practices led to suspicion and conflict with English Puritans and Scottish Covenanters.

Other factors

Character of Charles I

- In his youth, Charles suffered from poor health and a lack of parental affection. He had a fierce temper.
- Charles acceded to the throne in 1625 and, in many ways, cut a regal figure.
- His strong beliefs over his role as king, religion and the role of parliament brought him into conflict with parliament.
- There is debate about the extent to which he was dominated by favourites like Buckingham and his wife Henrietta.
- Charles tended to surround himself with people who agreed with him. This led to a lack of awareness and alienation from the developing opposition to his rule.

Economic issues

- Charles' desire to be financially independent of parliament led to conflict as he used a variety of methods to raise revenue.
- During the 1630s, Charles continued to collect tonnage and poundage, impositions and, in addition, revived ancient royal levies. All these violated the principle of no taxation without consent.
- An ancient custom, not enforced for 100 years, required that all men with landed income worth more than £40 p.a. should present themselves for knighthood at the King's coronation. In 1630, Charles fined those who failed to do so. This 'Distraint of Knighthood' was based on an Act of 1278.
- He levied fines for those encroaching on royal forests.

Political issues

- Charles sought to rule without parliament; from 1629 to 1640 he did so during the Eleven Years' Tyranny.
- Charles came into conflict with parliament as he did not really listen to them and did what he wished.

- His reliance on ministers, such as the Duke of Buckingham and the Earl of Stafford, reinforced his desire to rule in an absolute manner.
- Parliament sought to re-establish its authority on being recalled in 1640. This led to confrontation and the eventual Civil War.

Legal issues

- Charles used courts to enforce royal policy. This extended to the use of courts by his ministers to favour the government of Charles.

Legacy of James I

- It can be argued that Charles' belief in the divine right of kings and religion was a continuation of policy started under his father.

Scottish issues

- There was fierce opposition to the imposition of Laud's prayer book in Presbyterian Scotland. This led to the National Covenant and subsequent military failure in the Bishops' Wars, which further weakened Charles' authority.

Any other relevant factors.

20 How important was the role of parliament as a reason for the Revolution Settlement of 1688–1689? (20)

Context: Monarchy was restored in 1660. By 1688 the increasingly absolute rule of James II, among other factors, led parliament to ask his Protestant daughter, Mary, and her husband, William of Orange, to become joint monarchs.

The role of parliament

- Parliament resented James II's abuses of power but took comfort from the thought that he would be succeeded by his Protestant daughter Mary, but when James's wife gave birth to a Catholic son, parliament acted.
- Parliament wrote to Mary, by now married to the Dutch Prince William of Orange, offering her the Crown.
- In March 1689, parliament drew up a Declaration of Right, which legalised a new relationship between Crown and parliament in matters such as finance, law, the succession and religion. William and Mary agreed to this.

Political issues

- There was political conflict between parliament and both James and Charles during their reigns.
- Both rulers were frequently accused of misusing royal privilege. For example, James II's use of the Suspending and Dispensing Powers in 1687.
- Both kings supported the divine right of kings and had absolutist tendencies, ruling on their own without parliament.

Other factors

Charles II

- Charles theoretically agreed limitations on his power but, in reality, he was able to get round any restrictions.
- Charles was suspected of being sympathetic to Catholicism, which alarmed many MPs and subjects.
- Charles ruled alone for four years, dissolving parliament in March 1681 and ignoring the Triennial Act in 1684.
- In 1683, he imposed a new Charter for the City of London which said that all appointments to civil office, including Lord Mayor, should be subject to royal approval.

Religious issues

- The Declarations of Indulgence, 1687 and 1688, were two proclamations issued by the King, which gave greater religious freedom to those who did not conform to Anglicanism. It was feared that this was to encourage Catholicism and was opposed by many Anglicans. Presbyterians were suspicious of this.
- Charles declared himself to be a Catholic on his deathbed and had had a controversial religious policy during his life. He allied with his cousin, the Catholic King of France, during the Third Dutch War, for example.
- Charles was succeeded by his brother, James II, who was Catholic. James promoted Roman Catholics to key posts in government and the army.
- The birth of a Catholic heir for James directly precipitated the Protestant political elite of England to approach James's daughter, Mary, and her husband, William of Orange, who were Protestants, to be joint monarchs instead of James.

James II

- The leading Protestant nobility of England suspected James of trying to form an absolute government in England. He dismissed parliament.
- On his succession to the throne, James was faced by rebellion from Argyll and Monmouth. James increased his army's size as a result, which increased suspicion in England.
- James used his dispensing power to allow Roman Catholics to command several regiments without having to take the oath required by the Test Act; this further increased suspicion.

- James suspended laws against Roman Catholics and promoted Catholics to important positions, such as Sir Roger Strickland to be Admiral of the Royal Navy.

Any other relevant factors.

21 To what extent were the changes brought about by the Revolution Settlement, 1688–1702, significant? (20)

Context: A series of agreements made between 1689 and 1701 legalised the division of power between parliament and the Crown, and became known as the Revolution Settlement. This included the Bill of Rights, limiting the power of the monarch.

Religion

- The Toleration Act of 1689 provided for free public worship for all except Roman Catholics and Unitarians.
- Roman Catholics were still ineligible for elected posts in towns or parliament.
- Parliament now held more sway in religious matters, although the monarch still enjoyed the political advantages of being Head of the Church.

Finance

- It was impossible for the monarchy to exist financially independent of parliament.
- From 1689, parliament voted to give the Crown money as part of the Civil List system.

Legislation

- The legal settlement established parliamentary control over the legal system and courts.
- Judges could only be removed from their positions if parliament demanded this.
- Parliament now enforced its own control over judicial procedure. However, monarchs could still appoint judges who might be favourable to them.

Parliament

- The Triennial Act in 1694 was intended to keep MPs more closely in touch with public opinion.
- The Licensing Act was repealed in 1695, removing restrictions on the freedom of the press to report parliamentary criticism of the Crown.
- William and Mary had to agree to the Bill of Rights before they were given the throne, legalising the new relationship between Crown and parliament.

The succession

- The Bill of Rights declared that no Roman Catholic could become king or queen.
- Later, the Act of Settlement of 1701 stated that all future monarchs should be members of the Church of England.
- Parliament now governed the question of who ascended the throne.

Scotland

- The Claim of Right asserted that power flowed upwards from the people.
- The Settlement confirmed the position of the Kirk in Scotland as the Presbyterian Church.

The status of the army

- The Revolution Settlement meant that parliament gained partial control of the army. The monarch was not given enough money to maintain a standing army.
- Royal authority over military matters had now passed to the House of Commons.

Loopholes in the Settlement

- The monarch still held executive power and controlled foreign policy, declaring war and signing treaties. The monarch was still the source of patronage in the army and navy.
- The monarch still created peers, and could therefore control the House of Lords.

Any other relevant factors.

Part C – The Atlantic Slave Trade

22 *Financial considerations were the most important factor governing relations between slaves and their owners.*

How valid is this view? (20)

Context: As the Atlantic slave trade grew and became ever more profitable, the justifications for maintaining the trade became ever more self-interested, with an increased emphasis on defending the financial concerns of merchants.

Financial considerations

- The debate over conditions on board ship for transporting slaves, that is 'tight pack' or 'loose pack', was not based on humanitarian concerns, but what was the most effective way to successfully transport the most slaves to auction in the West Indies in order to make the biggest profit.
- The motivation of most people in the slave trade was financial; it was the quickest way to make big profits.
- There were many absentee plantation owners in the British Caribbean islands, which meant estates were managed by overseers. Their primary concern was often to amass as much profit as possible so they too could become property owners. As a result, the treatment of slaves was harsh.
- Although slaves were valuable as property, their replacement cost was not prohibitive. This meant slaves were cheap enough to be treated badly or worked to death. Slave owners referred to the human cost as 'wastage'.
- The health risks associated with long stays in the West Indies were well known: tropical diseases. White plantation owners sought to keep their stay on the islands as short as possible in order to minimise these risks and return to Britain to enjoy their money.

Other factors

Racism and prejudice

- There was widespread ignorance of African society and culture and a general assumption that if African societies were organised differently from European ones, they were inferior.
- There was virtually no awareness of Africa's rich history and an assumption that Africans were primitive in comparison to Europeans, which meant that Europeans widely assumed they were bringing enlightenment to the 'dark continent' through effective government.
- Africans were not regarded by Europeans as fellow human beings owing to the colour of their skin. This was used as an excuse for extreme brutality.
- A strong pro-slavery West Indies lobby produced books and newspaper articles justifying the slave trade from racial stereotypes.

Fear of revolt

- White owners and overseers were heavily outnumbered by black people. There was a constant fear of slave revolt both on ships and on plantations. The need for security of the ship's crew meant that slaves were kept under deck for long periods of time and usually shackled for the whole passage.
- Well-publicised revolts in islands like Haiti (Saint-Domingue), Antigua and Jamaica fuelled fear of rebellion.
- Day-to-day life on plantations was dominated by vigilance over the possibility of rebellion. Even minor 'offences' were harshly punished by draconian legal codes.

Humanitarian concerns

- Conditions varied on West Indian plantations. Where a planter's family lived with him, often small communities developed, with affectionate relationships between slaves and the free population. However, there was often little moderation of the realities of slavery.
- In Africa and on board ship, there was little personal contact between slaves and sailors. Slaves were treated as cargo, with little concern other than to keep them alive.

Religious concerns

- The existence of slavery in the Bible was used as a justification for the slave trade by traders and owners.
- Many prominent church goers were slave owners or traders. Their social status meant religious arguments were used to give slave trading respectability.
- Participants in the slave trade claimed that slaves were being exposed to the 'civilising influence' of Christianity. They also argued that slavery benefited slaves because through Christianity they had the chance to get salvation before God.
- The religious faith of some participants moderated their treatment of slaves.

Any other relevant factors.

23 How important was the slave rebellion in Saint-Domingue as an obstacle to abolition? (20)

Context: The early progress of the abolitionist campaign was slow owing to a range of vested interests. Fear of rebellion and loss of control in the event of emancipation helped ensure that there was also popular opposition to abolition.

Slave rebellion in Saint-Domingue

- Pro-slavery groups pointed to this rebellion as an example of what would happen if slaves were freed. The revolt began in 1791 and continued until 1804. An independent country, calling itself Haiti, was set up under the leadership of Toussaint L'Ouverture. It is estimated that as many as 200,000 people died due to this rebellion. The general fear of slave revolt was increased as a result.

- Unsuccessful attempts by colonial French troops to regain control of Haiti shocked the British Government. There were fears that the rebellion could spread to neighbouring British islands such as Jamaica. Any attempts to abolish the slave trade were banned because it was claimed that the West Indies could become unsafe and unstable.
- The British were humiliated when their attempts to regain control of Haiti were also unsuccessful.
- However, attitudes changed after the French Revolution when the Revolutionary Government attempted to regain control; once war was declared between Britain and France it was seen as a way of striking at the French.

Other factors

The power of vested interests

- Merchants from London, Liverpool and Bristol ensured that their MPs influenced successive governments to help maintain/protect the slave trade. They either bought votes or put pressure on others.
- The nature of politics at this time meant that there weren't distinct political parties but various interest groups. The House of Commons was dominated by the West India lobby, which for a long time was the most powerful. The Duke of Clarence, one of George III's sons, was a member of the West India interest group.
- Governments were often coalitions of different interest groups, often pro slavery. This ensured that opposition to the slave trade did not gather government support.
- Many absentee plantation owners or merchants held high political office or were MPs themselves. For example, William Beckford, owner of an estate in Jamaica, was twice Mayor of London. In the later eighteenth century, over 50 MPs represented the slave plantations.
- MPs who supported the slave trade vigorously opposed attempts to introduce laws banning the trade. They made powerful speeches arguing that the livelihoods of thousands of British people and the millions made by the slave trade necessitated its continuation.
- MPs used delaying tactics to slow down or prevent legislation to abolish slavery. For example, Henry Dundas, the unofficial 'King of Scotland', Secretary of State for War and First Lord of the Admiralty used his position to protect the interests of slave owners and merchants. In 1792, he effectively 'killed' Wilberforce's Bill banning of the slave trade by proposing a compromise that any abolition would take place over several years, which Dundas knew Wilberforce could not accept.
- Slave merchants would exert direct pressure on the government, for example, in 1775, a petition was sent from Bristol urging support for the slave trade.

The effect of the French Revolution

- Sympathy for the French Revolution disappeared with the execution of Louis XVI. Wealthy people reacted with horror to the idea that similar society upheaval could happen in Britain. Many wealthy people associated abolitionism with the dangerous radicalism in France.
- The abolitionist cause was associated with revolutionary ideas; for example, Clarkson openly supported the French Revolution.
- General fears about law and order led to laws limiting the right of assembly and protest. Even abolition campaigners like William Wilberforce supported these laws. The laws limited the growth of abolition societies.
- After Napoleon came to power in France, Britain became involved in the French Revolutionary Wars, leading to a decrease in support for abolition.
- Supporters of the slave trade argued that it was necessary to pay for Britain's involvement in the French Revolutionary Wars; it seemed unpatriotic not to support the slave trade.
- Radicals used similar tactics as abolitionists to win public support – associations, petitions, cheap publications, public lectures, public meetings, pressure on parliament, etc. This linked abolitionism with political radicalism in people's minds, which during the French Revolutionary Wars, they felt pressure to oppose.

Importance of the trade to the British economy

- The slave trade generated money – West Indian colonies were an important source of valuable exports to European neighbours.
- British people had become addicted to cheaper sugar and tobacco from the plantations and British cotton mills depended on the cotton crops raised by slaves.
- British shipbuilding benefited from the slave trade, as did associated industries.
- British industry received a boost from trading with Africa.
- Alternative funds would have to be raised in order to compensate for the loss of trade and revenue; taxes would have to be raised to compensate for the loss of trade and revenue.
- Britain's finance and insurance industry prospered on the back of the slave trade. Many individual fortunes were made.
- Abolition would help foreign rivals such as France as other nations would fill the gap left by Britain.

Fears over national security

- Abolition would decrease the number of jobs for sailors and the maritime industry – and so reduce the number of experienced sailors for the Royal Navy. Pro-slavery campaigners pointed out that Britain's global dominance was based on the strength of its navy; there was a possibility that Britain would lose its advantage over rivals.

Anti-abolition propaganda

- Lobbyists like the East Indies group conducted a powerful propaganda campaign to counter that of the abolitionists, producing countless letters and articles for newspapers.
- Pro-slavery campaigners produced books and plays supporting the slave trade. For example, in 1785, William Beckford wrote a book *Remarks Upon the Situation of Negroes in Jamaica*; Thomas Bellamy wrote a play in 1788 called *The Benevolent Planters*, telling the story of black slaves separated in Africa, but reunited by their owners.
- Slave owners and their supporters argued that the abolition of the slave trade was not legal because it would undermine a central tenet of British law: the right to private property. They successfully discouraged the Government from contemplating abolition without compensation because of the massive legal battle that would ensue.

Attitude of British governments

- Successive governments were more concerned with maintaining revenue and the rights of property of their wealthiest citizens rather than the rights of black slaves who had no political stake or influence in Britain.

Any other relevant factors.

24 To what extent was the effect of slave resistance the main reason for the success of the abolitionist campaign in 1807? (20)

Context: At the end of the eighteenth century, even as slave owning remained profitable, there were growing demands for the abolition of the trade and slavery itself.

Effect of slave resistance

- Successful slave rebellions like in Saint-Domingue (Haiti) increased the general fear of slave revolts.
- Abolition of the slave trade would mean slave conditions would have to improve because slaves would become more valuable. There were concerns that unless conditions improved, more slave revolts would follow.
- In Jamaica a substantial number of runaways lived in the mountains, outside the control of the authorities. Successive attempts to bring them under control had failed, which made it harder to maintain slavery without changes.

Other factors

Decline in economic importance of slavery

- As a result of the war with France, the slave trade declined by two-thirds.
- The industrial revolution had increased the importance of manufactured British goods and agriculture; Britain became less dependent on trading foreign goods.
- The slave trade became less important in economic terms – there was less demand for large numbers of slaves to be imported to the British colonies.
- There was a worldwide over-supply of sugar and British merchants had difficulties re-exporting it.
- There was growing competition from parts of the Empire like India, where crops like sugar were being produced on a bigger scale and more cheaply.

Military factors

- The abolition of the slave trade would undermine Napoleon's effort to restore French control in the Caribbean; the abolition campaign helped British interests.
- The 1805 Act banning any slave trade between British merchants and foreign colonies was aimed at attacking French interests by limiting their ability to engage in a lucrative trade.

Religious revival

- The religious revival of the late eighteenth century was at the heart of the anti-slavery movement. Many of the early leaders came from non-Conformist Churches such as Quakers and Methodists or Presbyterians and Baptists.
- Methodist leaders like John Wesley had criticised slavery, influencing abolitionists like John Newton.
- Early Quaker leaders translated their religious belief in the equality of all men before God into general humanitarian concerns. The Quakers were hugely important to the Society for the Abolition of the Slave Trade; nine of its original members were Quakers.
- In the eighteenth century, there was a religious revival that led to a rise in a fervent kind of Christianity: Evangelical Christianity. Evangelicals were concerned with morality and the impact of sin in causing mankind to fall out of God's favour.

Evangelical Christians were especially important in the abolition movement, for example William Wilberforce, Thomas Clarkson and Granville Sharp.

- Some Quakers had close links with the slave trade through banking and finance, for example Barclays Bank and Barings Bank.

- The Church of England had links to the slave trade through missionary organisations like the United Society for the Propagation of the Gospel (USPG), which owned slave plantations in Barbados.

Campaign of the Anti-Slavery Society

- Thomas Clarkson toured ports and cities connected with the slave trade to obtain witnesses for the parliamentary investigations of the slave trade which provided Wilberforce with convincing evidence for his speeches.

- The society published books and pamphlets, for example eyewitness accounts from former slaves such as Olaudah Equiano.

- The Anti-Slavery Society ran campaigns to boycott goods produced by slaves in the West Indies such as sugar and rum and supported the selling of products like sugar which had not been produced by slave labour.

- Public meetings and lecture tours involving those with experience of the slave trade, for example John Newton, were held and churches and theatres were used for abolitionist propaganda.

- The Anti-Slavery Society organised petitions and subscription lists supporting the abolition of slavery. Also, artefacts and illustrations with anti-slavery messages were produced, for example Wedgwood pottery.

- Members lobbied MPs to get promises that they would oppose the slave trade in parliamentary debates.

- Effective moderate political and religious leadership among the abolitionists influenced major figures such as Pitt and Fox to support their cause; abolitionists gave evidence to parliamentary commissions.

Role of Wilberforce

- Wilberforce spent eighteen years putting forward the arguments of the Society for the Abolition of the Slave Trade in parliament.

- Wilberforce's speeches in parliament were effective in drawing attention to the cause.

- Wilberforce's Christian faith had led him to become interested in social reform. He linked the need to reform factory conditions in Britain with the need to abolish slavery and the slave trade within the British Empire.

- Wilberforce collaborated with other abolitionists to achieve his aims, including the Quakers, Thomas Clarkson and Olaudah Equiano.

Any other reasonable factors.

Part D – Britain, 1851–1951

25 *Changing attitudes to women did more than any other reason to achieve votes for some women in 1918.*

How valid is this view? (20)

Context: Like men, women's social and economic status was changed by the industrial revolution. This led to changing attitudes which increased demands for political rights, but progress for many women was frustratingly slow.

Changing attitudes to women in society

- By 1868, women had advanced their legal status significantly; they could, in theory, divorce their husbands and keep custody of their children after divorce. They had also won the right to keep legal title over their property after marriage.

- By the beginning of the twentieth century, women had won the right to stand and take part in local elections, for example Poor Law Guardians and local council elections. Winning the vote in national elections was the next logical step.

- Millicent Fawcett, a leader of the NUWSS, argued that wider social changes were vital factors in the winning of the right to vote.

Other factors

Militant Suffragette campaign up to 1914

- Emmeline Pankhurst formed the Women's Social and Political Union (WSPU) in 1903. The WSPU adopted the motto 'Deeds Not Words'.

- The new strategy gained publicity. Newspapers immediately took notice, which meant the Suffragettes had achieved their first aim – to make votes for women an issue that couldn't be ignored.

- Violent protest escalated from 1907 and especially after 1911, for example the window smashing campaign and arson attacks.
  The Suffragettes aimed to put pressure on the government by provoking insurance companies.

- The prisons filled with Suffragettes, whom the government refused to treat like political prisoners.

- In retaliation, the women used starvation as a political weapon to embarrass the government. The government reacted by introducing the Prisoner's Temporary Discharge for Ill Health Act (the Cat and Mouse Act).

- Suffragettes divided public opinion for and against. On the one hand, it is unlikely the Liberal government would have looked at the issue of votes for women before the First World War without the Suffragettes. On the other, the militant campaign provided an excellent example for those who argued that women could not be trusted with the vote.

The women's suffrage campaign

- The National Union of Women's Suffrage Societies (NUWSS) believed in moderate, 'peaceful' tactics to win the vote, such as meetings, pamphlets, petitions and parliamentary bills.

- The largely middle-class members of the NUWSS made good use of family and social connections to lobby for their campaign.

- Membership remained relatively low at about 6,000 until around 1909 but grew to 53,000 by 1914 as women, angered by the Suffragettes, distanced themselves from their campaign.

Part played by women in the war effort

- At the outbreak of war, the suffrage organisations suspended their campaign for the vote. A WSPU pro-war propaganda campaign, funded by the government, encouraged men to join the armed forces and women to demand 'the right to serve'. This helped balance the negative publicity from the WSPU campaign and convinced public opinion that women were 'doing their bit'.

- Women's war work was important to Britain's eventual victory. Over 700,000 women were employed in the vital role of making munitions.

- The creation of a wartime coalition after 1916 made it more likely for change to happen; no one party could claim the credit.

- Politicians were anxious to enfranchise more men who had been conscripted to fight, but who were not eligible to vote. Women could be 'added on' to legislation that was happening anyway.

- Debates over the significance of the war in giving women the vote continue, however; those enfranchised were not the women who had worked long hours and risked their health and lives in the munitions factories.

- The war certainly acted as a catalyst but significant progress had been made towards female franchise before it started.

Example of other countries

- Women were already able to vote in other countries such as New Zealand, and in some American states. It made Britain look less progressive in comparison if former parts of the Empire had achieved votes for women before the 'mother democracy'.

Any other relevant factors.

26 To what extent were the social reforms of the Liberal Government effective in solving the main causes of poverty? (20)

Context: Thanks to social investigators, the main causes of poverty had been clearly identified by 1906. There were demands for government action to deal with these as the scale of social issues had grown too large for local action to cope with.

The young

- The Provision of School Meals Act, 1906, allowed local authorities to raise money to pay for school meals but did not force local authorities to provide school meals.

- After 1907, medical inspections for children were made compulsory but no treatment of the illnesses or infections found was provided until 1911.

- The Children's Charter of 1908 banned children under sixteen from smoking, drinking alcohol or begging. Special courts were set up for children accused of committing crimes. Young offenders' prisons – borstals – were set up for children convicted of breaking the law. Probation officers were employed to help former offenders in an attempt to avoid re-offending.

- It took some time to implement the Children's Charter reforms; it is debatable how much impact the reforms had on many children.

The old

- Rowntree had identified old age as the time when most people dropped unavoidably below his poverty line.

- The Old Age Pensions Act (1908) gave people over 70 up to 5 shillings a week. Once a person over 70 had income above 12 shillings a week, their entitlement to a pension stopped. Married couples were given 7 shillings and 6 pence.

- The level of benefits was low. Few elderly poor lived until their seventieth birthday. Many of the old were excluded from claiming pensions because they failed to meet the qualification rules.

The sick

- Illness was identified by Booth and Rowntree as a major cause and consequence of poverty.

- The National Insurance Scheme of 1911 applied to workers earning less than £160 a year. Each insured worker got 9 pence in benefits from an outlay of 4 pence – 'ninepence for fourpence'.

- Only the insured worker got free medical treatment from a doctor. Other family members did not benefit from the scheme. The weekly contribution was in effect a wage cut which may have made poverty worse in many families.

The unemployed

- Unemployment or irregular work was a major cause of poverty.

- The National Insurance Act (Part 2) only covered unemployment for some workers in some industries and, like Part 1 of the Act, required contributions from workers, employers and the government.

- For most workers, no unemployment insurance scheme existed.

Other reforms

- The 1906 Workman's Compensation Act covered 6 million workers who could now claim compensation for injuries and diseases which were the result of their working conditions.

- In 1909, the Trade Boards Act tried to protect workers in the sweated trades, like tailoring and lace making, by setting up trade boards to fix minimum wages.

- In 1908, the Mines Act and the Shop Act improved conditions by limiting working hours and allowing time off.

- In 1911, parliament broke the power of the unelected House of Lords, stopping them from vetoing finance bills and giving them power only to delay legislation from the elected House of Commons. Not only did this improve democracy, it gave future governments the ability to raise the money as well as the power to enact more social legislation.

Any other relevant factors.

27 To what extent were the Labour social welfare reforms, 1945–1951, successful in creating a welfare state 'from the cradle to the grave'? (20)

Context: The 1942 Beveridge Report was instantly popular on its publication. It identified key social problems and proposed solutions which seemed to offer meaning and hope in the fight against the Nazis during the Second World War.

The aims of the Welfare State

- The 1942 Beveridge Report identified the five 'Giants' of poverty: Ignorance, Idleness, Squalor, Disease and Want.

- Beveridge offered a vision of Britain's future offering help to all, 'from the cradle to the grave'.

- The Labour government also nationalised 20 per cent of industry – the railways, mines, gas and electricity. The government directly employed people in growth industries where success was measured by the amount of work done and people employed, not productivity.

Ignorance

- Reform was started by the wartime coalition government led by Churchill. The 1944 Education Act raised the school leaving age to fifteen. Wider measures to improve learning were implemented, with public health measures such as the introduction of school milk, etc.

- Labour introduced a two-tier secondary schooling whereby pupils were split at the age of eleven (twelve in Scotland) depending on their ability. The more academic pupils who passed the 'eleven-plus exam went to grammar schools (senior secondaries in Scotland) and the rest to secondary moderns.

- Those who went to grammar schools were expected to stay on past the age of fifteen and this created a group of people who would take senior jobs in industry, while those in the secondary moderns would leave, taking practical jobs, thus solving the skills shortages in the country.

- In theory, children of all backgrounds could get equal opportunities in life. In practice, the system created a bigger division between the poor and the rich because children from better off backgrounds got more help and support in passing the exam to get to grammar school. In many cases, the existing inequalities between the classes were increased rather than reduced.

- Labour kept to their promise of extending the school-leaving age, despite severe economic problems and pressure to postpone the measure.

- Labour expanded university education through the introduction of grants so all could attend in theory.

Idleness

- The need to rebuild Britain after the war meant unemployment was basically non-existent, so the government had little to do to tackle idleness.

- Expansion of university education after the war led to a 60 per cent increase in student numbers between 1945 and 1951. This provided more skilled workers and allowed people from less advantaged backgrounds to pursue a higher education, helping to keep unemployment down.

- The Labour government also nationalised 20 per cent of industry – the railways, mines, gas and electricity. The government directly employed people in growth industries where success was measured by the amount of work done and people employed, not by productivity.

Squalor

- There was a great shortage of housing as the war had destroyed and damaged thousands of homes. The housing shortage was compounded by limited attempts to improve housing in the inter-war period; most house building had been for private owners and little had been done about slum housing.

- The job of tackling the housing shortage was given to Bevan's Ministry of Health, which was already overstretched setting up the new Health Service.

- Labour's target for housing was to build 200,000 new homes a year. 157,000 pre-fabricated homes were built to a good standard, but the full target was never met.

- Bevan encouraged the building of council houses rather than privately funded construction.

- The New Towns Act of 1946 aimed to target overcrowding in the increasingly built-up older cities. By 1950, the government had designed twelve new communities.

- The Town and Country Planning Act attempted to get rid of slums by providing local communities with more power for building developments and new housing.

- However, by 1951 there was still a huge shortfall in British housing.

Disease

- The National Health Service (NHS) was set up in 1948 and was the first comprehensive universal system of health care in Britain.

- The NHS dealt effectively with the spread of disease. Some of Britain's most harmful diseases were almost wiped out by the NHS's programme of vaccinations.

- The NHS also offered childcare, the introduction of prescriptions, health visiting and provision for the elderly. Treatment was free at the point of need, which meant people did not have to pay to get medical help.

- The NHS was almost too successful. The demand from the public was overwhelming; the estimated number of patients treated by the NHS almost doubled. Costs could no longer be funded out of general taxations, so prescription charges were introduced by 1951.

Want

- The 1946 National Insurance Act provided comprehensive insurance to give sickness and unemployment benefits and covered for most eventualities. It was said to support people from the 'cradle to the grave' which meant people had protection against falling into poverty throughout their lives. This was very effective as it meant that if the breadwinner of the family was injured, their family was less likely to fall into poverty. However, a criticism of the Act was that the benefits were only granted to those who made 156 weekly contributions.

- The 1948 National Assistance Board was set up to provide help for those not covered by the National Insurance Act. This acted as a safety net to protect these people. However, many people still lived on incomes below subsistence level, showing the problem of want had not completely been resolved.

Any other relevant factors.

Part E – Britain and Ireland, 1900–1985

28 *The position of Unionists in the North was the most important obstacle to peace, up to the Anglo-Irish Treaty, 1918–1921.*

How valid is this view? (20)

Context: The First World War transformed the political situation in Ireland. The moderate Irish Parliamentary Party never survived the election of 1918 and radical Republicanism, in the form of Sinn Féin, emerged as the dominant political force. The Irish Unionist Alliance emerged as the main opposing political force in Ulster.

Position of Ulster Unionists in the north

- In the 1918 election, the Ulster Unionists became the second largest party in Ireland. By 1919, this organisation became the Ulster Unionist Party.

- The Unionists were closely allied with the Conservative Party and actively opposed Irish home rule. The Conservative party were the dominant political party in mainland Britain.

- Irish unionists had enthusiastically supported the British war effort and had paid a blood sacrifice on the battlefield, especially at the Somme.

- The Unionists expected this sacrifice to be honoured in any post-war Irish settlement.

Other factors

IRA tactics and policies

- The IRA evolved out of the Irish Volunteers. It fought a guerrilla campaign against the forces of the British government between 1919 and 1921.
- The IRA used ambush tactics as well as hitting remote RIC (Royal Irish Constabulary) barracks. They also assassinated British spies and intimidated local communities if they were not supporting the IRA.
- Militarily they were pressed badly by the British forces, but their success was in lasting so long and making parts of Ireland ungovernable, except by military means.

Legacy of the First World War – 1918 election

- The 1916 Easter Rising and the British government's reaction to it transformed politics in Ireland.
- People were disgusted by the treatment of the Easter Rising rebels and rejected the moderate policies of the Irish Parliamentary Party (Nationalists), instead turning to the more radical Sinn Féin.
- This transferred into a landslide election victory for Sinn Féin in the 1918 election. They won 73 seats. The Nationalists, in contrast, were reduced to just six seats.

Declaration of Independence and the establishment of the Dáil

- After the 1918 election, the Sinn Féin representatives refused to attend parliament in Westminster.
- Sinn Féin MPs met at Mansion House in Dublin and set up the Dáil Éireann (Assembly of Ireland).
- This was not recognised by the British, but the Irish set about creating a state building.
- The Dáil met with considerable success in this period, setting up rival legal systems and winning over the bulk of the Irish.
- The British administration in Ireland effectively collapsed.

Policies and actions of the British government

- To begin with, the British used force to impose their will.
- The British government used the vicious paramilitary Black and Tans to assist the Royal Irish Constabulary (RIC) during the Irish War of Independence. They did not endear the British to the Irish population owing to their drunken and indiscriminate behaviour. There were atrocities on both sides, for example the massacre at Croke Park after the murder of British intelligence officers and the sacking of Cork city.
- There were vicious reprisals on Irish communities.
- Some attempts were made by the British to impose martial law.

Any other relevant factors.

29 How important was the role of the IRA as a reason for the developing crisis in Northern Ireland by 1968? (20)

Context: By the 1960s, the issue of discrimination against the Catholic minority in Northern Ireland developed in political importance. The IRA emerged to defend Catholic communities.

Role of the IRA

- The IRA in the 1960s were heavily influenced by left-wing thinking. As such they developed a class-based political outlook.
- Before 1968, it had limited impact due to divisions over policies and priorities, and therefore there was little active engagement in defending Catholic communities.
- The organisation split in 1969 into the Official IRA and the Provisional IRA, which took a more active view of armed struggle and defence of Catholic areas against what they saw as the aggression of the British state.
- The Provisional IRA (PIRA) took an active role in protecting Catholic areas.

Other factors

The issue of civil rights

- The civil rights movement in Northern Ireland dates from the 1960s when there were moves to campaign against injustices and inequalities.
- The most important organisation established during this period was the Northern Irish Civil Rights Association (NICRA), established in 1967 to protest against discrimination in terms of voting rights, etc.
- NICRA initially used petitions and lobbying, but these were ineffectual.
- In 1968 there were civil rights marches by the NICRA from Coalisland to Dungannon, Londonderry (Derry) and Belfast.
- Marches were opposed by the Protestant dominated police and there were Protestant counter-demonstrations.

- Rioting took place during the Derry march.
- There were concessions from Prime Minister Terence O'Neill's government over housing and an appeal to be allowed time to deliver more civil rights.

The Unionist ascendancy in Northern Ireland and challenges to it

- Unionists dominated Northern Irish politics through the Ulster Unionist Party.
- Politics was dominated by issues like gerrymandering of constituencies to favour unionists. The right to vote in local elections was based on ratepayers who were more likely to be Unionists.
- The Unionist leader was Viscount Brookborough until 1963. The new Prime Minister after 1963, Terence O'Neill, was interested in building bridges with the nationalist community and with Eire but this was not popular with many unionists, such as the followers of Reverend Ian Paisley.
- O'Neill could not automatically count on support from the British government. The Labour party under Harold Wilson was in power and had links with the Northern Ireland Labour party.
- British developments such as the welfare state had implications as they allowed all sections of the Northern Irish community access to benefits and all levels of education. This had implications as to rights, etc.
- The emergence of the civil rights movement by 1968 saw more forceful political campaigns against inequality.

Economic issues

- There was Protestant domination of better jobs, such as in shipbuilding, government, etc. The decline of traditional industries in the 1960s had an effect, though government protected places like the Harland and Wolff shipyard.
- There were inequalities in terms of government investment between Catholic and Protestant neighbourhoods.
- Subsidies were given to Northern Irish landowners who were mainly Protestant.
- Attempts were made to reform the economy, but these were unsuccessful due to entrenched attitudes.

Cultural and political differences

- A strong Catholic sense of identity emerged, encouraged by the re-awakening of cultural interest and development of separate sporting culture, for example. Identity was strengthened through adversity.
- Catholic political representatives in parliament refused to recognise the partition of Ireland.
- On average, there were 10–12 Nationalists in the Northern Ireland Parliament compared to, on average, 40 Unionists. In Westminster, this was 10–12 Unionists to 2 Nationalists.
- There were splits in Unionism over O'Neill's attempts at compromise. Ultimately, this would lead to his resignation.
- There was violence in Derry when civil rights marchers were challenged by Unionists.

Any other relevant factors.

30 To what extent was the role of the Irish government the main obstacle to peace, 1968–1985? (20)

Context: Northern Irish politics became increasingly sectarian during this period. The developing trouble led to the deployment of British troops.

The role of the Irish government

- The Anglo-Irish Agreement of 1985 gave the Irish government a role in the governance of Northern Ireland for the first time. This led to improved co-operation between the British and Irish governments and paved the way for the Good Friday Agreement thirteen years later.

Other factors

The role of the British Army

- The British Army was initially deployed to improve security in Northern Ireland against a background of increasing communal violence.
- Aggressive tactics by the army led to disillusionment with them in the Catholic community.
- Examples of aggressive actions such as Bloody Sunday and the Fall Curfew encouraged support for the paramilitaries.

Economic differences

- Economic discrimination against the Catholic population existed for much of this period in terms of jobs, although this began to break down as the period went on, especially in the 1970s and beyond.
- Certain sectors favoured Protestants, such as engineering and shipbuilding.

Religious and communal differences

- Religious differences were significant as Northern Ireland was dominated by the Protestant majority, over its Catholic minority.
- Religious differences were enhanced by differing communal traditions as well as language and sporting differences.
- These differences were further compounded by political polarisation, frequently along religious lines: Catholic Sinn Féin and Protestant Ulster Unionist Party, for example.

Hardening attitudes

- Attitudes hardened from the late 1960s as intercommunal violence grew.
- Paramilitary groups formed to protect their own communities and attack their opponents.
- Paramilitary groups become more extreme with the emergence of the Provisional IRA, for example.
- There was loss of sympathy among some groups owing to the indiscriminate nature of the violence.

British government policies

- Government policy alienated many in Northern Ireland, especially in the Catholic community.
- Internment or detention without trial started in 1971 with little success.
- The number of violent deaths grew.

Direct rule

- Direct rule of Northern Ireland was imposed in 1972 after the British government decided to remove control of security from the Northern Irish government, which promptly resigned.

Any other relevant factors.

Section 3 – European and World

Part A – The Crusades, 1071–1204

31 How important was aid from Byzantium as a reason for the success of the First Crusade? (20)

Context: The First Crusade was a success due to a variety of reasons. It had been called to retake Jerusalem from the Muslims by Pope Urban II.

Aid from Byzantium

- The First Crusade had support from Byzantium in the form of guides and supplies. For example, as the Crusaders marched on through Anatolia, they were accompanied by some Byzantine troops under Tatikios.
- During the siege of Antioch in 1097–1098, the Byzantine navy helped keep the besieging army supplied with basic necessities.
- Alexius' army did not take part in the Crusade, but they did cause problems, diverting Muslim resources.

Other factors

The military power of the Crusader knights

- Muslim leaders underestimated both the intentions and power of the Christian knights.
- Previous Crusades were not as militarily experienced as the First Crusade.
- A fully trained and armed knight mounted on his war-horse was a formidable opponent for anyone, let alone the more lightly armoured Muslim warriors.
- Lengthy training meant that knights were skilled and aggressive in combat as well as disciplined when needed, for example at the Battle of Dorylaeum.
- Many Crusader knights had experience of fighting the Muslims already, for example Raymond of Toulouse who had fought in Spain.

Divisions among the Islamic states

- There were doctrinal splits in the Islamic world between Sunni and Shia. At the time of the First Crusade, Sunnis (Seljuk Turks) controlled Asia Minor and Syria, while Shia (Fatimids) controlled Egypt.
- Both sides would do deals with the Crusaders against what they saw as the greater enemy of their fellow Muslims.
- A unified Islamic response did not emerge. Divisions were even seen during battle, for example at Antioch in 1098.

The religious zeal of the Crusaders

- There was real belief that the Crusade was a result of God's will.
- While Raymond and the other leaders often quarrelled with each other over the leadership of the Crusade, The Papal Legate: Bishop Adhemar, was always recognised as the spiritual leader of the Crusade and was a crucial unifying force at times (before his death in 1098). He also led by example, for instance during the siege and Battle of Antioch.
- Religious belief was crucial at times for the success of the Crusade. For example, 'finding' the Holy Lance spurred the Crusaders on, as did the vision of Peter Desiderius urging the Crusaders to fast before the eventual taking of Jerusalem.

Misunderstanding of the Crusaders' intent

- The ideological nature of the Crusaders was not understood by the Muslim leaders. They saw the Crusade as a limited incursion, such as that practised by the Byzantines in Asia Minor. This undoubtedly helped the Crusaders as it contributed to the confused response of the Muslim leaders.

Any other relevant factors.

32 *Richard and Saladin were both great diplomatic and military leaders during the Third Crusade.*

How valid is this view? (20)

Context: The Third Crusade is famous due to the leadership of both sides: Richard I of England and Saladin, Sultan of Egypt and Syria. In practical terms, Jerusalem was not recovered, but the Crusaders fought well and concessions were gained from the Muslims.

Saladin's military strengths

- Saladin showed skill in counter-attack at Acre and Jaffa. His army destroyed the siege engines at Acre and swiftly moved to re-occupy Jaffa soon after his forces had been ejected.
- Counter-attack at the Battle of Arsuf saw many of the more enthusiastic Christian knights killed.

Saladin's military weaknesses

- Demands from his emirs meant it was difficult for Saladin to field a large army for any length of time.
- There was considerable criticism within the Muslim world that he was not able to drive the Crusaders into the sea.
- Militarily, the major actions were all defeats for Saladin, though the cohesion of his forces was maintained.

Richard's military strengths

- The two-year siege of Acre was ended swiftly after Richard's arrival. He gave greater purpose to the siege as well as bringing money and siege technology.
- Richard led from the front, and was also brutal, as seen by the massacre of Muslim prisoners taken at Acre.
- Richard's Crusaders showed skilled movement of troops in the Middle East from Acre to Jaffa. Military formations were skilfully placed and were supported by a fleet on their journey.
- The Battle of Arsuf saw the decisive defeat of Saladin's forces by Richard's army.
- Arsuf proved Richard's courage as a soldier and his skill as a commander.
- The taking of Jaffa and retaining it with a decisive amphibious attack showed Richard's military strengths.
- Richard realised that taking Jerusalem was not practical, though he did rebuild the fortress at Ascalon, threatening Saladin's communications with Egypt.
- Militarily, the Third Crusade transformed the chances of survival for the Crusader States.

Saladin's diplomatic strengths

- Saladin and Richard engaged in diplomacy throughout much of the Third Crusade.
- Saladin recognised the need to make a truce with Richard. In 1192, the Treaty of Jaffa was agreed which partitioned Palestine in return for a three-year truce.
- Saladin held together a large and diverse Muslim force.

Saladin's diplomatic weaknesses

- Saladin faced increasing discontent from his Muslim allies.
- He negotiated a truce over Jerusalem with Richard despite his strong position overall.

Richard's diplomatic strengths

- Richard began negotiations with Saladin, who sent his brother to meet with Richard after the taking of Jaffa.
- On 2 September 1192, following his defeat at Jaffa, Saladin was forced to finalise a treaty with Richard: Jerusalem would remain under Muslim control, unarmed Christian pilgrims and traders could visit the city.

Richard's diplomatic weaknesses

- Richard showed poor diplomacy with his allies, alienating Count Leopold of Austria, after Acre, and Philip of France, who left for home.
- He backed Guy de Lusignan as King of Jerusalem despite the fact Conrad Montferrat was more popular.

Any other relevant factors.

33 To what extent did the crusading ideal decline in the years up to the Fourth Crusade in 1204? (20)

Context: The Crusading movement was remarkably long lived historically. However, the movement had long been suspect in terms of the motives of some Crusaders. As time went on the Crusades became less successful.

The Fourth Crusade

- Instead of heading for the Holy Land as was originally intended, the Fourth Crusade ended up attacking Constantinople, the capital of the Byzantine Empire.
- Crusader leaders had been persuaded to help Alexios Angelos by diverting to Constantinople and placing his deposed father on the throne of Byzantium. The Crusaders would then continue to the Holy Land after picking up rewards.
- However, when payment was not made, the Crusaders and their Venetian allies attacked and plundered Constantinople. They set up a series of weak Latin kingdoms in parts of Byzantium in the aftermath of their successful attack.

Role of Venice

- Venice effectively managed to get the Fourth Crusade into debt by selling them huge amounts of equipment that they could not afford to pay for.
- The Doge of Venice proposed that the debt be paid off by the Crusaders attacking the city of Zara, a Christian city that had been Venice's, but was now controlled by the King of Hungary.

- The Venetians supplied the ships for the Fourth Crusade, but hoped to divert it to a more suitable target for their ambitions.
- Byzantium was a competitor for maritime trade in the Middle East.

Co-existence of Muslim and Crusading States

- The survival of the Crusader States, for up to 200 years in the case of the Kingdom of Jerusalem, shows that there must have been times of peace and co-existence between Muslims and Crusaders.
- Examples include the Treaty of Mutual Protection signed between King Alric of Jerusalem and the Emir of Damascus, prior to the Second Crusade.

The corruption of the crusading movement by the Church and nobles

- Popes were willing to use crusades against Christians, such as the Albegensian Crusade against the Cathar heretics of Languedoc (Toulouse and southern France) in 1209–1229.
- There are many examples of nobles using the Crusades for their own ends; for example, Bohemond and Baldwin in the First Crusade, and the hijacking of the Fourth Crusade.

Effects of trade

- Trade links directly into the Fourth Crusade and the influence of Venice in persuading the Crusaders to change their plans.
- Pisa and Genoa both had a lot of influence in events during the Third Crusade; they both used trade rights as a bargaining chip to get what they wanted.

Any other relevant factors.

Part B – The American Revolution, 1763–1787

34 To what extent did the views of George III represent British opinion towards the conflict in the colonies? (20)

Context: British opinion of the conflict in the colonies varied from support for the colonists' aims to outrage and opposition.

George III

- George wanted to see America pay for the protection Britain had provided during the Seven Years' War. He supported taxation of American products, such as tea, and the active application of the Navigation Acts.
- He introduced the Coercive Acts in response to events such as the Boston Tea Party, causing resentment.
- He was very interested in the American Wars, and intervened politically at home as well.

Edmund Burke

- Burke was a new MP in 1765. In general he was understanding of the colonists' motives and critical of British policy. For example, he spoke out against the Stamp Act. However, he did not wish the colonists to leave the British Empire.
- In 1769, he published a pamphlet that blamed the British government for creating policies that stirred the conflict.
- He understood the need for good relations with the Americans, but was criticised at home.

Thomas Paine

- Paine's pamphlets were widely read, but not necessarily supported. He attacked the monarchy and was something of a radical.
- Published in 1776, his highly popular (in America) 'Common Sense' was the first pamphlet to advocate American independence.
- His support for American independence put him at odds with prevailing thought in Britain.

Parliament

- Through the Proclamation Act in 1763, Stamp Act in 1765, Declaratory Act in 1766, Tea Act in 1773 and Coercive Acts in 1774, parliament enforced British authority over the colonies.
- The majority of lords and MPs endorsed the views of the King.
- Parliament used military enforcement as a tool to control America between 1763 and 1776.
- Prime ministers through this period supported active prosecution for the War against America.

Earl of Chatham

- William Pitt, Earl of Chatham, had effectively been Britain's leader during the Seven Years' War.
- He was sympathetic to the colonists and didn't like the Stamp Act, for example. He sought to find compromise with the Colonists.
- Pitt felt that Britain could not win once war broke out.

Differing British views of the situation in the colonies

- Lord Grenville, Prime Minister 1763–1765, represented the rights of British merchants and attempts to raise revenue in America.
- Lord Rockingham, Prime Minister 1765–1766, advocated British parliamentary sovereignty over America.
- The Duke of Grafton, Prime Minister 1768–1770, believed in the superiority of the British Parliament over America.
- Lord North, Prime Minster from 1770 until 1782, believed parliament should enforce British interests and supremacy in the colonies. He believed the war could be won.
- John Wilkes was elected as an MP in 1768, was a radical and spoke out against British policy on America.
- Businessmen favoured the Navigation Acts, but wanted the war to end as it disrupted trade.
- There was some sympathy for colonists in Scotland and Ireland in terms of resentment at the power of their bigger neighbour.

Any other relevant factors.

35 How important was British military inefficiency in explaining why the colonists won the American War of Independence? (20)

Context: The American War of Independence took place between 1776 and 1781, between Britain and its thirteen colonies of North America. There were a number of factors that contributed to the colonists' victory.

British military inefficiency

- Britain military forces struggled with by poor communication and operating at such a long distance from their political masters. It sometimes took months for troops to reach North America, and orders were often out of date because the military situation on the ground had changed by the time they arrived.
- There were many examples of poor military planning and operation. For example, General John Burgoyne's Saratoga campaign.
- There were practical logistical problems, for example British flints could fire only six rounds before requiring re-sharpening, while American flints could fire 60 rounds before re-sharpening.
- The British suffered from a manpower shortage and could not hold ground even if it had been won in battle.

Other factors

French entry into the war

- The French had been on the losing side in the Seven Years' War so looked for revenge on Britain during the American War of Independence by siding with the colonist rebels.
- The Franco-American Treaty was signed in 1778, recognising the United States.
- France provided valuable physical support in terms of material, troops and naval vessels.
- There was important French military contribution to the war, such as defeat of the British fleet at the Battle of Chesapeake and the supplying of siege equipment at Yorktown.

Washington's military capability

- George Washington had prestige, military experience, charisma and was known as a strong patriot when he became Commander-in-Chief of the Continental Army.
- He led, organised army training and found capable officers to lead them, for example General Daniel Morgan who had fought in the American–Indian wars.
- Washington had served with the British and was aware of their systems and procedures.
- He benefited from having a very motivated army.

Washington's leadership

- Washington was a respected businessman who had entered politics and served with distinction in the Seven Years' War.
- He was a popular choice as Commander-in-Chief of the Continental Army.
- He enthused his men, listened to advice and was able to ensure logistical support for them. He trusted the men that he found to lead the army and gave them the latitude to do what was necessary.

French contribution worldwide

- The French got into massive debt owing to their participation in the American War of Independence.
- French naval forces ensured that British naval units were spread thinly as they could not now be concentrated on America, for example action in the Indian Ocean.

- French navy made a significant contribution through action at the battles of Chesapeake Bay and Ushant.
- The French contribution encouraged others to join the war to get at the British, for example Holland and Spain.

Local knowledge

- The war was mostly fought on American soil, giving an immediate advantage to the American Continental Army.
- Most locals favoured the rebels and did not actively help the British, even burning their crops at times. The distance between Britain and the colonies already meant that supplies were slow in arriving at the front.

Any other relevant factors.

36 *The American Revolution made little political impact.*

How valid is this view? (20)

Context: The American Constitution was supposed to be the antidote to the tyranny that had passed for British rule of the Colonies. Its system of checks and balances was designed to ensure that no one part could dominate.

The experience of rule by Britain

- British rule seemed unfair to colonists as they were ruled by the King and parliament with no representation of their own and no way to influence decision making.
- There was a real fear of tyranny by monarchy, so the American system was designed to prevent this.

Significance of the Constitution

- The deliberate separation of Legislature, Executive and Judiciary was designed to create the checks and balances the system needed.
- The Bill of Rights established the rights for individuals in states within a federal union of all states. It set out clear lines of authority between federal government and individual states. This would avoid central government exerting a controlling power over people's lives.
- The Constitution was aimed at men and excluded women and slaves from notions of equality.

Executive: the role of President

- Executive power was vested in the elected President, and his Vice-President and Cabinet.
- The President acted as Head of State and Commander-in-Chief, but would have no vote in the law-making process, although he could suggest and veto legislation.
- Members of the Executive could be removed from office by the electorate or the other branches of government (impeachment) if it was felt they were not doing their job properly.

Legislature: Congress

- Legislative power lay in the hands of an elected Congress which was divided into two Houses, the Senate and the House of Representatives.
- Congress passed laws and raised taxes, as well as having responsibility for international trade, war and foreign relations.
- Congressional elections were held regularly to ensure that congressmen remained in touch with the people they served.

Judiciary: Supreme Court

- Judicial power was granted to the Supreme Court of the USA.
- The Supreme Court acted as the highest court of appeal in the country. It also debated the legality of new laws passed by Congress.
- Supreme Court judges were nominated by the President and their appointment was ratified by Congress after a rigorous checking process. Appointees to the Supreme Court could be removed from their position if they acted improperly.

Any other relevant factors.

Part C — The French Revolution, to 1799

37 How important was the character of Louis XVI as a reason for the failure of constitutional monarchy, 1789–1792? (20)

Context: In the aftermath of the 1789 Revolution, the monarchy clung to a limited amount of power. This was bitterly resented by Louis, who sought to overturn the Revolution.

Character of Louis XVI

- Louis was not good at making decisions and tended to appoint 'yes' men to important positions.

- He did not support reforming ministers when he had the chance.
- He was weak and indecisive.

Attitudes and actions of Louis XVI

- Louis disliked the idea of a constitutional monarchy and was obstructive, which made him even more unpopular.
- He had vetoed key Assembly demands such as decrees against 'refractory' priests and émigrés.
- His actions on attempting to flee the Revolution in the 1791 flight to Varennes confirmed his lack of loyalty to the new government. The fact he was fleeing to join émigré nobles was also not in his favour.
- Rumours of attempts to contact émigrés and the Austrian Emperor to overturn the Revolution seemed to be confirmed.

Other factors

Weaknesses in the constitution and the government

- Louis disliked the restrictions on his power.
- The Legislative Assembly members such as the Girondins and Jacobins disliked the way Louis used his veto to block legislation. Many members were increasingly radicalised.
- Political factionalism at Assembly level increased with many groups unhappy with the political settlement after 1789.

Financial problems

- The economy was in trouble before 1789 and did not improve with the Revolution.
- Inflation spiralled out of control.
- Increases in the price of basic food stuffs like bread made workers in urban areas restless.
- There was continued heavy taxation.

Foreign affairs and the outbreak of war

- The Holy Roman Emperor, Leopold, was the brother of Marie Antoinette and increasingly viewed events in France with concern.
- He, along with the Prussian king and French émigré nobles, announced the Declaration of Pillnitz, which stated that European leaders were concerned about the well-being of Louis and his family. This was viewed with alarm by the French government, who perceived it as a threat to French sovereignty.
- The Legislative Assembly with Louis' support declared war on Austria.
- The French invasion of the Austrian Netherlands was a shambles.
- A Prussian–Austrian army, under the Duke of Brunswick, invaded and issued the Brunswick Manifesto, declaring their intention to restore Louis to the throne.
- Louis' position was now fatally undermined in the eyes of the mob.
- Louis and his family fled the mob and he was arrested on 13 August 1792. The constitutional monarchy was at an end.

Any other relevant factors.

38 *Political instability was the most important reason for the establishment of the Consulate.*

How valid is this view? (20)

Context: Political chaos characterised the Revolution, with change from the monarchy to constitutional monarchy, to radical republican terror to the Directory and eventually to the Consulate and Napoleon. The reasons for the formation of the Consulate were many.

Political instability

- France had undergone a series of increasingly radical governments since the Revolution of 1789. People were tiring of the political uncertainty.
- Political factions in France viewed each other with suspicion.
- France suffered from the destruction of what had become a civil war.
- France was threatened with invasion by other European powers who did not want to see the Revolution spread to their countries.

Other factors

The role of Napoleon

- Napoleon was the hero of the Revolution in many people's eyes after successfully campaigning in northern Italy against the Austrians and in Egypt against the Mamluks.

- In fact, he left his troops in Egypt after the destruction of the French fleet by Nelson, but he did return to France in October.
- It was hoped that he could bring stability to France.
- Napoleon had political aims along with Sieyès.
- Napoleon had strong support in the military and led the coup against the Directory.

Army involvement in politics

- As the French army improved in performance it came to be used more within France. Bonaparte, for example, as a young artillery officer had been involved in the famous 'whiff of grapeshot' incidents to put down disturbances in Paris.
- Army success in the Revolutionary Wars, such as Napoleon's conquest of Italy, made generals into heroes.
- The Directory had been protected by the army from a Royalist insurrection in 1795.

The Constitution of 1795

- The Constitution of the Year III (1795) is the constitution that founded the Directory.
- The Constitution of 1795 was intended to found a republic with a franchise based on the payment of taxes; a bicameral legislature (Council of Ancients and a Council of 500) to slow down the legislative process; and a five-man Directory. It all aimed to provide a stable system that could not be dominated by one area.
- In reality the checks and balances in the Constitution slowed down decision making and made strong and decisive government difficult to achieve.

Role of Abbé Sieyès

- Sieyès was an important theorist of the French Revolution who had been involved from its beginning. He had wanted to set up a bourgeois constitutional monarchy and was no fan of the way the Revolution had radicalised.
- He became increasingly concerned to make France stable and thought he had found the right man to support him in Bonaparte. After the overthrow of the Director, he became Second Consul, but his planned constitution never came to fruition as Bonaparte imposed his own ideas.

Any other relevant factors.

39 *The peasantry was most affected by the French Revolution.*

How valid is this view? (20)

Context: The French Revolution made a huge impact on French society. It made profound changes to the way society was organised and had varying impacts on the various groups that made up society.

The peasantry

- The peasantry did make some gains due to the French Revolution.
- The ending of feudalism in August 1789 freed the peasants from the legal and financial burdens placed on it.
- The nationalisation of Church land as well as the transfer of land from the nobility and clergy to the peasantry was an advantage to peasants who could afford to buy the land.

Impact on other groups in French society

The urban workers

- The urban workers made up the feared Parisian mob, which roused itself at various times during the French Revolution. Examples include the storming of the Bastille and the march on Versailles, which had a huge symbolic and actual impact on the power of the monarchy.
- Longer term, although the Revolution enshrined certain rights, the urban workers were affected by military service, inflation and food shortages.
- Economically they gained little as trades unions were banned after the passing of the Chapelier Law in May 1791.

The bourgeoisie

- The bourgeoisie probably benefited the most from the French Revolution.
- Most of the political forms of the Revolution, starting with the Declaration of the Rights of Man, saw political power put into the hands of the bourgeoisie through this period. Most voting qualifications were based on property ownership, for example.
- Economically, they benefited from the ending of feudal practices as they could afford to exploit the new commercial opportunities that arose.
- Promotion based on ability benefited the educated middle classes.

The First Estate

- The Revolution had a huge negative impact on the better-off clergy as their economic rights and political status were lost.
- The Civil Constitution of the Clergy passed in July 1790 meant that the Church was now subordinate to the French Government.
- Earlier the Church had been stripped of its land holding and the tithe had been abolished.
- The monastic orders were devastated and the clergy became state employees.

The Second Estate

- Aristocratic tax and status privileges were removed by the Revolution.
- The ending of feudalism in August 1789 saw the status of the nobility in France collapse.
- In 1790, outward displays of 'nobility' such as titles and coats of arms were forbidden by law.
- In 1797, after election results suggested a pro-royalist re-emergence, the Convention imposed alien status on nobles and stripped them of their French citizenship.

Any other relevant factors.

Part D – Germany 1815–1939

40 *Austrian strength was the most important obstacle to German unification, 1815–1850.*

How valid is this view? (20)

Context: Although nationalism grew throughout the period there were powerful forces that opposed the integration of the Germanic states.

Austrian strength

- Throughout this period, Austria dominated 'Germany' politically.
- Austria was president of the Bund after the Congress of Vienna and this helped its leaders to oppose nationalism and promote the interests of the individual German states.
- There was active opposition to nationalism, through censorship and repression, as it threatened the multi-national Austrian Empire. Examples include the Karlsbad Decrees and Six Articles.
- In fact, the military power of Austria was waning, but could still be potent, as seen by their actions in Italy in the 1848 revolutions.
- The Treaty of Olmütz, 1850, signalled the political triumph of Austria over Prussia. In the short term, nationalism had been contained.

Other factors

Resentment towards Prussia

- The economic dominance of Prussia across Germany was supported in the sense that German states joined the Zollverein, but there was resentment of that power as seen by their behaviour in the Bund, where smaller states tended to side with Austria.
- Austria resented their rejection from the Zollverein and the failure of their own customs union.
- The growth in Prussian power threatened Austrian dominance of the Bund as seen by the Treaty of Olmütz where Prussian proposals for the Erfut Union were firmly rejected.

Divisions among the nationalists

- There were disagreements about what a united Germany should be like, especially between the *grossdeutsch* and *kleindeutsch* arguments.
- Divisions and weaknesses of the movement were seen in the 1848 risings where the Frankfurt Parliament talked much, but acted little.
- The decision of the Prussian king to oppose the parliament after initially being sympathetic showed where the real power lay.

German princes

- Organisations like the Bund enhanced the power of individual rulers as decisions had to be unanimous.
- Rulers of the independent states had little interest in unification as it had implications for their rule and power.
- There were strong regional differences which were fiercely defended by the individual rulers across the Germanic states that were enhanced by long periods of independence. For example, the Kingdom of Bavaria had existed in some form since 1623.

Religious differences

- The Treaty of Westphalia that ended the devastating religious wars (termed the Thirty Years' War) across Germany left the northern Germanic states following Protestantism and the southern Germanic states following Catholicism. It also left lingering resentment.
- The religious difference exacerbated existing resentments and feelings of being different across the German states.

Economic differences

- Commercial trade developed across the Customs Union, but there were significant economic differences even within the Union.
- Prussia itself was very varied compared with the industrially more developed Rhineland given to it at the Congress of Vienna, but the eastern estates of the Junkers in the East were largely rural and bred the conservative Junker class who still had some influence at this time.

Indifference of the masses

- Through this period the mass of the population were peasants with some industrial workers. They were largely indifferent to the idea of a unified Germany, though there was some stirring of cultural pride.
- Nationalism had most effect on the middle classes. The upper classes had little interest.

Any other relevant factors.

41 To what extent were the weaknesses of the Weimar Republic the main reason why the Nazis achieved power in 1933? (20)

Context: the Nazis were invited to form a government in 1933. It was a remarkable transformation for a political movement that only had twelve seats in the Reichstag in 1928.

Weaknesses of the Weimar Republic

- Initial enthusiasm for the Republic waned in the aftermath of its acceptance of the Treaty of Versailles.
- The Weimar Republic electoral system was proportional, which, though great in a democratic sense, was a disaster for such a politically polarised parliament.
- The use of Article 48 by the President could be abused and meant people got used to such a method of decision making.
- There was a lack of support from the key institutions of state, such as the judiciary, civil service and army, and an unwillingness to reform these institutions.
- The alliance between the reactionary *Freikorps* and democratic government showed the weakness of the government.

Other factors

Role of Hitler

- Hitler was seen as young and dynamic when compared with the other leaders of political parties in the Weimar Republic.
- He was an excellent public speaker who used his opportunities well to advertise his beliefs, such as the trial for his part in the Munich Beer Hall Putsch.
- He gave scapegoats the blame for the condition Germany was in and had a clear message about making Germany great again.
- He knew what he wanted, power, and was willing to wait and plan for it, but to act decisively when needed; such as 'holding his nose' and going into parliament after the failure of the Munich Beer Hall Putsch, and using the opportunity of the Reichstag Fire to further his cause.

Resentment towards the Treaty of Versailles

- The key problem for the democratic politicians was their acceptance of the Treaty of Versailles.
- The German people believed they had been fighting a war of defence and the peace settlement would be based on Wilson's fourteen points.
- Germans felt betrayed by the terms of the treaty, especially the land loss.
- The right blamed the democratic politicians and created the myth of 'stab in the back' as well as the term 'November Criminals'.

Social and economic difficulties

- Reparations were bitterly resented and were blamed for the country's economic woes.
- The hyperinflation crisis of 1923 had a particularly significant impact on the country's middle classes, a group whose support the Weimar Republic needed.
- The Great Depression of 1929 transformed the political situation in Germany. It led to businesses shutting and rising unemployment. The people blamed the Republic, turning to radical alternatives as an easy answer to difficult issues.

Appeal of the Nazis after 1928

- The Nazi message had not changed, but people began to listen during the Depression.
- Its anti-communist, anti-Versailles, make-Germany-strong message had appeal among the middle classes who feared a 'Red' government.
- The Nazis also gave desperate people someone to blame: the Jews, communists, Democrats and 'November Criminals'.
- Josef Goebbels orchestrated an effective use of propaganda.

Weaknesses and mistakes of others

- There was a lack of unified opposition to Fascism within the Weimar Republic, especially between the left-wing parties of the SPD (Social Democratic Party) and KPD (German Communist Party).
- The traditional right wing, in the form of Von Papen, made mistakes, for example thinking that they could make Hitler do their will.
- The age and infirmity of Hindenburg was a weakness.

Any other relevant factors.

42 How important was propaganda as a reason why the Nazis were able to stay in power, 1933–1939? (20)

Context: The Nazis ruled Germany with a mixture of oppression and popular policies.

Propaganda

- Joseph Goebbels co-ordinated the manipulation of the media to sell the Nazi story.
- Radio, cinema and rallies disseminated Nazi propaganda to every community.
- A cult of personality existed around Hitler.

Other factors

Crushing of opposition

- Once elected to power, the Nazis moved swiftly against their political opponents.
- The Communist Party was crushed.
- The SPD (Social Democratic Party) and other political parties were banned.
- State governments were brought into line.
- The Nazis used the SA and concentration camps against opponents.

Success of economic policies

- The Nazis claimed economic success with a massive reduction in unemployment.
- Huge public works were undertaken, such as the autobahns.
- Re-armament stimulated the economy.
- Long term, the artificial stimulus of the economy was probably unsustainable.

Success of social policies

- The Nazis implemented a range of social policies to control all sections of society.
- Trades unions were banned and the German Labour Front, under Robert Ley, was created.
- Huge investment in youth organisations, such as the Hitler Youth, were made.
- Education was controlled.
- The Strength through Joy movement was created.
- A concordat with the Catholic Church was reached; a reichsbishop was appointed as Head of the Protestant Churches.

Success of foreign policy

- Military re-armament took place.
- Re-occupation of the Rhineland occurred.
- Anschluss, the annexation of Austria into Nazi Germany in March 1938, took place.
- The Nazis occupied the Sudetenland.
- Breaking the terms of the Versailles Treaty was popular.

Establishment of a totalitarian state

- Between 1933 and 1934, the Nazis converted a democracy into a totalitarian state; only the Nazi Party was allowed.

- The Gestapo, SS (an elite force of troops) and SA were used to police Germany and remove opponents to the regime.
- Anti-Nazi judges were dismissed and replaced with those favourable to the Nazis.
- An all-embracing law which allowed the Nazis to persecute opponents in a 'legal' way was enacted: Acts Hostile to the National Community (1935).

Fear and state terrorism

- Fear/terror, through the Nazi police state and the Gestapo, was widespread.
- Concentration camps were set up to detain opponents.
- The SS was used to control the German public.

Any other relevant factors.

Part E – Italy, 1815–1939

43 How important were social, economic and cultural divisions as an obstacle to Italian unification, 1815–1850? (20)

Context: By 1850, the forces of nationalism had grown in Italy. The revolutions of 1848 showed this. However, there were many obstacles which prevented unification from happening before1850, such as the dominant position of Austria and her dependent duchies.

Social, economic and cultural differences

- Italy was a geographically divided country.
- There were divisions between the north and south of the country in terms of regional dialects, thus creating cultural differences.
- Regional identity remained strong with most identifying primarily with their local area.
- There were significant economic differences, with industry located in the north, and the south being a largely poor, agrarian-based economy.
- Italians in the north perceived southerners as being backward, ignorant and superstitious.

Other factors

Attitude of the Papacy

- Pope Pius IX came out against nationalism in 1848; he was unwilling to fight against Austria as it was a leading Catholic power.
- The Roman Republic was set up in 1849 and was denounced by the Pope, who called on the Catholic powers of Europe to restore him. French forces were duly despatched and the city fell after three months of resistance. The Pope had sided with autocracy.

Dominant position of Austria and her dependent duchies

- After the 1815 Vienna Settlement, the Austrian Emperor had direct control over Lombardy and Venetia. Fellow Habsburgs were in charge in the duchies and he had agreements with the Papacy and other states.
- Lombardy and Venetia were ruthlessly run with what was effectively a police state. Government jobs could only be gained if you spoke German.
- The Austrian army was well protected behind its defensive frontier, known as the 'Quadrilateral'.
- The Austrian Commander was the elderly Joseph Radetsky, who was a very capable military commander.
- He fell back on the Quadrilateral, waited for reinforcements and then routed the pro-unification forces of the Piedmontese monarch, Charles Albert at the Battle of Custozza.
- He besieged Venetia until the Republic of St Mark surrendered on 22 August 1849.
- The Austrian army swiftly re-established control.

Political differences/divisions among the nationalists

- The nationalists were divided in what they wanted when the opportunity arose.
- Mazzini wanted a democratic republic, while people like Gioberti wanted a confederation of princes led by the Pope.
- Many moderate nationalists were fearful of the ideas of people like Mazzini.
- The secret societies lacked specific aims and were poorly organised.
- The 1848 Revolution was a missed opportunity, but did show divisions between leaders and states. For example, when Piedmontese soldiers 'liberated' Lombardy and Venetia they were disappointed that the people of these regions seemed to want a republic rather than to be ruled by Piedmont.

Italian princes

- The rulers of the many Italian states were going to oppose nationalism in any form as it would mean they were out of a job. For example, King Ferdinand in Naples/Sicily was threatened by rebellion in 1820. He initially promised reform, but when he had the chance he asked for Austrian help to crush the rebellion. Metternich was only too pleased to help.

Indifference of the masses

- Italy was a relatively poor European country. The mass of population were peasants who were simply not that interested in nationalism. For example, some felt that Mazzini was inspirational, but in reality he had relatively few members in his Young Italy organisation.

Any other relevant factors.

44 *The role of Mussolini was the most important reason why the Fascists achieved power in Italy, 1919–1925.*

How valid is this view? (20)

Context: By 1925, Mussolini and the Fascists had gained power in Italy. Many factors contributed to the Fascist rise to power in Italy, such as the weakness of the political system and the determination of Mussolini and the Fascists.

Weaknesses of Italian governments

- Parliamentary government was weak and corrupt in Italy.
- Since unification, Italy had been governed by middle class Liberals who formed coalitions.
- After 1919, elections were by proportional representation. This encouraged the growth of small parties and weak governing coalitions were the norm.
- The weakness of the system can be seen in the speed of its collapse.

Other factors

Role of Mussolini

- Mussolini took the Fascists on an extreme right-wing political journey, seeing parliamentary democracy as weak and degenerate. Their message proved seductive.
- He was an effective orator.
- Mussolini had a significant role in the March on Rome, which made him the constitutional Prime Minister of Italy.
- Mussolini's active foreign policy as Prime Minster helped increase his popularity, easing the way to dictatorship.
- Mussolini helped manipulate the electoral system, which gave the Fascists a landslide victory in 1924.

Economic difficulties

- At the beginning of the First World War there was a boom in war-related industries.
- War was financed by extending government debt. Inflation hit the lira.
- After the war, unemployment rose to 2 million. Many unemployed were ex-soldiers who were increasingly resentful.

Resentment against the Peace Settlement

- In 1915, Italy entered the war on the side of the Entente. They had been promised land in Europe and a share of land abroad, as well as a share in any reparations after the war.
- In fact, Italy was a military liability and had to be helped by Britain and France. The war did cost 600,000 Italian lives, however. After the war, Italy was largely ignored at the Peace Conference.
- Italy got most of the European land it had been promised, but no colonies and no share of the reparations. This caused a lot of resentment.

Appeal of the Fascists

- The Fascists promised to end political chaos and oppose the 'Red menace'. There was a focus on order, reliability and power which appealed to many in the middle and upper classes.
- The Fascists were nationalistic which was popular and promised to make Italy great again.
- *Squadristi* (paramilitary militia) violence was directed against socialism so gained the support of industrialists and many of the middle class.

Role of the King

- At key moments the King gave in to the Fascists. Initially a state of emergency and imposition of martial law was agreed as the Fascists marched on Rome, but the King changed his mind.
- Mussolini demanded to be made Prime Minister. The King agreed to this.
- Even after the murder of Matteotti and the Aventine Secession, the King was unwilling to dismiss Mussolini.

Social and economic divisions

- Political divisions were exacerbated by social and economic inequalities. For example, membership of trades unions and the PSI (Italian Socialist Party) rose – strikes, demonstrations and violence occurred.
- Industrialists and the middle classes were fearful of revolution – they were concerned about a breakdown in law and order.

- In the countryside, there was seizure of common land – peasant ownership increased.
- The brutal behaviour of Fascists across the north of Italy in 1922, under Italo Balbo, was not stopped by the police.

Weaknesses and mistakes of opponents

- Political opponents were divided. Liberals were split into four factions, for example.
- There was not the political will to oppose Mussolini in the end.
- Government weakness was seen in actions like the failure to stop D'Annunzio's seizure of Fiume.

Any other relevant factors.

45 To what extent was foreign policy the main reason why the Fascists were able to stay in power, 1922–1939? (20)

Context: Mussolini was the Fascist leader of Italy between 1922 and 1939. His control of Italy was a mixture of repression and acceptance.

Foreign policy

- Mussolini was initially extremely popular with a successful foreign policy, up until 1938.
- Foreign policy successes in 1923, such as the Corfu Incident, which led to the Italian occupation of the island with little fighting.
- Mussolini's prestige was boosted by the invasion of Abyssinia in 1935, giving the appearance of his developing an Italian empire.
- Participation in the Spanish Civil War enabled Mussolini to boost Italy's pretensions as a military power.
- Mussolini's foreign prestige was boosted by his role as key negotiator in the Munich Agreement of 1938 between Germany and the Western Allies.

Other factors

Social controls

- Control of the workers and the economy was achieved through the 22 corporations that were set up in 1934.
- Workers were provided with a wide range of benefits, such as insurance, but strike action was banned.
- For most people the regime offered stability and, for the middle classes, protection from communism.
- The young were encouraged to join youth movements, such as the Avanguardista, which aimed to create energetic soldiers and willing mothers.

Fear and intimidation

- Secret police, the OVRA, was established in 1927 and the death penalty was reintroduced. Brutal tactics were used, but relatively few people were imprisoned and killed.
- Local blackshirt militias terrorised those inclined to oppose the Fascists. Made up of ex-soldiers, tactics involved forcing people to drink castor oil and making them eat live toads.
- Creation of a special tribunal of army and militia officer to try even minor offences, which controlled the population.

Establishment of the Fascist State

- Emergency powers were given to Mussolini in 1922. He set up alternative power structures that opposed the parliament, such as the Fascist Grand Council.
- Acerbo law transformed Italy into a single constituency that Mussolini could manipulate in the 1926 general election.
- Democracy was ended in 1926 when all opposition parties were banned. By 1929, all the trappings of a Fascist dictatorship existed.

Crushing of opposition

- Opposition was weak and divided. The Liberals divided into four factions and the Left three.
- Groups were unlikely to work together against the Fascists.
- Opportunities to move against the Fascists were lost, such as after the murder of Matteotti.
- The King backed Mussolini at key moments.

Propaganda

- Fascist control of the media meant the populace heard a pro-Fascist message.
- Mussolini developed a cult of personality as the great leader.
- Slogans such as: 'War is to a man, what childbearing is to a woman' transmitted Fascist ideas, reinforcing the macho stereotype.

Relations with the Papacy

- Lateran treaties/concordats with the Papacy enabled acceptance of the Fascist regime by the Catholic majority. Many Catholics supported Mussolini's promotion of 'family values'.
- Priest salaries were paid for by the government.

- Religious education in schools could be given only by Church-approved teachers.
- The appointment of bishops had to have government approval.

Economic and social policies

- Fascists developed the Italian economy in a series of public works and initiatives, for example the 'Battle for Grain' and the 'Battle for Land'.
- Fascism crushed organised crime, with most Mafia leaders in prison by 1939.
- Wars in Ethiopia and Spain cost huge amounts of money for a poor country like Italy.

Other relevant factors.

Part F – Russia,1881–1921

46 *Between 1905 and 1914, the Tsarist government successfully regained its authority.*

How valid is this view? (20)

Context: The 1905–1907 Revolution seriously shook the Tsarist state. However, once the shock of revolution had worn off, the state swiftly reasserted itself with the Tsar more determined than ever to maintain his absolute autocracy.

Stolypin

- Pytor Stolypin was appointed Prime Minister to the Tsar in 1906, replacing Sergei Witte. He aimed to restore Tsarist autocracy but also prevent further discontent by enacting limited political and economic reforms. Stolypin was assassinated in 1911 before his land reforms had begun to take full effect.

Repression

- Stolypin was given the job of restoring control after the events of 1905. He used military courts to issue death penalties. The punishment of hanging was used so frequently it was known as 'Stolypin's necktie'. Opponents of the Tsar were also sentenced to hard labour in Siberia. The Okhrana and censorship were used to silence any public criticism of the Tsar.

Land reforms

- Stolypin's main plan for restoring order and stability was through agricultural reforms. The most important reform was the cancelling of the redemption payments which had kept peasants tied to their villages for 40 years. Each peasant was given the right to sell his plot of land and leave the village. The power of the village *mir* (council) was reduced in order to boost Tsarist control.
- Stolypin also introduced reforms in education, which became compulsory, aiming to give access to more skilled jobs.
- However, the land reforms did not change agriculture as much as was hoped. In practice, the reforms did little more than reduce the number of rural disturbances.

Industrial reforms

- Stolypin introduced improvements in industrial working conditions and pay. More factories came under the control of inspectors and there were signs of improving working conditions. However, conditions actually worsened after 1906 as more peasants flooded into the city searching for work. After 1910, there was an increase in strikes and disturbances in all major cities.
- In 1912, a workers' sickness and accident insurance scheme was introduced.

Political reforms

- Stolypin wanted the support of the middle class so he tried to work with the Duma (elected legislative body) rather than against it. He changed the franchise in 1907 which prevented many national minorities, peasants and workers from voting, although they did still have a say in the Zemstvos. This allowed him to obtain a more co-operative Third Duma which passed his land reforms.
- Stolypin's work with the dumas helped to strengthen the Tsarist state as he helped secure the support of the middle class for the state. However, few urban workers had the right to vote – excluded from any political power, workers increasingly started to act on their own.

Other factors

Nature of events in 1905

- **October Manifesto:** Sergei Witte had been Finance Minister since 1893. He had been responsible for reforms which had boosted Russian industry and encouraged foreign investment from France. He had also been responsible for beginning the Trans-Siberian Railway. He was seen as the 'architect' of Russian parliamentary democracy when he became the first Prime Minister of the Council of Ministers and forced the Tsar to issue the October Manifesto, in which the Tsar made political concessions. Witte was sacked soon after as he lost support in court circles and the Duma.

- **The Duma:** Elections were allowed for a representative political body known as the State Duma. This new body could discuss matters and had minor law-making powers; however, the Tsar retained ultimate control by appointing all ministers who were solely responsible to him. Nicholas II rejected all suggestions for universal suffrage and never accepted the Duma as a legitimate political body. These political reforms may have saved the Tsarist regime in 1905, but the subsequent curbing of any political influence by the Duma merely stored up trouble.

- **Peace with Japan:** Sergei Witte's brilliant negotiations enabled the Russians to sign the Treaty of Portsmouth in 1905, ending the war with Japan. The Russians lost little from the Treaty and the ending of the war enabled the Tsarist government to return home loyal soldiers to repress rebellion at home. However, even Witte said that while the necessary political stability had been achieved, the 'peasant problem' remained.

Role of the Tsar

- The Tsar's role during 1905 had essentially been passive but, control having been restored by his ministers, he reasserted his authority with the Fundamental Laws of 1906. He also sacked ministers like Witte who had required him to make political concessions.

- The Fundamental Laws of 1906 placed further restrictions on the Duma. They reasserted Nicholas II's power to veto any legislation passed by the Duma.

Russification

- Stolypin also enforced russification and disenfranchisement to suppress the national minorities. Opposition and discontent were ruthlessly repressed and this acted as a deterrent, thereby strengthening the Tsarist state.

Opposition to the Tsar

- Revolutionary soviets (councils) had been set up in 1905; however, these were slow to pick up the mood of the people and lost the brief opportunity to topple the Tsar's regime. For example, the St Petersburg soviet was only set up in October 1905. After 1905, revolutionary parties continued to strive for mass workers' support, but their isolation from the Duma and surveillance by the Okhrana kept them underground until 1914.

- The 1914 General Strike in St Petersburg was a reflection of a vigorous trades union movement.

- Lenin's criticism of the Duma allowed the Tsar to treat it with further disdain.

- Middle-ground politicians like the Kadets and Octobrists were willing to turn a blind eye to the Tsar's use of terror in return for the limited reforms of the Duma.

Any other relevant factors.

47 To what extent were the weaknesses of the Provisional Government the main reason for the success of the October Revolution, 1917? (20)

Context: The abdication of the Tsar in February 1917 had led to a largely middle- and upper-class provisional government being formed. However, the working class, isolated from political power, was represented by the revolutionary parties. Divided political power was to prove a major issue in 1917.

The weaknesses of the Provisional Government

- The Provisional Government, as its name suggests, was never intended to be a permanent authority, which undermined its credibility.

- The Provisional Government was an unelected government; it was a self-appointed body made up from the remnants of the Tsarist Duma, which had been elected on a highly restricted franchise, thus not representative of public opinion.

- The Provisional Government decided to continue to pursue victory in the war. This was largely due to the social makeup of the Provisional Government – middle and upper classes who had supported the fall of the Tsar because they believed it was the only way to achieve victory for Russia in the war. There was also pressure from Russia's allies to continue and Russia's dependence on foreign loans which would be withdrawn if Russia did not continue to fight.

- The Provisional Government's social makeup meant that it did not see the urgency of economic and social reforms to satisfy the workers and peasants. As a result, the Provisional Government steadily lost support as public opinion backed the Soviets.

- The Provisional Government issued an eight-point programme including amnesty for all political offences, freedom of speech and elections for a Constituent Assembly. This was counter-productive as revolutionaries left jail and were able to work against the Provisional Government.

- Kornilov Revolt: In September Kerensky had to ask the Soviets and Red Guards to help defend Petrograd when the Supreme Commander of the Russian Army sent troops back to Petrograd, after falling out with Kerensky. The Bolsheviks controlled these organisations and were able to act as protectors of Petrograd. The Bolsheviks did not return their weapons to the Provisional Government after they had persuaded Kornilov's troops not to attack the city, strengthening their grab for power in October.

Other factors

The appeal of the Bolsheviks

- **Leadership of Lenin:** Lenin's return in April 1917 immediately broke the initial co-operation of the Bolsheviks with the other revolutionary parties after the February Revolution. He called for a second socialist revolution.

- Lenin refused to allow the Bolsheviks to work in coalition with the other revolutionary parties and insisted that the Bolsheviks work for a complete workers' revolution.
- Kerensky's announcement on 25 November of elections to the Constituent Assembly (the body that would decide the future government of Russia) prompted Lenin to return to Russia after the July Days. After a heated debate, he convinced the other Bolsheviks to seize power immediately. Without Lenin's leadership, it is doubtful that the Bolsheviks would have acted decisively. Lenin knew that they would not get a majority in the Constituent Assembly.
- **Propaganda:** Lenin's April Theses quickly became Soviet policy, with persuasive slogans such as 'Peace, Land and Bread' and 'All Power to the Soviets'.
- **Policies:** Lenin foresaw that the Bolsheviks could achieve power through the Soviets; Bolshevik power in the Soviets would be followed by Bolshevik takeover of the state. The Bolsheviks kept attending the Petrograd Soviet when most of the others stopped doing so and this gave them control of the Soviet, which they could then use against the Provisional Government.
- **Leadership of Trotsky:** In Trotsky, Lenin had found an energetic and motivational organiser who laid the plans for the October Revolution.

Dual Power – the role of the Petrograd Soviet

- The Petrograd Soviet reconvened immediately after the February Revolution. This was an organisation built up from the grass roots as each factory and soldiers' unit formed their own mini soviets and sent delegates to the city Soviet. This gave the Petrograd Soviet a popular mandate and political authority.
- The Petrograd Soviet issued Order No. 1 in March 1917 which stated that soldiers should only obey orders that were acceptable to the Petrograd Soviet.
- In September 1917, the Bolsheviks won majorities in both the Petrograd and Moscow soviets with Trotsky becoming Chairman of the Petrograd Soviet.

The decision to continue the war

- In April 1917, Paul Miliukov sent a note to Russia's allies assuring them that Russia would continue to fight. Publication of this note led to widespread protests and loss of support for the Provisional Government.
- The war continued to go badly, with failure of the July offensive and a disastrous defeat at Tarnopol.
- Mutiny and desertion increased as military failures continued. The continuation of the war caused further misery for people in Russia.

Economic problems

- With the war ongoing, food shortages and inflation had continued.
- Factory owners took advantage of the Bolshevik 'defeat' in the July Days to re-impose strict discipline in factories.
- Strikes increased again and productivity declined. Wages did not keep pace with price increases and fuel shortages continued. Pro-Bolshevik propaganda condemned the Provisional Government for extending the 'bony hand of hunger' from the winter of 1916–1917.
- The Provisional Government appointed the Land Committee in May 1917 to direct and supervise land reform but it accomplished little, leading to the peasants resorting to land seizure. This in turn increased desertion from the army as soldiers rushed home to ensure that they got their share.

Political discontent

- The Kronstadt Mutiny, July 1917: Sailors and workers attempted to set up a Soviet-style government at the naval base outside Petrograd. This event triggered the confused political uprising of the July Days.
- The July Days were strikes and demonstrations in Petrograd inspired by, but not led by, the Bolsheviks. The uprising was put down by troops loyal to the Provisional Government. Trotsky was arrested and Lenin was forced to flee to Finland in disguise. Kerensky was able to brand the Bolsheviks as traitors.
- Throughout 1917, the countryside was effectively in a state of turmoil and chaos.

Any other relevant factors.

48 *Disunity among the Whites was the main reason for the victory of the Reds in the Civil War.*

How valid is this view? (20)

Context: The Bolsheviks managed to cling on to power after the October Revolution. However, after the signing of the peace treaty with the Germans at Brest-Litovsk in April 1918, growing opposition led to civil war.

Disunity among the Whites

- The Whites were an un-coordinated series of groups whose morale was low. In the Ukraine, there was a separatist nationalist opposition nicknamed the 'Greens' and in Siberia, there was a Social Revolutionary controlled government that opposed both the Whites and the Reds.

- The Whites were a collection of socialists, liberals, moderates, etc. who all wanted different things and often fought among themselves due to their political differences. All of the Whites shared a hatred of communism but other than this they lacked a common purpose.

- There were at least three important White generals, Kolchak, Yudenich and Denikin, but no overall Commander-in-Chief or clear chain of command.

- No White leader of any measure emerged to unite and lead the White forces, whereas the Reds had Trotsky and Lenin.

- The Whites were too spread out geographically to co-ordinate attacks and put consistent pressure on the Reds. As a result, the Reds were able to fight one attacking force at a time.

- The Whites were not as well supplied and fed as the Reds because they did not have easy access to supplies or credit.

Other factors

Role of Trotsky – organisation of the Red Army

- Trotsky supervised the formation of the Red Army, which became a formidable fighting force of 3 million men.

- He recruited ex-Tsarist army officers for their military expertise, but had them and their families monitored by political commissars to ensure their loyalty.

- Trotsky's headquarters was a heavily armed train, which he used to ceaselessly travel around the country.

- He used conscription to gain troops and would shoot any deserters.

- Trotsky helped provide an army with great belief in what it was fighting for, which the Whites did not have.

Use of terror

- The Cheka was set up to prevent opposition to the Reds and fight counter-revolution after 1918.

- Chekist agents could act as they pleased; there was no need for proof of guilt for punishment to be exacted.

- There was persecution of individual people who opposed the Reds as well as whole groups of people, which helped to reduce opposition due to fear.

- The Cheka often brutally murdered their victims, for example packing the lungs and mouths of victims with mud.

- Some of the first victims of the Cheka were leaders of other political parties.

- In 1921, Lenin gave the Cheka more latitude in how they operated. Estimates vary as to the number of victims during the Civil War, up to 250,000.

Propaganda

- The revolutionary slogans of the Reds were more persuasive than those of the Whites, who offered a return to the old Tsarist regime. Many ordinary Russians preferred to support the Reds as they offered at least the possibility of improvement. Peasants were especially fearful of the loss of their land.

- The Whites were unable to take advantage of the brutality of the Reds to win support as they often carried out similar atrocities.

Superior Red resources

- The Reds were in control of a concentrated area of western Russia, which they could successfully defend due to the maintenance of their communication and supply lines.

- Once the Reds had established defence of their lines, they could repel and exhaust the attacks by the Whites until they scattered or surrendered.

- The Reds controlled the major industrial centres in their land (Moscow and Petrograd), so had access to factories to make weapons. Control of the railways meant they could transport troop supplies quickly and efficiently and in large numbers to the critical areas of defence or attack.

- The decisive battles between the Reds and Whites were near railheads.

- Having the two major cities of Moscow and Petrograd in their possession meant that the Reds controlled the administrative centres of government.

Unity of the Reds

- The Reds were under the leadership of Lenin, who was responsible for the introduction of War Communism. He was a skilled delegator and ruthless political operator. The cult of Lenin as an infallible leader grew at this time.

- Lenin imposed War Communism; this was the relaxation of strict communist economic policies to improve industrial and agricultural production. Peasants were forced to sell their grain to the Reds, so the communists were able to ensure that their troops were well supplied.

Effects of foreign intervention

- The British, French and Japanese all sent forces in 1920, supposedly to help the Whites fight against the Reds. However, the calibre of the soldiers was not high. The Japanese never left Siberia and the British and French headed for areas which contained industrial assets lost in the October Revolution. For example, the British headed for Baku, centre of the Russian oil industry. Few foreign troops directly engaged with the Reds.

- The supplies and number of soldiers given by the allies was not enough to make a significant difference to the outcome of the war.
- Foreign intervention was a propaganda coup for the Bolsheviks, who were able to claim that the foreign 'invaders' were imperialists trying to overthrow the revolution and invade Russia.

Any other relevant factors.

Part G – USA, 1918–1968

49 *Weaknesses in the US banking system were the main reason for the economic crisis of 1929–1933.*

How valid is this view? (20)

Context: After the First World War, the American economy seemed to have emerged unscathed, even enhanced. The USA emerged as a significant creditor nation, lending money internationally. However, the banking system had weaknesses, which led to problems when the economic crisis hit.

Weaknesses of the US banking system

- A major problem was lack of regulation, specifically the lack of rules on the money reserves that banks had to keep in relation to the money lent.
- The banking system was made up of hundreds of small, state-based banks. Often, whole communities deposited their money with one bank. These banks speculated on the stock market to try to maximise profits and lending to the community it served.
- When one bank collapsed, it often led to a 'run' on other banks, resulting in a banking collapse and national financial crisis. Twenty per cent of those banks operating in 1929 had closed down by 1932.
- Bank closures led to the collapse of the finance industry which supplied credit to businesses. Without credit, businesses were unable to operate, leading to their closure, even if the business was viable.

Other factors

Republican policies in the 1920s

- The USA experienced a period of prosperity after the First World War. It was believed that government should only intervene when requested to do so by business, therefore leading to the Republican administration's policy of *laissez-faire*.
- There was a failure to help farmers who did not benefit from the 1920s' boom.
- Low capital gains tax encouraged share speculation which resulted in the Wall Street Crash.
- The depression was also due to the actions – or inactions – of President Hoover. Politicians and the government were slow to realise the seriousness of the crisis. As a result, action was 'too little, too late' and focused on the needs of businessmen, not the wider American society.

Over-production of goods

- New mass-production methods and mechanisation meant that production of consumer goods had expanded enormously.
- Cars, radios and other electrical goods had flooded the market and more was being made than people could buy, for example 1.9 million cars were made in 1920, 4.5 million in 1929.
- By 1929, those who could afford consumer goods had already bought them. Many people had bought them on credit.

Under-consumption – the saturation of the US market

- Throughout the 1920s, businesses and the better-off had benefited from low tax policies. The result of this was that the bottom 40 per cent of the population received only 12.5 per cent of the nation's wealth. In contrast, the top 5 per cent owned 33 per cent of the nation's wealth.
- Incomes did not keep up with rising productivity. For example, between 1920 and 1932, the income of farmers dropped by 70 per cent. Many Americans could not afford the new consumer goods.
- Some Americans did not benefit from the economic boom in the 1920s. For example, in 1928 an estimated 42 per cent of Americans did not earn enough money to supply their food, clothing and housing needs.
- By the end of the 1920s, demand for new consumer goods was met and the car industry was forced to lay off workers owing to falling demand.

International economic problems

- The impact of the First World War on European economies was enormous; it had turned creditor nations like Britain into debtor nations. After the First World War, Britain was unable to pull itself out of financial problems because of the loss of markets like Germany for its export-led economy. Germany's economy was experiencing real problems after its defeat. The 'loss' of two major trading partners meant demand for American goods was reduced further.

- All European states, except Britain, placed tariffs on imported goods.
- US tariff barriers meant that other countries found it difficult to pay back loans because they could not sell to America. Often these countries, for example Germany, had to refinance their loans which meant they became increasingly indebted.

Wall Street Crash

- Throughout the 1920s, share prices rose. However, this demand was fuelled by people buying 'on margin': only paying a fraction of the value in the hope that the share price would continue to rise before having to sell. Unfortunately, this meant that share prices began to outstrip the real value of the company shares being sold.
- There was an atmosphere of uncertainty in October 1929 and shareholders began to sell their stocks, believing that prices had reached their peak.
- 24 October 1929 – Black Thursday: the Wall Street Crash began as prices fell dramatically. 29 October 1929 – Black Tuesday: the stock market collapsed completely, causing panic. Many ordinary Americans were ruined, still more lost their jobs as businesses folded.
- The stock market crash did play a role in the depression but its significance was as a trigger because it caused the collapse of credit and of confidence.

Any other relevant factors.

50 How important was the experience of black servicemen in the Second World War in the development of the Civil Rights campaign, after 1945? (20)

Context: The upcoming centenary of Lincoln's emancipation of slaves in 1963 highlighted the lack of progress black Americans had made in the century since they had been offered freedom and equal rights.

Experience of black servicemen in the Second World War

- Black soldiers experienced freedoms from segregation in Europe and witnessed German prisoners of war receiving better treatment than they did in American military camps.
- Black soldiers were influenced by the 'Double-V-Campaign': victory in the war and victory for civil rights at home.
- Philip Randolph highlighted the problems faced by black American workers during the Second World War. He led the 'March on Washington' movement in 1941 to protest against racial discrimination. This convinced Roosevelt to issue Executive Order 8802, banning discrimination in the defence industries.
- The 'March on Washington' group also successfully pressured President Harry S. Truman to issue Executive Order 9981 in 1948, ending segregation in the armed services.
- Roosevelt also established the Fair Employment Practices Committee to investigate incidents of discrimination.
- The creation of the Congress of Racial Equality (CORE) 1942, was the beginning of a mass movement for civil rights.

Other factors

The continuation of prejudice and discrimination

- The experience of war emphasised freedom, democracy and human rights, yet in the USA, Jim Crow laws still existed and lynching went unpunished. Between 1896 and 1968, over 200 anti-lynching bills were introduced into Congress but none were passed owing to the opposition from southern states.
- The 1955 Emmet Till murder trial and its publicity. Till was a fourteen-year-old boy who was lynched after supposedly flirting with a white woman. None of the murderers were convicted despite strong evidence. His treatment was well publicised and outraged black Americans.
- High-profile legal cases advanced the cause of equal education for blacks: 1954 Brown v. Board of Education of Topeka; 1957 Little Rock Central High School. This encouraged more campaigning for wider change.
- The success of the 1955 Rosa Parks and the Montgomery Bus Boycott encouraged more campaigning.

Formation of effective black organisations

- In 1960, a group of black and white college students organised the Student Non-violent Co-ordinating Committee (SNCC) to help the Civil Rights movement. They started by targeting segregated lunch counters and their continued use of non-violent protest won many supporters across the country.
- They joined with young people from the SCLC (Southern Christian Leadership Conference), CORE and NAACP (National Association for the Advancement of Colored People) in staging sit-ins, boycotts, marches and Freedom Rides. Media coverage of the attacks on Freedom Riders shocked the American public and won them much support.
- Combined efforts of the civil rights groups ended discrimination in many public places including restaurants, hotels and theatres.

Emergence of effective black leaders

- Inspirational, but more confrontational, Malcolm X was the articulate voice of the Nation of Islam. He spoke against Martin Luther King's non-violent campaign and rejected the involvement of whites in the campaign for civil rights. Malcolm X was one of the first to highlight the particular problems of crime and unemployment experienced by black Americans in the ghettos.

- Stokely Carmichael drew his ideas from Marcus Garvey. He believed in black separatism and Black Power, and rejected much of Martin Luther King's non-violent approach. His ideas were very attractive to young black Americans.
- The Black Panther Party for Self-Defense was formed in 1966 by Huey P. Newton and Bobby Seale. They followed the ideas of Malcolm X and Stokely Carmichael. They were popular with young black Americans from the ghettos but membership of their group was relatively low. The Black Panthers attracted attention but lost support as a result of their confrontational tactics.
- All leaders attracted media coverage, large followings and divided opinion across the USA, but some leaders and organisations were overshadowed by the media focus on the main personalities.

The role of Martin Luther King

- Martin Luther King had key skills and attributes as an inspirational speaker and was prepared to put his own life at risk for the cause of civil rights.
- Martin Luther King believed in non-violent protest to achieve civil rights goals. His belief in patient persistence to wear down the arguments of white racists was influential in enabling the American government to justify its concessions and support of civil rights.
- Martian Luther King presented a positive media image, which persuaded white Americans to join him on his campaign.
- King became President of the Southern Christian Leadership Conference in 1960, co-ordinating the work of different civil rights groups. This gave him a national platform, making him well-known.
- One of the first campaigns on which King became well-known was the 1955 Montgomery Bus Boycott. During this campaign, he motivated the black population to maintain their year-long boycott and force significant concessions from the bus company. His personal effectiveness during this campaign enhanced his reputation.
- King achieved worldwide renown with his 1964 civil rights march and 'I Have a Dream' speech, one of the modern era's most influential speeches.
- He won the Nobel Peace Prize in 1964, gaining more national and international recognition for his role.

Any other relevant factors.

51 The Civil Rights movement was effective in meeting the needs of black Americans, up to 1968.

   How valid is this view? (20)

Context: The Second World War had stimulated renewed demand for black civil rights. By the 1960s, these demands were becoming more vocal.

Aims of the Civil Rights movement

- The Civil Rights movement was mainly peaceful and intended to bring civil rights and equality in practice, not just in the Constitution, to all non-white Americans.
- Some Black Radical movements had more separatist aims.

Role of the NAACP in desegregation – methods and tactics

- National Association for the Advancement of Colored People (NAACP) lawyers fought the Brown v. Topeka Board of Education, 1954.
- The NAACP helped organise the Montgomery Bus Boycott, 1955.
- The NAACP was important in mobilising student demonstrations.

Role of CORE in desegregation – methods and tactics

- The Congress of Racial Equality (CORE) organised sit-ins and Freedom Rides during 1961.
- CORE helped organise the March on Washington.
- CORE was instrumental in setting up Freedom Schools in Mississippi.

Roles of SCLC and Martin Luther King in desegregation – methods and tactics

- Martin Luther King was leader of the Southern Christian Leadership Conference (SCLC), set up in 1957 after the success of the Montgomery Bus Boycott (1956) to co-ordinate the actions of local protest groups.
- Birmingham, Alabama 1963: use of water cannon: Reaction of Kennedy, role of Martin Luther King in pressuring the administration.
- In August 1963, a March on Washington took place. Martin Luther King made his famous 'I Have a Dream' speech amid massive publicity.
- Martin Luther King encouraged non-violent protest, as exemplified by sit-ins and Freedom Rides.
- Martin Luther King believed that the Civil Rights Act of 1964 'gave Negroes some part of their rightful dignity, but without the vote it was dignity without strength'.

- In March 1965, King led a march from Selma to Birmingham, Alabama, to publicise the way in which the authorities made it difficult for black Americans to vote easily.
- Little Rock, Arkansas, saw desegregation in 1957 following national publicity.

Changes in federal policy

- Truman used presidential executive orders to appoint black candidates and to order equality of treatment in the armed services. Kennedy signed an executive order in 1962 outlawing racial discrimination in public housing.
- The president ordered the use of the army/National Guard to uphold the law: examples include Eisenhower at Little Rock to protect nine African-American students enrolled in a Central High School; Kennedy at Oxford, Mississippi to protect black student, James Meredith.
- Landmark legislation was passed: Johnson and the 1964 Civil Rights Act banning racial discrimination in any public place; the Voting Rights Act of 1965: by the end of 1965 over 250,000 black people were newly registered to vote, There was also government support for Affirmative Action.

Social, economic and political changes

- The Civil Rights Acts of 1964 and 1965 improved political rights but were irrelevant to black people in the cities of the North who already had these freedoms.
- There was little improvement in the economic rights for black Americans in the North, for example in equal pay.
- The Watts riots, Los Angeles, were shocking because rioters burnt the homes in their own neighbourhood.
- There were splits in the Civil Rights movement and increasing criticism of Martin Luther King by Black Radical movements.
- The SCLC non-violent campaign was met by race riots. The promised housing initiative by the Mayor of Chicago (1966) to ease tension never started.
- Urban poverty and de facto segregation was still common in cities. Martin Luther King's campaign to attack poverty largely failed.

Rise of Black Radical movements

- After 1966, there was a divergence in the Civil Rights movement between non-violent versus more radical action.
- Stokely Carmichael and Black Power.
- Malcolm X publicised the increasing urban problems within the ghettos of America. He became famous for the slogan: 'By any means necessary.'
- The Black Panthers were involved in self-help schemes providing food, clothing and other services in poor black neighbourhoods.
- The Kerner Commission of 1968 recognised that US society was still divided.

Any other relevant factors.

Part H – Appeasement and the Road to War, to 1939

52 To what extent were attitudes to the Paris Peace Settlement the main reason for the British policy of appeasement, 1936–1938? (20)

Context: The First World War had a profound impact on Britain. Not only did it have to cope with unprecedented military losses, but also deal with the psychological impact of the war and adapt to the much changed post-war Europe.

Attitudes to the Paris Peace Settlement

- The Peace Settlement had been subject to serious intellectual criticism by the likes of John Maynard Keynes, the eminent economist of the day. It became a common assumption in government circles that parts of the Versailles Treaty needed revision.
- Britain was reluctant to act as the League of Nations' 'policeman' and enforce Treaty provisions that had no direct benefit for Britain.
- By the 1930s, the Peace settlement was perceived to be harsh by many people in Britain.

Other factors

Economic difficulties

- The post-First World War economic slump had led to industrial problems and disputes which had culminated in the 1926 General Strike. The political and social divisions resulting from this event led to a conservative economic and political outlook, which emphasised holding on to the assets and lands Britain already possessed.
- Britain was preoccupied with dealing with domestic political problems arising from the impact of the 1929–1932 economic crisis and depression.
- Conservative economic policies dictated that budgets should be cut, which meant that it was 1936 before Britain started developing new weapons.
- Germany was a valuable trading partner and there was a reluctance to further damage international trade and commerce.

Public opinion

- The First World War had a continuing psychological impact on the people of Britain. Everyone knew someone who had died or come home injured from the war. Disabled ex-soldiers, either begging or selling matches, were a common sight in many towns and cities. The public did not want a repeat of the horrors of war for the next generation.
- Many political leaders shared public attitudes to another war, also having lost close relatives, for example Neville Chamberlain.
- Most people were pre-occupied with Britain's social and economic problems. This led to isolationist feelings, such as those expressed in Chamberlain's pre-Munich speech in which he deplored the idea that Britain should be facing war 'over a faraway place'.

Pacifism

- 1935 Peace Ballot. This was a five-question survey of the British public's attitudes to the League of Nations and to economic or armed foreign intervention. The results were widely interpreted by the press and the government as showing an unwillingness to take action unless in agreement with other countries.
- 1933 Oxford University Union 'King and Country' debate. The debating society overwhelmingly voted in favour of the motion that 'under no circumstances' would it vote for King and Country. This debate was well publicised and discussed.
- 1933 Fulham East by-election. The unexpected result here showed the strength of anti-war feeling when a 'safe' Conservative seat was won, instead, by a pacifist Labour candidate.

Concern over Empire

- The Empire was thought to be essential to British economic well-being and to her status as a great power.
- Fears were raised that Britain could not defend the Empire against simultaneous threats, according to a review by the Chiefs of Staff. It was thought essential to do a deal with at least one of the aggressive Fascist powers.
- There were genuine worries as to whether the Empire would assist Britain in the event of another war. The 1937 Imperial Prime Minister's Conference refused to give a firm undertaking to aid in resisting Hitler. Britain's own army was small and help would be necessary to take on Germany's army.

Lack of reliable allies

- There was a failure by most countries in the League of Nations to act in anything other than their own self-interest. Disarmament and Collective Security seemed to be empty slogans. Specific examples of self-interest include Manchuria and Abyssinia.
- The unreliability of the French, owing to its own political divisions, meant Britain was lacking one of its key allies.
- US isolationism had a similar effect.
- New democratic countries in middle and Eastern Europe seemed weak military allies. Only Czechoslovakia had a decent armaments industry, Skoda Works.

Fear of the spread of communism

- After the Russian Revolution, there was greater fear of the spread of communism than Fascism. The communists' seizure of foreign assets in Russia created suspicion of Soviet Russia.
- Nazi Germany was seen as a buffer and it was thought that destabilising the Nazi regime might lead to questions over communist revolution in Germany – as had nearly happened in 1919.
- There was fear of communism spreading into Western Europe, for example fear of the French Popular Front government and worries about a communist victory in the Spanish Civil War.

Beliefs of Chamberlain

- Chamberlain believed strongly in his own negotiating skills and that any problem had a rational, negotiable solution.
- Chamberlain dominated his government. He controlled foreign policy and in his roles as Chancellor and then Prime Minister prevented any re-armament that could not be classed as defensive spending in order not to provoke a reaction from the Germans. For example, spending on the new Spitfire and Hurricane planes was limited.

Any other relevant factors.

53 To what extent can it be argued that the Munich agreement was a success? (20)

Context: Created after the First World War, Czechoslovakia promised to be the hallmark of success for the Paris Peace Settlement. Containing several different nationalities, it nonetheless settled down to operating as an effective democracy. However, it contained about 3 million Sudeten Germans within its borders and, in the 1930s, Hitler exploited this in his search for territorial gains. Agreement was reached in September 1939, between Germany, Britain, France and Italy to give the Sudetenland to Germany – the Czechs themselves were not consulted.

Arguments for the Settlement

- The Agreement was the pragmatic recognition that Czech defences were vulnerable to attack after the 1938 Union with Austria.
- The location of Czechoslovakia meant that neither Britain nor France would be able to prevent a German attack or provide significant support were there to be an attack.

- Public opinion showed that Britain was reluctant to risk war over mainly German-speaking Sudetenland. Chamberlain's pre-Munich speech struck a chord with many.
- The immediate British public reaction to the Munich Agreement was that of relief and rejoicing that war had been averted. Chamberlain got mobbed on his return to Downing Street and received the honour of being received on the balcony at Buckingham Palace by the King.
- A minority of opposition politicians, like Clement Atlee, and mavericks, like Winston Churchill, openly opposed the Agreement. There were some anti-Munich demonstrations in the weeks following the Munich Agreement but these were dwarfed by those in favour.
- Britain was not militarily ready for war, especially in her air defences – or even for offensive action.
- Failure of the League in earlier crises meant that there was a lack of alternative; there was no unified international response to Hitler.
- There was reluctance from the French to commit to intervention in Czechoslovakia, and no desire for Britain to take the lead.
- There was a lack of engagement of the USA in European affairs.
- Chamberlain's suspicion of Soviet Russia meant that he was happier to see Germany extended eastwards rather than the Russians expanding westwards.
- The unwillingness of the British Empire and Dominions to commit to supporting Britain in any war was well known.
- Poland and Hungary were willing to benefit from the dismemberment of Czechoslovakia rather than aid their neighbour.
- Munich bought Britain another year for re-armament.

Arguments against the Settlement

- Britain had been seen to surrender to Hitler's blustering and threats at an international conference, with the whole world watching.
- It was the final 'nail in the coffin' for the Paris Peace Settlement, which as co-creators and signatories, Britain and France should have been defending not tearing up.
- It could be argued it was a cynical betrayal of Czechoslovakia and democracy.
- The removal of the Sudetenland deprived the Czechs of natural border defences and left it vulnerable to further German aggression, as happened in March 1939.
- German manpower and resources were greatly enhanced by the addition of Czechoslovakia's industry and armaments factories.
- The Agreement facilitated Hitler's influence and ambitions in Eastern Europe.
- The failure to even engage the Russians in discussions about preventing German expansion created more suspicion and alienation of the Soviet Union. It convinced Stalin that the West was trying to divert Hitler's ambitions in Western Europe by encouraging him to move east. The Munich Agreement was undoubtedly part of Stalin's calculations in the signing of the Nazi–Soviet Pact in 1939, which gave Hitler the 'green light' for war.
- Poland was left very vulnerable to attack.

Differing views of the Munich Settlement

- Initially there was pro-Munich euphoria over the avoidance of war.
- A minority of opposition politicians, like Clement Atlee, and mavericks, like Winston Churchill, openly opposed the Agreement. There were some anti-Munich demonstrations in the weeks following the Munich Agreement but these were dwarfed by those in favour.
- Chamberlain was criticised for his role in the Settlement in the 1940 book, *Guilty Men*, by Michael Foot, Frank Owen and Peter Howard.
- The settlement is criticised by Winston Churchill in his post-war memoir, *The Gathering Storm* (1948) in which he accepted that Chamberlain had honourable motives but that these were mistaken; Hitler should have been resisted and more effort should have been made to work with the Soviets.

Any other relevant factors.

54 *The occupation of Bohemia and the collapse of Czechoslovakia were the main reason for the outbreak of war in 1939.*

    How valid is this view? (20)

Context: By 1939, Appeasement had failed to settle German grievances and Hitler showed no sign of letting up in his demands for more territory.

Occupation of Bohemia and the collapse of Czechoslovakia

- After the German invasion of Czechoslovakia in March 1939, the British and French governments could no longer fool themselves and had to admit that Hitler's word was worthless and his aims went beyond the incorporation of ex-German territories and ethnic Germans into the Reich.

- Support was promised to Poland and Rumania.
- The British public accepted that all attempts to maintain peace had been exhausted.
- Chamberlain felt betrayed by the Nazi seizure of Czechoslovakia, realised his policy of Appeasement towards Hitler had failed, and began to take a much harder line against the Nazis.

Other factors

Changing British attitudes to Appeasement

- Czechoslovakia did not concern most people in Britain until the middle of September 1938, when some began to object to a small democratic state being bullied. Most of the press and the population went along with the Munich Agreement out of relief at the avoidance of war; however, levels of popular opposition are often underestimated.
- German invasion of the remainder of Czechoslovakia in spring 1939 consolidated growing concerns in Britain.
- The German annexation of Memel (largely German, but in Lithuania) further showed Hitler's bad faith.
- Actions convinced the British government of the growing German threat in south-Eastern Europe.
- Along with France, Britain gave guarantees to Poland and promised action in the event of threats to Polish independence. However, the British government was well aware that it was unlikely to be able to honour promises made to the Poles.

Developing crisis over Poland

- Hitler's aims for the destruction of Versailles included regaining Danzig and the Polish Corridor.
- The British and French made a decision to stick to their guarantees to Poland.

British diplomacy and relations with the Soviet Union

- Stalin knew that ideology and geography would inevitably lead to Hitler's attack on Russia.
- Stalin invited Lord Halifax, the British Foreign Secretary, to go to Russia to discuss an alliance against Germany.
- Britain refused as they feared Russian communism, and they believed that the Russian army was too weak to be of any use against Hitler.
- In August 1939, the British and French eventually sent a low-level military mission to discuss an alliance with Russia. Owing to travel difficulties it took five days to reach Leningrad. The talks broke down over the issue of Russian troops in Poland.
- Stalin was unimpressed with the lack of status of the mission; this confirmed Stalin's suspicions regarding the British, that they were willing to try any tactic to ensure the Germans attacked eastwards instead of west. He felt they could not be trusted, especially after the Munich Agreement, and that they would leave Russia to fight Germany alone.
- The failure of the Franco-British mission to Russia led directly to Stalin opening talks with the Nazis who seemed to be taking the Russians seriously, sending Foreign Minister von Ribbentrop and offering substantive concessions.

Position of France

- France had signed an agreement with Czechoslovakia offering support if the country was attacked. However, Hitler knew that the French would do nothing without British support.
- The French military, and particularly their air force, had been allowed to decline in the years after 1919.
- After Munich, the French were more aggressive towards dictators. In 1939, they were keen to reprise their military alliance with Russia; however, French foreign policy was tied to the British and their actions.

Nazi–Soviet Pact

- The Nazi–Soviet Pact was unexpected – it was the result of Hitler and Stalin's self-interested motives.
- The Pact established diplomatic, economic and military co-operation, and the division of Poland.
- Hitler was freed from the threat of Soviet intervention and war on two fronts.
- Hitler now felt able to attack Poland because he rightly assumed that Britain and France would not go to war over Poland without Russian assistance.
- Hitler's foreign policy aims, the destruction of the Versailles settlement and *lebensraum* in the East probably mean the Nazi–Soviet Pact should be seen more as a factor influencing the timing of the outbreak of war rather than one of its underlying causes.
- In the longer term, Hitler would probably still need to expand eastwards to sustain Germany's militarised economy.
- Hitler believed that the British and French were 'worms', whose promises over Poland would turn out to be empty because of their previous policy of Appeasement and avoidance of war at all costs.
- Hitler believed that delaying war would mean the balance of military and economic advantage would shift against Germany.

Invasion of Poland

- On 1 September 1939, Hitler and the Nazis faked a Polish attack on a minor German radio station in order to justify a German invasion of Poland. An hour later, Hitler declared war on Poland, blaming the 'attack'.
- France and Britain had a defensive pact with Poland. This forced France and Britain to declare war on Germany, which they did on 3 September.

Any other relevant factors.

Part I — The Cold War, 1945–1989

55 To what extent was Khrushchev's domestic position the main reason for the Cuban Missile Crisis of 1962? (20)

Context: The success of the Cuban Revolution was a surprise to both East and West. Castro's regime sought to reform their political and economic system, causing America to put pressure on. This and pressures on Khrushchev allowed the Cuban Missile Crisis to develop.

Khrushchev's domestic context

- Khrushchev was coming in for criticism from hardliners over de-Stalinisation, and from China over perceived ideological weakness.
- Khrushchev's domestic agricultural reforms had failed; a foreign policy victory would be a useful diversion.
- The possible use of missiles could be seen as a bargaining counter over the presence of French, British and US troops in Berlin.

Other reasons

The arms race

- President Khrushchev of the Soviet Union was fond of showing off and saying that the Soviets were producing ICBMs (intercontinental ballistic missiles) 'like sausages'. In reality the Soviets had fallen behind the USA in the arms race, and both sides knew it.
- The Soviets did have a lot of MRBMs (medium – range ballistic missiles), however. If these could be stationed on Cuba, then just about all the major cities of the USA were within range.
- The Soviets had lived under the threat of American missiles based in Turkey and Italy, so felt that placing missiles on Cuba was fully justified.

The Cuban Revolution

- The removal of the pro-American Batista regime by Fidel Castro did not automatically mean Cuba would be communist.
- However, Castro's policies soon worried the Americans, especially the nationalisation of land and businesses, many of which were US owned.
- The USA refused to buy Cuba's sugar crop, but the Soviets did instead. Castro was pushed towards Khrushchev.

American foreign policy

- Under Eisenhower's administration, plans were made for an invasion of Cuba by US-trained exiles.
- Kennedy inherited the plan and doubtfully agreed to it.
- The Bay of Pigs debacle confirmed to Castro that his government was under threat.
- There were several American plots to kill Castro and remove him: Operation Mongoose, etc.

Kennedy's domestic context

- Kennedy had recently been elected on a very thin majority.
- He could not afford to be seen to be weak on communism, hence his agreement to the CIA invasion plan.

Khrushchev's view of Kennedy

- Khrushchev met Kennedy at the Vienna conference. Kennedy was not his normal self, owing to medication. Khrushchev was bombastic and felt Kennedy was inexperienced.
- Success in building the Berlin Wall led Khrushchev to believe the USA would do nothing about the missiles.

Ideological differences

- The Cuban crisis was symbolic of the broader ideological struggle.
- Khrushchev wished to spread revolution to Central and South America from Cuba.

- America wanted to contain and roll back what it saw as the expansion of communism.

Any other relevant factors.

56 *The economic cost of the arms race was why the superpowers attempted to manage the Cold War, 1962–1979.*

How valid is this view? (20)

Context: As the Cold War developed, the dangers of nuclear conflict soon became apparent. This and associated issues such as cost and a desire for economic development led to attempts to 'manage' the Cold War.

Cost of the Cold War

- Developing nuclear technology in terms of ever-increasing destructive power and delivery systems was expensive.
- There was a desire to diversify the Soviet economy, which was geared to heavy industry and armament production.
- The American desire to build their 'Great Society', for example, required funds that could be diverted from armaments.

Other factors

Policies of co-existence and détente

- The Soviet Union became embroiled in an ideological argument with China that spilled over into conflict. The desire to fight a war on two fronts focused their minds.
- East European leaders such as Erich Honecker in East Germany looked to access western economic skill to develop their economies.
- The USA was embroiled in Vietnam as well as dealing with an increasingly violent Civil Rights campaign at home. This made better relations with the Soviet Union desirable.
- West European allies in NATO sought engagement with the East to lessen tension. Willi Brandt, as Mayor of Berlin then Chancellor of Germany, sought engagement with the East for practical reasons.

Danger of mutually assured destruction

- As the superpowers developed their nuclear arsenals, so their ability to destroy each other grew.
- The development of technologies that would allow second strike capability led to the chances of mutually assured destruction.
- There was a realisation that if war happened it could lead to the destruction of the world.

1962 Cuban Missile Crisis

- The 1962 Cuban Missile Crisis began when the Soviets attempted to place medium-range ballistic missiles on Cuba.
- This crisis saw the world come close to nuclear conflict and focused the minds of both superpowers, resulting in the introduction of the hot line between the Kremlin and White House as well as nuclear testing bans.

Development of aerial surveillance technology

- Both sides developed far greater capability to see what the other was doing as the Cold War progressed.
- This allowed each side to verify what the other was doing and made the completion of agreements, such as SALT I, easier to police.
- An example of the good use of surveillance technology was the identification and monitoring of the Cuban missile site development.

Any other relevant factors.

57 How important was the defeat of the Soviet Union in Afghanistan as a reason for the end of the Cold War? (20)

Context: As the 1970s and 1980s progressed, it looked as if the Cold War may reform with the new leadership of Gorbachev, but no one foresaw the collapse of communism in the late 1980s.

Defeat of the Soviet Union in Afghanistan

- The Soviet Union intervened in Afghanistan to rescue a sympathetic Marxist government.
- They got bogged down in a war with the Western funded and armed Mujahideen.
- The war was expensive and used up valuable resources.
- Eventual Soviet withdrawal showed the limits of Soviet military power.

Other factors

Western economic strength

- The economic strength of the West allowed it to sustain large military spending as well as show the East a better quality of life.
- An example of Western economic strength is the threat of the Strategic Defence Initiative. While militarily a little implausible, it was backed by formidable finance and technology.
- The Marshall Plan was important in the immediate post-war period in ensuring economic stability and growth in the West.

Soviet economic weakness

- The Soviet economy was geared to heavy industrial production and servicing its large military.
- The lack of quality consumer goods did not demonstrate a superior economic model.
- Some East European states looked to the West to modernise their economies and even borrowed large sums of money during détente, which was not encouraging economically.
- When another arms race beckoned, Gorbachev recognised that the Soviet Union could not compete.

Role of Mikhail Gorbachev

- Gorbachev became leader of the Soviet Union in 1985.
- He wished to reform the communist system to better the lives of the people.
- His policies of Perestroika and Glasnost encouraged people to criticise the political system.
- He engaged with the USA in a desire to reduce the risk of conflict, so he could readjust the Soviet economy.
- He was behind the decision to withdraw the Soviet military from Afghanistan in 1988.
- His decision to withdraw Soviet military support for the satellite state regimes was very important.

Role of Ronald Reagan

- Reagan rejected détente and brought a combative approach to the Cold War.
- Openly critical of the 'evil empire', his presidency saw growth in military expenditure as well as the proposed 'Star Wars' programme, which threatened a new arms race.
- Reagan could be personally charming and changed tack after meeting Gorbachev and receiving intelligence that the Soviets genuinely believed they were going to be attacked.

Collapse of communism in Eastern Europe

- With the loss of Soviet military support, the Eastern European states rejected communism.
- Poland elected Solidarity into government in 1989. Other states soon followed.

Any other relevant factors.

[End of marking instructions for Practice Paper C]